C000090095

Sam

A novel by Gerald Jones

Copyright © 2021 by Gerald Jones

All rights reserved. No part of this book may be reproduced or used in any manner without written permission of the copyright owner except for the use of quotations in a book review.

ISBNs:
Paperback: 978-1-80227-284-0
eBook: 978-1-80227-285-7

For my grandchildren Corey, Connor, Colebien,
William, Harvey and Evlynne

Appalachia 1933

When a puny child in Appalachia complained of being hungry her teacher told her to go home and eat. "I can't," the girl replied, "it's my sister's turn to eat."

Acknowledgements

Many thanks to Kevin Wilson for his editing and contribution to this book.

Ian Williams for his computer skills.

Fiona, Peter, Clare and Colin who passed comment having read it before going to print and Beryl for her infinite patience and ability to type faster than myself.

Cover picture, David Goodman, Graphic Design.

Author's note

'Sam' became a sequel to 'The Consequence' as an afterthought, mainly due to so many people requesting "a second book". So to this end I give you 'Sam'. I hope you enjoy reading it as much as I have enjoyed writing it.

1

Tucked away in the valleys of Mid Wales a village church bell rings out, its peal reaches across grazing meadows and rolling hills. Crows in nearby trees disturbed by the sound lazily lift their wings and fly to other trees close by. Gathered beneath the church's spire people chatter discussing the past week's events before entering and asking God to forgive them for their sins.

Llandyssil, like other villages in the valleys, is unseen and seemingly insignificant to outsiders, insignificant in so far as if it ceased to exist it wouldn't really matter. But the reality was that this village had a life and that this life integrated with the lives of other seemingly insignificant villages would form a network of activity that spread from village to village and from village to towns.

Life in these communities was mundane and predictable. On a certain day of the week, every week, the church would fill with people and the pub would be empty of them. It was a treadmill of routine but the sameness produced a reassuring way of life and the people were happy to live it. This was the way it was until the year of 1914 when the country called for volunteers to fight in a war that proved to be catastrophic. Only when it was over would the people begin to count the cost, only then, realizing things would never be the same. But the churches would still keep their congregations, as they would pray for the souls of lost victims, and the pubs would sell more beer, as pints would be raised in memory of the same.

"I've heard it said that boys should have heroes," Megan said, with a smile as she handed Sam a piece of bread pudding. Sam looked at the portion his Aunt handed him. It was a generous piece he noticed, cut from a slab that Megan had made that morning and Aunt Megan's bread pudding was something to behold. Aunt Megan wasn't really his aunt but for the last three years she had become more and more of an influence in his life, ever since his father and Uncle Bill had arrived home from the war. Uncle Bill wasn't his uncle either, it was the close relationship between him and Sam's father, that over the years had created a situation where to call him Uncle Bill seemed a natural thing to do and when he married Megan the blacksmith's sister, she became Sam's Aunt. They had married soon after the death of Michael Gill, three years ago.

As he ate, Sam for no reason thought of Michael Gill. He remembered him as an old man, a man of substance, a man who had been a big influence on his Aunt Megan's teenage years. He remembered him sitting on the very chair where he now sat at and eating from the same table that the crumbs from his bread pudding now fell on.

"And you, Sam, do you have heroes?" Sam looked up, his thoughts of Michael immediately forgotten by Megan's question.

"Heroes?" repeated Sam.

"Yes heroes, do you have any?" Megan said, as she laid a damp tea towel over the slab of bread pudding before carrying it to the pantry.

"I suppose I do," said Sam, quickly thinking of who his heroes were.

"And whom may they be?"

"Uncle Bill, and Michael Gill," Sam said without hesitation.

"Bill?" said Megan, "he's my hero too."

"Maybe," Sam replied, "but not for the same reason as he is mine."

"And Michael Gill?" Megan spoke sounding somewhat amused, "you hardly knew him."

"I do remember him," Sam said swallowing the last of his bread pudding. "I was ten when he died, and the stories you have told me about him since, make me think that he was someone special."

"He was," Megan answered recalling the memory of a man that had meant everything to her. Even now at the age of thirteen Sam knew how much his Aunt Megan missed Michael. He was her mentor, her father figure, and her guide in life.

Sam often called at Aunt Megan's home usually after school and sometimes at weekends and now as he walked to his own home he pondered on her question about heroes. Was it amiss of him not to have mentioned his own father in that regard? Of course, he loved his father and had the greatest admiration for him. Did he not go to war with his Uncle Bill and Jack and fight side by side with them, did he not watch out for them as best he could while they were away? As he was some years older than them the sense of responsibility was a burden he felt he could carry. Sam even had a feeling that his father was their hero, a man who they both looked up to, a man they could trust. The more he thought about his father the more Sam realized that he didn't know him that well. Even his mother told him that he wasn't the man that he used to be. Sam couldn't really talk about how he used to be as he couldn't remember a lot about him before he went away, and when he came back it was like starting all over again. He also didn't talk a lot, especially on the subject of the war, saying that it was a bad time for them all, even asking Sam not to mention it.

Sam did remember how he used to go shooting with his father but that didn't happen so often these days, so his father's shotgun hung above the fireplace rarely used. Preferring now to go ferreting or to catch rabbits with wire snares saying that there were ways to get rabbits other than shooting them.

Bill on the other hand did not mind talking about the war. If Sam asked questions about it, Bill would answer. Bill knew that questions would be asked, but for some reason he was more honest with his answers to Sam than with anyone else. He liked Sam, he liked him a lot, even telling him about the nightmares he had when he first arrived home and about walking the hills at night. But now he had less trouble sleeping, or so he said. Maybe that wasn't altogether true and even if he did wake up with the sweats, he didn't tell Sam, only his Aunt Megan would know the truth and she wasn't telling.

As for Michael Gill, Megan was right in saying that Sam hardly knew him, but what with the tales of his adventures and the kind of man that he was Sam could be excused into thinking that he knew him and knew him well.

Four months after Megan had posed the question regarding Sam's heroes Sam turned fourteen years of age. He left school and started work as an apprentice carpenter to the local undertaker. He was not an indentured apprentice as his employer wasn't sure he was able to keep Sam in full time employment. Continuity of work was the big problem, so the arrangement was that if there was no work Sam could be laid off, and if Sam wanted to leave, he could do so, or he could help the undertaker with general building work, until someone died and another coffin was needed.

Four years later Sam was still there and in those four years he had grown, not only in stature but in maturity. He had a gentle way about him, maybe his Aunt Megan's influence and the nature of his work had something to do with it. He would often think of those grieving families as they said their last goodbyes to a loved one who would depart this world in one of his coffins. Sam stood five feet ten in his socks, with a lean body that according to his father was in need of a few more pounds of meat wrapped around his bones before he could be called a man. Sometimes Jim would have to check himself when talking to his son, as it wasn't that many years ago when he had fought side by side with men of Sam's age, and the thought of it all was an obscenity that he prayed would never be repeated. Sam's thick black wavy hair and skin colour a shade darker than most, could cause people to mistake him for someone not of these parts, but he was of these parts and proud to be so.

It was on a Sunday morning in early January when Sam stood with his Uncle Bill on a hill. They leaned on a gate, casting their eyes on the valley below. The air was crisp and dry as Sam took deep breaths of the cold morning air. Thoughts of the previous day crossed his mind. The whole village had turned out to see Miss Mavis' fishtail coffin being lowered into the grave that Sam had dug the day before. It wasn't the first coffin he had made, but it was the most important one. He realized that when his coffin disappeared into the grave with Miss Mavis inside, people did not see the hours of work that went into the making of a coffin. The half inch oak boards would have been cut from selected trees. They would be clean grained, with few branch knots. The boards would then be laid down to dry for up to two years before being made into the shapes and sizes of coffins required. The fishtail and shoulder bends for the side boards were fashioned with the help of fires making it easier to get the desired shape. The use of putty mixed with cocoa powder to match the varying colour of the oak when filling in nail holes and fine shakes in the coffin boards. The sanding, oiling and polishing were the things people didn't see, but there amongst the bowed heads may well have been someone who knew a good coffin from a poor one, and Sam's coffins were as good as any.

During the four years that Sam had worked at the undertakers he had become a young man with plans, and those plans didn't include the surroundings that he was familiar with. He, like his Aunt Megan, was an avid reader. He read of far off lands, of people that lived a different life to his, people with different customs and with a diversity of living that sometimes baffled him. What with the stories Megan had told of Michael Gill and Miss Mavis telling of her experiences, including a few bawdy tales of living in the City of London, Sam was determined to go out into the world to see and do things that he would never see or do at home. The alternative was to live a life he didn't want, and he knew the kind of life that would eventually befall him if he stayed.

In the last six months of Sam's seventeenth year Megan had detected an uneasiness in Sam and it was at this time that he told of his wish to follow in Michael's footsteps and go to America. He told her that he had been thinking about it for a long time and had been saving money for the past two years. In those years Sam hadn't changed his mind, the yearning to travel just got stronger. His only concern was that he wouldn't have enough money for the voyage and to keep himself for a week or so until he got himself a job.

"I'm a coffin maker," he said to himself, "and people don't stop dying even in America. I'll always have something to bury."

Megan was distraught at Sam's wanting to go to America but not totally surprised, but she did feel responsible for this young man's wonder lust.

"Well, you have been filling his head with Michael's tales of adventure," Bill said with a laugh. He could sense the anxiety in Megan as she sat down.

"What will Violet and Jim say when they learn of his wanting to leave?"

"They already know, Megan my dear," Bill said as he placed a hand on her shoulder. "You are the last to know." Megan turned in her chair, eyes wide open. "He mentioned it to them some months ago and he didn't want to tell you as he knew you would blame yourself." Megan stood up tears filling her eyes.

"And you knew?" Megan asked. Bill felt the dejection in her voice.

"Yes, I knew, I didn't tell you in case he changed his mind. Violet told me that he had been hinting about going for the last twelve months."

"Why didn't she tell me? Maybe I could have put such thoughts out of his mind, they must be devastated," Megan said as she lowered her head.

"Violet didn't tell you as she had told Sam that he had to tell you himself and they are not devastated, in fact,

Jim is quite proud of him, he told Violet that at least he is not going to a bloody war."

"And you Bill, what do you think?"

"Me? I think Sam must do what Sam must do. We both think a lot of him and you know him better than most so enjoy his adventure Megan, be part of it. Now as it's a nice evening I suggest you take a walk and go and see Violet. Miss Mavis is getting the kids ready for bed, so you go and have a chat."

As Megan closed the door to her home and walked the few yards to the road she felt suddenly alone and as her footsteps passed the cemetery a sense of nostalgia passed over her. She stopped and looking over the stone wall of the graveyard she saw Michael Gill's headstone. She closed her eyes remembering the words written on it.

> **"Here lies Michael Barry Gill**
> **1841 – 1920**
> **Loved by all"**

That is all it said. There was no 'husband of', or 'father of anyone', just the words 'loved by all'.

"Not such a bad epitaph," Megan said to herself as she set off again down the steep hill road and into the village turning left at the pub and on to Violet and Jim's home.

As Violet opened her door and saw Megan, she immediately embraced her friend. Violet knew the reason for Megan's visit as Sam had told his mother that he had mentioned his wanting to go to America to Megan that morning.

"Now before you say a word Megan Jones," Violet said as she released Megan from her embrace, "I will not have you feeling any guilt for Sam wanting to go away. Come in and have a cup of tea."

Over the next hour Violet told Megan of her fears and expectations for her eldest son, Megan apologizing for her part in his decision to leave saying that if she had known what was going on in his head, she would have tried to dissuade him from making such a decision.

"Megan, you know Sam better than anyone, maybe better than me," Violet placed two cups of tea on the table and sat next to Megan, "but always keep in mind, to Sam you are his Aunt and his friend, to me he is my son and this is not a criticism of you. Goodness knows me and Jim see you as an Aunt from heaven so don't you Goddamn change."

As Violet spoke Megan looked at the china teacup she held, she noticed it had a little chip on the rim.

"How old are you Megan? Twenty nine?"

"And I'm nearly forty. Tell me, what will you say when your son, Michael Gill's namesake, my godson, comes to you when he's eighteen and tells you he's going away to climb Mount Everest or fly to the moon? Sooner or later we must let our children go and it seems my time has come to let one of mine go and there will come a time when your Michael will be gone. He may not go to the end of the earth but in one way or another he will go and when that time comes, I pray to God that he will have had the love and all that goes with that word. In fact, everything you have given our Sam and I thank you for that. Now," Violet continued, as she stood, "please don't think you are anyway responsible for him wanting to spread his wings. As Jim says, he is not going to fight in a bloody war as our men had to."

Megan stood, as they gave each other a hug. Violet half whispered in her ear, "We have him for another six months. Let's make the most of it."

Megan walked home with mixed feelings in her head and heart and as she again walked past the graveyard, she looked at the wall surrounding it and thought to herself, "Behind that wall there is another man, another man that I must let go of."

Bill, now standing with Sam scanned the valley below. It was a scene he knew well but one he never got tired of looking at. Sam was the first to speak.

"Life's not going to be the same with Miss Mavis gone," there was a despairing edge to Sam's voice as he spoke, "and Aunt Megan will miss her terribly. I don't know" Sam hesitated, "but she seems to have had a lot of bad luck in losing people she has loved."

As Sam spoke, Bill, who apart from the years of being away at war, that now seemed such a long time ago, had seen Sam grow into the confident and mature young man he now was. Sam's concern and respect for Bill's wife had always been evident. They were alike in many ways and what Bill saw in his wife he also saw in Sam. They both seemed on a level that, to a point, excluded others. It wasn't an intentional exclusion, it was just the way it was.

With Sam now speaking of Megan's bad luck in losing her loved ones, Bill thought that she was about to lose another. Maybe Megan was in some way responsible for the way Sam wanted to seek adventure. Could it be that they were all collectively responsible? Michael Gill, Miss Mavis, even his father, Jack, and Bill himself, as going to war in itself was an act of adventure.

"So, you'll be away on Wednesday?" Bill said, looking at Sam, "we will miss you." Sam turned, pushing his fingers through his dark windswept hair. "You will write," added Bill.

"Of course, I will," answered Sam, "I made a promise to my mother and Aunt Megan".

"Has Megan given you any money?" Bill muttered.

"Yes, she has, and Miss Mavis gave me ten pounds before she died, she was a kind lady."

"You talked about Megan being unlucky in losing people she loved. Well in some respects your Aunt Megan is a lucky lady."

"Lucky?" said Sam.

"Yes, you see, the people that Megan has loved and lost, loved her in return and the people she loves today also love her and the people in future years that she will love, will love her back. She's that kind of lady."

"Never thought of it like that," Sam said, smiling at his uncle.

"I will probably see you before you leave Sam, but if I don't, I would like to shake your hand and wish you well." Then again looking at his surroundings, he added "Your father and I over the years have walked these hills many times, so it is fitting that I walk them once more with his son before he goes away, and maybe, maybe we will walk them again on your return."

"I'd like that," said Sam.

2

A flurry of snow swirled under the platform roof of Princess Station, blown in by a persistent wind that hadn't relented since Sam's last change of train, mid-morning. Sam had travelled on three different trains since leaving Montgomery Station early that morning. The experience of encountering so many strangers on the trains and railway stations made him a little uneasy. Everyone seemed to be in a hurry, oblivious to the people around them. He made mental notes of some of the well-off stepping into and out of the first class carriages. Men wearing fedora hats, tailored suits and fashionable overcoats. He smiled to himself as he noticed their women folk wearing similar dresses that he had only seen Miss Mavis wear. In the second class carriages he was amongst his own, the working class, travelling on trains for purposes unknown to him.

He heard several languages being spoken and English, in accents ranging from Scottish where he could hardly understand a word that was spoken, to Geordies, whose accent brought a smile to his face. He picked up on other dialects spoken, but from where, he knew not. A fish out of water came to mind, as he pondered their way of life. They laughed, slept, ate sandwiches, and drank tea like himself, but in everything else it seemed, his life was probably far removed from theirs. For a moment he thought of his own accent. He was Welsh, and although he didn't speak the language, up until this moment hadn't really thought of himself as speaking any different, from anyone else. He was aware that people from North and South Wales spoke with a different accent. And people from Montgomeryshire, their accent was different again.

On the last leg of his journey to Liverpool several men, whom he presumed to be from the Orient, boarded the train. He wondered if they were sea farers and as they passed him in the corridor, they spoke in what he guessed to be Chinese, which he found amusing. They in turn were followed by a group of men that smelt of the sea. They were in working clothes wearing thick woolen jumpers, corduroy trousers, and cloth caps, looking every bit like the gangs of Irish navies that sometimes worked on the railway lines at home. But these men were not Irish as they spoke with Liverpool accents. Sam wondered if these men were Dockers.

Several times he had heard people speak of the *Laconia* and each time he would look to see who had mentioned the name of ship that he was to board the following day. The last was a man seated by the open door of a carriage he shared with other passengers. Sam, standing in the corridor opposite, noticed that seated by the gentleman was a lady upon whose knee sat a little girl. The child, maybe six years of age had curly blond hair with a black ribbon threaded through it. Turning his gaze to the man, Sam noticed he was drumming his fingers on his knee, a nervous habit thought Sam. He would be in his thirties, well dressed in a black leather trench coat with a deep fur collar, the trilby, also black, he wore on a slight angle. That along with a pencil moustache, made him look like the film stars he had seen at the Scala picture house, Newtown. His wife, a good looking woman, wore a coat not unlike her husbands, but with the addition of fur around the cuffs and hem. She sat upright, looking elegant and demure, yes, he thought, together they looked like they had just walked off a film set. The little girl was looking at Sam and when she caught his eye, she immediately slid off her mothers' lap and stood by the doorway where her father was sitting. With her hands on her father's knee, she looked at Sam and with a smile said "Hello." Sam looking into eyes that could melt the moon smiled back and acknowledged her hello with one of his own.

"Hello little girl and what is your name?"

For the remaining forty minutes of the journey Sam's time was spent in the company of Joe Fleming, his wife Pageant and daughter Billie. Sam occupied an empty seat opposite them when an elderly woman rose and waddled up the corridor brushing past Sam as she went. From the start he felt at ease in Joe's company. He had a warm and comforting voice. Sam guessed them to be in a financially comfortable position but this did not come through in their conversation. As it turned out the Flemings were like

Sam, emigrating to America, but unlike Sam they were to be expected, awaiting them was accommodation, a job and all that goes with it.

Joe had connections in New York through his job as a newspaper reporter. He had worked for the Birmingham Echo when through a friend of a friend a position to work for the New York Times came his way and throwing caution to the wind he took it. Sam queried Joe's ability to get a position of reporting for this newspaper, asking why they would want a reporter from the Birmingham Echo when surely one could be found from within the company. Joe smiled.

"I am good at my job Sam and I have connections. Suffice to say they were not looking for anyone else."

"And you Sam?" Joe still drumming his fingers on his knee, "what do you do for a living?" Sam unsure of how to answer Joe's question without his job sounding boring said the first thing that came into his head.

"My work," Sam said with conviction, "is to fulfill the final needs of people".

Joe looked at Sam with a curious frown.

"Let me think," he said with a smile, "you look far too young to be in the legal profession," then hesitating added "are the people you deal with elderly?"

"Not necessary," said Sam, a smile spreading across his face.

"I'm intrigued," laughed Joe, "go on, tell me what do you do for a living?"

"I make coffins," said Sam still smiling.

"You make coffins?" Joe echoed, putting an emphasis on the word coffins as he spoke.

"Yes," said Sam with a shrug, "it's not a big thing making coffins."

"I beg to differ," Joe answered looking at his wife who was smiling having overheard the conversation. "I mean, a coffin will be the last resting place for all of us. And by the way, may I say that the definition you gave of your work, to fulfill the final needs of people, is a sobering statement. With your permission I would like to use it sometime."

"Feel free," said Sam, "I didn't think it meant anything more than what it was."

"It has connotations," said Joe. Sam was thinking of the word connotations when the train's whistle sounded. Sam looked out of the window as the train slowed down. There was an air of expectancy in the carriage, as rows and rows of houses passed by. He had never seen so many in his life. From his seat he could see two church spires, numerous large buildings and the rooftops of more houses being interrupted by more tall buildings. Large areas of land that ran alongside the railway line slipped past, where hundreds of sleepers were stacked. Then there were piles of coal and hills of granite ballast. Endless passenger and freight carriages, some being shunted, by trains into sidings, made it all a sight to take in. The train stopped and people were getting up from their seats. Carriage doors were opened as people stepped out onto a cold uninviting platform. Feet of all sizes were heading for the station's exits and once clear of these, questions were asked about the whereabouts of hotels, boarding houses and rooms that could be let for the night. A lot of people like Joe had already booked rooms and a lot, like Sam, had not. Having collected his suitcases from a carriage intended for the purpose of storing baggage, Sam made his way to Princess Dock, a short walk from the station. There he found the booking office for the Cunard Shipping Company and along with other passengers that would board the ship, he stood in a queue and waited his turn to be booked in.

On presenting his ticket and other relevant documents including his passport he was given a cabin number and was informed that he would be sharing a cabin with three other men. He was told to report for boarding at any time after eleven am the following day, as the *Laconia* would be sailing at four thirty in the afternoon. He had left one of his suitcases with the shipping line to be placed in the hold of the ship, the other containing clothes and personal effects that he would be needing, he would carry with him.

Sam spent the night in a room above a bar in a public house called The Admiral Rodney. He had walked the wet cobbled street that led away from the booking office and at the end of it, at a junction to his left, an inn, he looked up. He smiled to himself when he saw the sign. It hung on an elaborate wrought iron frame bolted to the brickwork above the door. It swung, creaking loudly in the sleet squalls that were now becoming more frequent. For a moment Sam looked at the imposing figure of Admiral Rodney all decked out in his naval uniform. Admiral

Rodney was someone Sam knew something of, and a pub near Liverpool docks named after him came as a surprise. Admiral Rodney was a British naval officer instrumental in numerous escapades on the high seas. Being an Admiral of the white, a senior rank in the Royal Navy, he had commands in the American War of Independence and was victorious over the French in the Battle of the Saintes. On Breiddon Hill some twelve miles from Sam's home, stands a monument to Admiral Rodney, having been erected by the gentlemen of Montgomeryshire who supplied Welsh oak for the building of British Navy ships.

"So that's what he looked like," he glanced at his watch before entering, a quarter past four. It would be dark in half an hour. When Sam closed the door he was greeted by the warmth of the room and a big smile from the barman who was pulling a pint.

"And what can I do for you young man?" he said as he placed the drink alongside two other pints of porter already on the bar. Three men dressed in oil skins and sou'wester hats standing at the bar picked them up and walked over to a table situated by an open fire.

"I was wondering if you had a room I could rent for the night?" asked Sam with a tinge of hope in his voice.

"Well, I do have one," he said as he threw a tea towel over his shoulder, then adding, "it's one that nobody wants." As he spoke, he looked up, Sam followed his gaze.

"You have one above the bar?"

"Nothing wrong with the room, but it can get a bit noisy sometimes."

"I'll take it," said Sam without hesitation.

"Hang on a minute," said the barman raising his bushy eyebrows, "I haven't told you how much it is and you haven't even seen it yet."

"Do I really need to see it?" asked Sam with a smile, "as this is a respected establishment, I don't think you would over charge me."

"Respected establishment, whoever told you that?" the barman laughed as he spoke. Then turning to the men seated at the table by the fire, and still laughing, told them that as The Admiral Rodney was now a respected establishment, there was to be no more cursing, farting or fighting and that all drunken persons would be forcibly removed from the premises. With that the men burst out laughing, with one asking George, the barman, if the new rules applied to them. The banter went on as George led Sam upstairs, opening the door to the room he was to spend the night. George asked Sam if he had eaten and if he was hungry he would get him something and to come down to the bar once he had settled in.

Sam looked around the room. It was sparsely furnished with a wardrobe, a rocking chair, and a small bedside table on which stood an oil lamp and a box of matches. He had placed his suitcase on a threadbare rug that covered most of the floor. He gazed at the pictures that hung on the wallpapered walls. There were four of them, one on each wall, all of which showed scenes of tall ships in full sail. A single bed placed in the corner of the room was an iron bedstead much like the one he slept on at home, except that this one had four brass knobs, one on each corner of the bed's frame. He sat on the bed, the candlewick bedspread sank beneath him. It was comfortable enough he thought, as peals of laughter from the bar below came through the floor and into the room. He distinctly heard a voice asking how such a respected establishment could serve such shit beer, this being followed by a roar of approval. In any event his comment must have inspired the locals to question the suitability of such a place to slake their thirst.

Sam found the bathroom, ran some cold water into a sink and washed his face. After using a towel that hung on a hook behind the bathroom door, he replaced it and closed the door behind him. In his bedroom Sam lit the oil lamp. An orange glow filled the room as he lay on the bed, making sure his boots hung over the edge to not dirty the bedspread. His mind was on the day's events and the thought of not seeing his family again for many years brought him close to tears. It was surreal, he thought, lying on a strange bed in a strange room in unfamiliar surroundings. He closed his eyes and listened. He could clearly hear the goings on in the room below, the cussing was loud but unthreatening. It crossed his mind that he didn't have to board the ship the following day, he could just as easily catch a train and go back home to carry on with the life he knew, as opposed to a life of uncertainty and the unknown that awaited him. The thought of going home was a fleeting one, and his thoughts now turned to his being where he was. Had he lived his life with the subconscious thought that he was preparing himself for the moment he was to step foot on the gang planks of the Laconia? If it was, then to that end he must do what he must do.

Sam lay on his bed for half an hour before opening the door of his room and from the landing descended the stairs. At the bottom stood George the landlord with a tray in his hands.

"Just thought you may like some beef broth," he said with a smile. He turned and placed the tray on the kitchen table. There were shouts for service, coming from the bar, as George, with a little laugh said, "You've bloody well started something in there Sam, considering this was known as one of the roughest pubs in the area. You come along and upgrade our standing without consulting the clientele. When you have finished that, come on in and meet the boys."

"Will it be safe?"

"You won't have to worry about that," replied George, "these boys think you're a bloody hero."

With some bread and butter, Sam ate his beef broth with relish. Then, taking a deep breath, he stepped through a curtained doorway and stood beside George at the pumps, the bar separating them from the pub's customers, whose numbers had increased somewhat since he had left the bar to go to his room.

George introduced Sam to his locals as a young man who may have been a little hasty in his remarks regarding The Admiral Rodney as being a respectable establishment.

There seemed to be a jovial atmosphere in the room, as Sam, with a little apprehension and a big smile, apologized to anyone that may have been offended by his comments. A rough looking individual standing at the bar was the first to speak.

"No Sam, I think you've got it right, there isn't a soul in this room that doesn't respect this place for what it is."

"And what is it?" asked Sam.

"It's a shit hole," answered the man. George's customers howled their approval. "But," said the man raising his voice and his hand at the same time, "it's the best shit hole this side of the Liver Birds." Again, the pub was in uproar, with men raising their glasses to drink a toast to the popularity of The Admiral Rodney. "Give this man a drink George," he said, pointing his finger at Sam, "Fred will pay for it." Sam glanced at Fred standing beside the man who suggested he buy a drink for him. He was a big man, probably in his forties, having cauliflower ears, a bent nose and two missing teeth, looking like he had just gone ten rounds with Jack Dempsey.

The door to The Rodney, as the locals called it, opened and closed many times during the evening. Once, while Sam was measuring up Laurel and Hardy for coffins, Sam had them lying down on the floor side by side and was on his knees with a tape measure when in walked George's wife Mary and daughter Grace, both carrying shopping bags. Mary stopped and for a second, thinking that a fight had taken place, not an unusual occurrence at the Rodney, then soon realizing that there hadn't been a fight, she smiled. Grace walked straight past, her stern face reflecting that fighting in her parent's public house was something she disapproved of, even, when on discovering that there hadn't been a fight her attitude to grown men behaving in a manner as they do when drunk, was none the less unacceptable to her.

The Laurel and Hardy incident happened when Sam came from behind the bar and as rough as they were, he found George's customers friendly and humorous. Unsurprisingly they were all dockworkers working different shifts, some having a few beers before going to work, some a few beers after work and others would be there until closing time. Fred and his mate being amongst the latter. They all pretty much guessed that Sam would be boarding the Laconia the following day and wanted to know all about him, as it was rare that any discerning person would come anywhere near The Admiral Rodney let alone be welcomed as Sam was. Not that Sam was a discerning person, he was just a naïve young man finding his way in an unfamiliar world. Knowing that he was Welsh he was asked to give the boys a song. He said he couldn't sing, then someone asked if he was a fighting man, to which he answered that he didn't fight, but he made friends with men who did. Then a man on unsteady legs sided up to him and after snorting some snuff from the back of his hand said, "If you don't sing and you don't fight what do you do?"

"I make coffins sir," replied Sam. Once again everyone rolled about with laughter. Sam couldn't understand what was so funny about his making coffins for a living, he wasn't offended just bewildered. Then from nowhere he was handed a tape measure and asked to measure up Tim Smith, an old man that was slumped over a table in the far corner of the room, as they all doubted he would make it till morning.

It was at this point, when in front of him stood Laurel and Hardy, not their real names of course, in fact they looked nothing like the men on the silent screen. The only thing in common with both was that one was taller than the other. Sam was then asked if he could cost the price of a coffin for each of them.

All the time this was going on the beer flowed, mostly down the throats of the men gathered and sometimes onto the floor. Sam, having drank more than maybe he should have, directed the men to take off their boots and lie on the floor. There was encouragement coming from all sides as the men, without too much persuading, proceeded to do Sam's bidding and as they were in working clothes it mattered none in getting them a little dirtier. It was then, when Sam was on his knees doing the business that Mary and her daughter walked in. Sam noticed the look on Grace's face as she walked past, but he carried on measuring the men, something he had done many times, before but not on people that were still breathing!

"Hardy is six feet four inches," said Sam.

"And Laurel?" shouted someone.

"Well, he's five foot one inch."

The shorter man got up protesting that he was taller than Sam had suggested he was. With all three men now standing, Sam looked at both men, then walked around them sizing them up.

"Well," said Fred, "and how much is it going to cost us to put these two in the ground?" Sam now stood in front of both men looking them up and down for the last time. There was, for the first time that night silence, as Sam pointed to the taller of the two.

"A coffin for this one will cost," Sam paused, "will cost...." he paused again, "will cost twice as much as a coffin for this one," he said pointing to the short man. Once more the pub erupted with the sound of laughter. After the laughter had died down, Mary, who had been standing behind the bar with George, disappeared behind the curtain, only to return a minute later carrying a roasting dish. Placing it on the bar she removed a tea towel covering its contents, then, with the smell of roast rabbit drifting through the room, men started to form a queue. Grace followed her mother holding a large wooden cutting board and placed it alongside the dish. Mary, with a meat fork in her hand, lifted the first of the three rabbits onto it. She then, with no airs and graces started to rip it apart. Table manners went out of the window as men with dirty hands grabbed pieces then moved away to let others in. The rabbits were gone in minutes, it was a frenzy, akin to feeding time at a zoo. Sam stood back and watched in amazement. On looking up he saw Mary beckon him and as he got to the bar, she lifted the hatch and let him through.

Unbeknownst to Sam, George had been telling Mary about the young man who had sought a room for the night. He told her that Sam would be boarding the *Laconia* and would be sailing to New York the following afternoon.

The room above the bar had in recent weeks been the subject of some controversy within the family, ever since a local man, who with the approval of Grace, had been allowed to stay the night. Grace, whose room was next door, awoke during the night to find him sitting on her bed. She called her father and together they took him back to his room. He was an elderly gentleman with no harmful intentions, but the question of Grace's safety was paramount as the room above the bar was sometimes used by the waifs and strays that would end up at The Rodney.

Grace had lived with her parents at The Admiral Rodney for nine years. Her mother had lost both her brothers at the Battle of Passchendaele. Soon after being informed of their deaths Mary vowed that she would dedicate her life, as best she could to help, in whatever way, the men that would be coming home from the war. George, an ex-Docker himself, stood by her. They borrowed from friends and family and bought The Admiral Rodney. They were warned by many that beer and returning soldiers was not a good mix but Mary would not be dissuaded, saying that the needs of these people were unlike the needs of men who had not seen and done the things that these men had. If it was to mean that these men could have a drink or even get drunk in the company of their fellow soldiers they could do so in an environment that was safe and uncondemning.

In those nine years they had raised money and sought the help of big business to convert unused buildings into food kitchens, and to provide beds for the homeless. Many times they were condemned for taking money from returning soldiers who drank at their pub, in effect making a profit from the vulnerable. This accusation was vigorously denied by George, saying that profits after expenses were given back to their customers in many ways. Even the police approved of the way they ran their business. They held letters from the magistrate's courts praising their concern for the veterans of the war. Often, they went to court to defend the innocence of some of their customers, after being accused of stealing, causing an affray and other misdemeanors. Sometimes they won, sometimes they lost, nonetheless in those nine years their name had become respected by most.

Sam sat at the kitchen table. On a plate in front of him was a rabbit leg and some roast potatoes. He looked up, and Grace smiled as she handed him the saltshaker. He smiled back and shrugged in an apologetic manner.

"I'm sorry," he said looking down at the rabbit leg.

"Sorry for what?" she answered in almost a whisper.

"For the way I acted in the bar, I saw the look on your face when you walked in."

"Sam," she said, as she pulled out a chair from under the table and sat opposite him, "you are a stranger to me as I am to you and I have seen far worse behaviour in that bar than someone fooling around on the floor. Eat your food Sam it's getting cold."

Sam looked at his food and stuck his fork into a roast potato. As he ate Grace carried on, "At first I did think there had been a fight and was relieved when I heard laughter come through the curtain. When I pulled the curtain aside and saw a tall young man with a grin that would make anyone smile, I smiled too," she raised her eyebrows "as you may have gathered by now this pub is not like others, all our customers, well most of them, have a low standard of education having left school at fourteen and some before that, with most working on the docks like their fathers before them. Scoundrels, vagabonds, thieves and liars come through that door Sam, along with sailors, stevedores, crane drivers and everyone in-between."

Sam looked up. Grace seemed to be looking through him and he noticed how strikingly beautiful she was. He lowered his eyes then placed his knife and fork together on an empty plate.

"So, your door is open to anyone?" said Sam, looking Grace in the eyes.

"No," she said with a chuckle, "we do have standards. We have no harlots coming in and anyone that offends my mother."

Sam stood as Mary slid back the curtain and entered the kitchen, carrying the roasting pan that had held the rabbits.

"Is there anything I can do to help, Mrs. Holloway?" Sam asked as he stood aside letting her pass.

"Well, if you're asking, you can wash this pan for me." she placed the pan in a large sink.

"Not a problem Mrs. Holloway."

Mary stood back and looked at Sam, "And how do you know our surname is Holloway."

"It's on a little plaque above the door, advertising that you are licensed to sell alcohol. Mind you, it didn't say anything about you serving roast rabbit. I suppose it's in the small print." he said as he rolled up his sleeves.

"Very observant of you Sam."

"Not really, it was there so I read it."

"Grace, pour some hot water in the sink for Sam, I'll start collecting glasses in the bar, we will be closed in fifteen minutes." As she got to the curtain she stopped and turning asked how much beer he had drunk.

"Not enough," answered Sam with a grin, "I have declined a lot more than I have drunk."

"I suspected as much," she said as she joined George behind the bar. Sam stayed at the sink, not leaving it until the last glass stood on the draining board. Grace stood by his side drying everything he had washed, changing when needed a wet tea towel for a dry one. Standing side by side at the sink with Sam, reminded Grace of her own parents, when her mother would put bubbles on her father's nose and he in return would playfully grab her bum only to be repulsed by the flick of a tea towel. She would of course be shocked if Sam would do such a thing, after all he was a total stranger. Grace felt comfortable in Sam's company, he had a polite manner, interesting to talk to and not pretentious in any way.

"Well, that's another Friday night over with," said George sounding relieved. He placed the bar till on the table, "Don't worry about counting up tonight Grace, I'll do it in the morning."

"That's alright dad, I'll do it before going to bed."

Mary brought over four mugs of tea, and laid them on the table, on each one was a coloured print with a nautical theme, a ship's wheel, anchors, sailor's rope knots and the like.

"Yours has crossed harpoons on it, Sam, help yourself to sugar and milk." For the next half hour, they sat and discussed the night's events, Sam looking a little sheepish a little on the mention of Laurel and Hardy.

"I'm not normally like that," said Sam as he lifted his mug and drank the last of his tea.

"You were very entertaining, I wish every Friday night was fight free."

"You don't have fights every Friday night, do you?" asked Sam looking at George.

"No not every Friday night," quips Mary, "Sometimes it's a Saturday night." They all laughed and as they did George rose from his seat and reached for a candle, one of many that were on a shelf that ran along the wall adjacent to the door leading to the stairs.

"I'll be bloody glad when we have electric lights, it will save a lot of bother, I'm off to bed."

"Me too," said Mary, "we'll leave you two, it isn't often Grace has someone her own age staying the night." They both bade Sam and Grace goodnight and climbed the stairs.

For two hours Sam and Grace talked of their families, of their hopes and dreams. Sam spoke of his anxiety about his decision to go to America. Grace listened, saying, that she was a little envious of him, saying, that every time a ship sailed out of the harbour she would wonder…

"Wonder what?" asked Sam as Grace delved into the till her father had placed on the table, scooping out coins and stacking them in bundles.

"Oh, I don't know," she said, "wondering if I will ever do something as brave as to leave home." From out of the till Grace brought a little book and jotted down the night's takings before placing it back in its little drawer. Grace told him that she worked in an accountant's office three streets away saying that when they moved into the pub, she would every night count the takings and log them in a book like she had that night. Over the years her ability to present the pubs accounts to their accountant for tax purposes was acceptable, even to the point of being better at it than her father. Sam listened intently as Grace spoke, he had never really been in the company of a young woman before and not in a situation like this. There was something about her that made him feel, that at this moment, he needed her company as much as she needed his. He stayed silent as she sat opposite him clasping the empty mug, the one with the ship's anchors on it.

"I love my parents dearly Sam and my mother is the soul of discretion, her work for the returned servicemen leaves me in awe sometimes, but the war is over Sam and has been for some time, she can't save them all. I know for some the war will never be over, but I'm getting tired of all this." Sam looked up, Grace's hands had left her mug and she held them out, palms face down on the table. "This Sam, I want more than this. I am not ungrateful, I have a lot more than most of my age, I am an only child, and my mother had two miscarriages before I came along so I am not unaware of what I have." Grace fell silent holding again the mug in front of her then speaking softly, her voice breaking in places and with tears in her eyes. "My father is a hardworking man, an ex-dockworker. I have lived amongst dock workers most of my life and if I ever saw one again it would be too soon."

Sam had not expected this! Grace's outpouring of dissatisfaction with her life made him feel uncomfortable. Why would she be telling him of her unhappiness, a few hours ago neither knew of each other's existence and yet there must have been something in him that made her say the things she was saying?

"Say something Sam," she whispered. He reached across the table and praised her fingers free of the mug she held.

"My Aunt Megan," he said struggling for words, "Once told me that time was a precious thing, in fact she told me many things, but time was here and now and you cannot go back and change things. We are the same age

Grace and have lived very different lives, but there is one thing that is the same for all of us and that is our destiny. Our parents, friends and surroundings can shape our lives but our destiny is ultimately in our own hands. These words are not my words Grace, I am only relaying to you what my Aunt Megan has told me and sometimes I find it hard to understand the meaning of what she says, but she did tell me that in time I will. In any case, I have not lived long enough to be that smart. I don't know if your parents know of how you feel, I expect they don't and I think that maybe I am the first person that you have confided your worries to. If so, I ask myself why, why me?"

Grace shifted in her seat, she looked up and pursing her lips, spoke with a little more assertiveness.

"I'm sorry that I have involved you in my problems, I have no right to, but as you and I have little in common except our age, and that after tomorrow we will never meet again, I thought that you would not judge me."

"Judge you! Whatever made you think I would judge you, or even have the right to? It seems to me Grace that we are both finding our way and what we have in abundance is time and we must be careful how we use it but use it we will."

"Another quote from your Aunt Megan?" Grace said smiling broadly. Soon after they rose from their seats, Sam picked up the two empty mugs and placed them in the sink. Grace lifted the Tilley lamp off the table and held it up as Sam opened the door at the foot of the stairs. On the landing he turned and looked at Grace. She didn't move, the soft light from the lamp lit up one side of her face. He reached up and brushed her auburn hair away from her shoulder, for a moment they just stood facing each other. There were clouds at Grace's feet as Sam reached and took her in his arms, he bent his head, whispered "Goodnight" and kissed her cheek. Grace with one arm around Sam whispered the same.

"Goodnight Sam and thank you."

"There's nothing to thank me for Grace,"

"You will never know," Sam kissed the top of her head, turned and taking the candle that George had left on the shelf on the landing, opened the door to his bedroom and walked in. Grace stood and looked at the door then turned and walked the four steps to her bedroom, she slowly closed the door to her room. On pushing the door closed she watched the flat bar of the latch rise and drop making a click sound, she then looked at the bolt on the door, it had been placed there by her father after the incident of the intruder in her room. Her father had told her that whenever there was a man staying in the guest room, she must bolt the door. As she looked at it, she smiled. Sam would never come into her room she thought, Sam was too much of a bloody gent.

3

That night they both went to sleep with the same thought on their mind, what might have happened if Sam were to stay? The following morning he found everyone in the bar cleaning up.

"Mind where you walk," said Mary, "there's some glass on the floor,"

Sam looked in the direction Mary was pointing.

"Is there anything I can do?" Sam enquired.

"No thanks Sam, we're about finished, well I am." George joked. Sam looked over to where Grace was mopping up an area of floor where some beer had been spilt.

"Go and make Sam some breakfast Grace." Mary said, as she gestured for Grace to give her the mop. Grace looked up and smiled.

"Did you sleep well Sam?" she asked.

"Very well," lied Sam, "by the look of it it's going to be a nice day."

"Come into the kitchen Sam," said Grace, "I'll make you some bacon and egg." Sam followed her and sat down at the table. Nothing was said about the night before and as Sam ate his food Grace talked as though nothing had happened. At eleven o'clock, Sam brought down his suitcase and asked George how much he was in his debt. George looked at Mary and Grace, they smiled, and when George told him that he owed them nothing, Sam with his hand already in his pocket refused George's generosity saying that he would not leave until he had paid his dues.

"Sam it isn't often we have people like you in our home."

"Like me!" said Sam, "there is nothing about me that warrants you not charging me for board and lodgings. If I leave here without paying, I will feel guilty."

"I tell you what I'll do Sam, when you come back from America after making your fortune, I would like you to call on us and that's when we will settle up." Sam shook his hand.

"I don't know what to say, except thank you and if or when I return, you can rest assured that I will repay your hospitality." Mary handed Sam his suitcase, gave him a little hug and wished him well, saying that they had enjoyed his company.

"I'll get my coat," said Grace as she went into the bar taking it off the coat stand that the customers used. The coat she wore was much like the one the lady on the train wore and when she stood in front of Sam, he wanted to remember the image of her, her height, her slim figure, the colour of her hair and her smile.

"Are you going to walk with me to the docks?" Sam said with a lump in his throat.

"How could I not?" she answered with a smile, a smile that lifted Sam. Mary noticed the look on her daughter's face, was this the little girl that would run around the bar taking sweets off men that would bring them in especially for her, the little girl that wanted to marry a Prince? Mary looked at them both, was this her Prince she thought?

"Are you ready?" Sam asked.

"After you Sir," Sam stood at the bar and said his last goodbye to Mary and George. As they looked at the closed door, a tear ran down Mary's face, George looked at her.

"And what's the matter with you?"

"Good God George, are you blind, can't you see what has just happened here?" George never answered, he just shrugged and followed his wife into the kitchen where Mary started to wash the breakfast dishes for the second time.

Outside they had walked but a few yards when Sam stopped and turned, he glanced up, Admiral Rodney was still there looking down on them, as he looked down on everyone that happened to pass.

"Would you mind if I hold your hand, Grace?" she didn't answer, she just slipped her hand into his and as they walked Grace wanted to keep walking, down this road and then another and another, she didn't want him to go, never mind catching a boat that would take him God knows where. At the gate that Sam was to go through they stopped and faced each other. Grace's heart was breaking as she held him.

"Goodbye Sam," she said, as tears ran unashamedly down her face.

"Goodbye Grace," he whispered into her ear, "and I hope you find whatever you are looking for." Grace's mind was numb as they broke apart. She watched him, along with the dozens of other people, walk through the gate and out of her life. She watched him disappear amongst the throng of heads that were all going where he was going. Grace turned; she didn't want to go home, so she walked to the end of the street and then walked another then another. It was two hours later when she walked through the door of The Admiral Rodney, her mother was in the bar waiting for her. As they hugged each other, and through their sobs, she told her mother that she would never forget Sam.

"I know Grace, I know." Mary said as she held her daughter, stroking her hair as she spoke.

"Good God, she's only just met the lad." George said coming into the bar. Mary raised her head from Grace's shoulder and looked at him with disgust.

"Go and chop some bloody sticks or something." George disappeared,

"Now Grace," Mary said, holding her at arm's length, "I want you to go to your room and have a good cry. I understand even if your father doesn't." Grace ran up the stairs and into her room, she threw herself onto her bed not even taking her coat off. I hope you find what you're looking for, were Sam's last words to her. "I had found what I was looking for Sam," she said out loud, and inside Grace was screaming her answer, "I had found and lost it, everything, everything in less than twenty four hours."

"Excuse me." Sam heard someone say as he stood still amongst the crowd of people all moving toward what could only be described as a mustering point, being directed by a man in a yellow coat. His mind was a blur of thoughts and emotions, his thoughts were of Grace and his emotions were the result of knowing her. He shuffled forward trying to focus his mind on what was happening around him.

"Sam, Sam, come here." an anguished voice called out. Sam stood frozen, as a little boy pushed past him followed by a lady who had called his name. In silence he moved forward oblivious to the excitement around him, all he wanted was to be alone with his thoughts.

"This way, this way." The man in the yellow coat kept saying. They were directed into an enclosure then filed into a customs building. From there, up several steps onto a large landing, and at one end of this was a set of double doors which led to a gantry that led from shore to ship. In two lanes people traversed this gantry some stopping to look over the railings. Stopping for a moment Sam did the same, shifting his shoulder bag onto his other shoulder, he glanced over the side. Many feet below, the wharf was busy with men loading stores into the side of the *Laconia*. He noticed the water lapping the side of the ship and the harbour wall. Thick ropes crisscrossed from the ship to steel mooring bollards on the wharf, preventing the ship from drifting.

Sam entered the ship through the Purser's office, where he was given a key to Cabin 316. He was informed that he would be sharing with three other gentlemen and would be allocated a table at meal-times, first sitting. Opposite the desk in the Purser's office was a staircase. Three decks down and along numerous corridors, passing suitcases left outside passengers' doors, he found Cabin number 316. The door was ajar and on entering was met by a lad who had entered minutes before. His hand reached out.

"Hi, my name is Edward and it looks like you will be one of my travelling companions."

Sam introduced himself.

"I thought I would come early, as I could pick my bed. I'll take this bottom bunk," said Edward, placing his suitcase on the one he had chosen. "Have that one," he gestured with his hand to the bottom bunk opposite. "Whoever comes in now will have to take the top bunks."

"That sounds reasonable," said Sam as he threw his suitcase on the bottom bunk. They talked for half an hour or so, then Sam suggested they explore the ship before four o'clock. Throughout the ship they walked and talked, going from one deck to another, poking their heads through the doorways of libraries, rest rooms, lounges, dining rooms and everywhere where they, as second class passengers, could go. The top deck was reserved for first class passengers. But there were plenty of places they could go, as to stay in his cabin for days on end would drive him crazy. They were on the lower deck when the ship's siren blew. People were milling around looking for places to stand on the wharf side of the ship, to wave at the people who were gathered below.

For half an hour Grace lay on her bed staring at the ceiling, she felt a little embarrassed about her feelings getting the better of her and realized that the young man she had walked to the dock with was on the verge of a new life. For him she was a distraction that he could do without. She got up and washed her face. Still with her coat on she decided that she would go back and see him off. Her mother was in the kitchen. She hugged her and told her of her intentions saying how silly she felt.

"Silly," said her mother, "I fell in love with your father the first time I laid eyes on him. It happens sometimes. I'll get my coat and come with you, although the chances of seeing him amongst all those people are pretty slim." George was in the bar. Mary told him that she was going with Grace to the dock.

"You'll never see him," said George as he kissed his daughter, "but you will never know unless you go," he added, as he patted her backside. They got to the dock as the ship's siren sounded. Hundreds of people had gathered, some with banners with the names of those that were sailing.

"He'll never see us," said Grace.

"Come with me." Mary grabbed Grace's hand and led her to the far side of the dock where there were fewer people. All the time straining their eyes, looking along the ship's railings. On the decks the passengers had lined up, some with banners of their own. The ship's siren sounded again, as the heavy ropes were slipped from their bollards crashing into the sea where they were winched aboard the *Laconia's* decks. Slowly she started to drift clear of the harbour walls. Grace started shouting Sam's name and waving, her mother following suit. They couldn't see him. Then Mary glanced at the people at the rear of the ship.

"There he is," she shouted, pointing to where Sam was standing. Grace couldn't contain herself, she was screaming his name and ran as far as she could along the quay with her mother by her side. Then they saw him look their way and to their amazement he started to wave back, he had seen them. There was someone with him and he started, like Sam, to wave in their direction. Grace and Mary didn't know that he was also waving at them, to people that knew someone that he had just met.

All the time this was going on, the Laconia was moving further away, being pulled by the tugboats that would take it to a point where the ship, under its own power, would take it across the Atlantic Ocean. They stood for some time watching the ship drift further away. People were starting to walk away, some with handkerchiefs drying eyes that had shed tears for loved ones that they may never see again.

"Do you think we will ever see him again Mum?" Grace said.

"I have a funny feeling about that," answered Mary, "he said that if he was ever to come back, he would settle his debt. I have no reason to disbelieve him."

It would be impossible to find her, even if she were to come down to see him off thought Sam and why should she, all he had done was spend a night in a room at a pub. He had met a girl who he liked and who he guessed liked him. She had seen him to a ship that would take him where he wanted to go and that was it. But it wasn't like that. Up until the moment she started to cry, Sam thought that his relationship, if you could even call it that, was one of meeting a friend he didn't know. But now with his hands clutching the ship's railings, he searched the crowd in front of him wanting to see her for the last time. He saw the ropes fall into the water and felt the ship slowly move, but Grace was nowhere to be seen. He didn't tell Edward of the possibility that an attractive young lady might be there to see him off, as in all probability she wouldn't be. As the excitement built up, they walked to the rear of the ship, away from where it seemed the entire ship's passengers had gathered. There were less people where they now stood and as he looked again at the crowds below, he noticed two women running clear of them and as they did, he saw them waving in his direction. Immediately he raised his arms. It was Grace and her mother, they had seen him. He heard them call but their words were lost amongst the calls of others.

"Who are you waving to Sam?" shouted Edward, "I thought there was no one to see you leave."

"There," said Sam, pointing to Grace and Mary who were now standing by the last bollard on the wharf. "Wave to them Edward, wave to them. It's the people I stayed with last night, they have come to see me leave." Sam waved and waved until the Laconia turned and gradually Grace and her mother disappeared from view behind a lifeboat that was hung ready to be deployed in case it was needed.

"You're a dark horse," said Edward, "only been away from home one night and already chasing a bit of skirt, a pub landlord's daughter at that."

"It wasn't like that Edward, listen would you mind if I were to call you Eddie. It seems less posh and it suits your face."

"I don't mind," said Edward, "all my mates at home call me Eddie and some call me other things, but we won't go into that." Sam then told him about meeting Grace at the pub where he spent the night, then wishing he hadn't mentioned her and the attraction he felt for her, but it was already in the past. However the experience did emphasize the fact that there were girls in this world, a fact he really hadn't paid much attention to, at least not up until then.

When they arrived back to their cabin, they were greeted by the sound of the raised voices of their fellow travelling companions. When they entered, they were met by two men, both of whom smiled and held out their hands in friendship.

"My name is Martin and this is my son Colin. We have placed our suitcases in the rack and are now going dockside for a drink." With that they left and closed the door behind them.

"What was all that about," said Eddie, raising his eyebrows.

"I have no idea," said Sam, "but I hope they work out their differences before they come back."

On the first day at sea the rain came. Sam slept soundly and although his mind was in a state of excitement and not one of doubt or worry, the throbbing off the ship's engine and the gentle rise and fall of the Laconia was enough to send his tired mind and body to a slumber that was welcomed.

4

In the early hours of the 15th of April 1912 R.M.S Titanic sank on its maiden voyage, sailing from Liverpool to New York. Over one thousand five hundred people perished. Fourteen years later, Sam looked at the same ocean responsible for their deaths. His knowledge of the sinking was only what he had read about but his appreciation of the tragedy only came to the fore as he looked upon the mighty waves that crashed upon the bow of the *Laconia*. Time and again the ship would lurch from side to side, sometimes the stern would be dragged down sinking into a trough that would seemingly hold it until, another wave rolled under the ship causing it to rise, setting it free. Those poor people Sam thought, as his white knuckles held firmly the guard rail on the port side of the ship. Sam was surprised that during the twenty four hours that the storm had lasted he had not been affected by sea sickness, unlike a lot of the passengers and all three of his fellow travellers that shared his cabin.

Fifty three year old Martin Sanders and his son Colin, thirty, were violently sick during the height of the storm. The effects of their sickness would last another day before they were well enough to start the bickering and petty arguments that had been going on for the days before the storm, in fact ever since they both had set foot on the *Laconia*.

At first Sam found this bickering amusing, but it didn't take long before both he and Eddi grew tired of their constant rows. Eddi suggesting that the less time spent in their company the better. So they never really got to know there travelling companions. "Rather sad," thought Sam.

It was Eddie who was to acquire another cabin for himself and Sam. Eddie was twenty seven, a steel erector from Newcastle and his explanation to Sam regarding their new accommodation was quite simple. On his arrival at the Cunard offices he had overheard a conversation concerning a family cabin that due to the sudden death of a family member, Cabin 439, would now be vacant. Unbeknown to Sam, Eddie asked a few questions, thinking that the chances of it still being empty would be slim. To his surprise the room was still empty, and with some skillful debate Eddie got to turn the key to Cabin 439.

For the rest of the voyage Sam was to spend a lot of his time in the company of Eddie whom he got to know well. Sam would learn of Eddie's life, his hometown, his dreams and aspirations, his longing to work on the skyscrapers of New York. He told Sam of the Mohawks and Iroquois, Canadian Native Indians, who were instrumental in the erection of the steel girders that formed the skeleton of the skyscrapers of New York. Sam listened intently to Eddie's story of his wanting to be part of the building of New York's skyline. When asked of Sam's experiences in life Sam was hard put to make his life sound any more exciting than maybe someone being killed by the kick of a horse, or the excitement of having to release a few sheep that had got stuck in a hedge, at which point Eddie interjected saying that a few sheep getting stuck in a hedge where he lived, where incidentally there weren't any hedges, would be released only to be strung up in someone's back yard, relieved of their lives and dispatched to neighbour's pantries within hours. They both laughed at this but it told of the difference in how they both lived. Eddie, was both streetwise and sceptical to people's words and motives, and Sam who wasn't streetwise, as where he lived there was no need to be. Eddie listened as Sam told him of how a man was viewed where he came from.

"A man," said Sam, "was only as good as his word and his actions spoke as to his character."

Eddie tilted his head and smiled.

"My God Sam, we come from two different worlds. Your world, as idyllic as it sounds, is not the world you will find yourself in. Out there are people that will take you for everything you have, and don't tell me you don't have people like that even where you live." Sam thought for a moment. Eddie was right, there were such people, but they were well known to everyone so it wasn't a problem. "All I'm saying Sam, is be careful. Everyone you meet from now on will be strangers to you as they will be to me, so

I hope you don't mind me saying don't be too casual in whom you place your trust."

That night Sam lay awake dwelling on the advice, if that was what it was that Eddie had given him. Everything that he had said made complete sense. The problem was, could he change from being who he was? He doubted if he could.

5

It was mid-morning, when Sam on a cushioned seat opened the book his Aunt Megan had given him.

"Just a little something to read, when you have time," she had said, as she handed him the novel wrapped in a brown paper bag. The morning was grey and uninspiring. Sam gazed through the sea sprayed windows of the reading room that was situated on one of the ship's upper decks. The salty brine had left long streaks on the glass, making it a little difficult to see through. From where he was sitting, there was some ten feet of open decking before the ship's outer railing and beyond that, the open sea. The sea was choppy and the clouds were low in the sky. The threat of rain, Sam thought, as he thumbed through the pages of the book he held. He looked at the page in front of him, the first paragraph, then he started to read.

"Call me Ishmael. Some years ago, never mind how long precisely, having little or no money in my purse and nothing particular to see on shore I thought I would sail a little and see the watery part of the world."

Sam stopped reading and turned the book to its front cover, he read again for the umpteenth time, its title and the author's name; Moby Dick, by Herman Melville. He had heard of the book but was unfamiliar with the story. He smiled to himself as he thought of his Aunt Megan buying him a book about a sea adventure, knowing that to enhance a good story, the reader would be better served in being immersed in the book's descriptive surroundings and nothing could be more descriptive than the sea and himself in a big boat floating about on it. Did she really have this in mind when she bought the book, he wondered.

Two hours later Sam looked up. It had started to rain and the rise and fall of the ship became more noticeable. He looked at the sea, the white capping of the waves as they reached their peak seemed to hang for a moment before crashing down in front of the wave that had created it, then to rise again in the wave behind. He was fixated by the turbulent water, realizing that since its conception the sea had never been still.

"Hello Sam."

On hearing his name being called, Sam turned in his seat and was pleasantly surprised to see Joe Fleming, the gentleman whose company he shared on the train before they were to part company at Princess Station. Joe, casually dressed, but nonetheless smart enough to be noticed, wore a pair of black and white spats, black trousers and a burgundy fair isle knitted jumper, under a tweed jacket.

"Have I interrupted your reading Sam?" he asked.

"No not at all." Sam replied folding back the corner of the last page he had just read and closed the book. "Please join me," indicating the two empty seats at his table. Joe placed a newspaper on the table before sitting and with a sigh murmured, "I don't know but I think I have just left the company of two of the most boring men I have ever had the misfortune to meet."

Sam raised his eyebrows, "Really."

"Yes really, you would think that educated people would have some regard for the views of others that don't agree with their thinking." Joe suddenly stopped speaking, then looked at Sam. "I'm sorry Sam, I do apologize, and here I am going on about two total strangers, when indeed the last time I saw you was when we got off the train at Princess Station, which was, "he paused," three days ago, my goodness it seems a lot longer than that."

"And how are Mrs Fleming and Billie?" Sam asked with a smile.

"Pageant is well, but Billie has been in bed for the last two days. I'm afraid messing about on boats doesn't agree with the workings of her tummy, but she will be alright, and you Sam, how are things with you?" Sam told Joe all about what had happened since they had parted company, his rented room above the bar at The Admiral Rodney, the banter that went on with the landlord's customers and his meeting with the landlord's daughter, although he didn't spend time telling him of any feelings he had for the girl. He explained the situation regarding his cabin companions and of how he and one of the lads managed to get another cabin, so now everything was dandy.

It was refreshing for Joe meeting up with Sam again. He listened intently as Sam told him about his experiences of the last few days and as he listened, he became aware of a young man, who much like himself, would take on a challenge that life had presented him, a kindred spirit, such that he felt sure, would shadow them both in the coming years.

"And the book?" Joe asked nodding his head at the novel on the table. Sam looked down.

"Moby Dick," he said without further prompting. "Just started to read it."

"And how are you finding it?"

"Not sure," said Sam pursing his lips as he spoke, "Will probably finish it though, if only for Aunt Megan's sake. And you Joe, I see you have brought along the newspaper that you will be writing for in the not too distant future." Although the paper that Joe had placed on the table was upside down, Sam looked at it, and could see it was the New York Times and its date, the third of January 1927. "Anything of interest?" he asked with some amusement in his voice.

"Of interest", Joe smiled as he started drumming his fingers on the table. "Well, there is an article about prohibition."

"Prohibition!" Sam interrupted, "isn't that about the non-sale of alcohol in America?"

"It is," said Joe as he opened the paper and turned it around for Sam to read. "There it is." He pointed to the column on the right hand side of the front page. Sam lifted the paper and silently read the article.

"Padlocks close cafes, but rum keeps flowing. Injunctions that have closed four hundred speakeasies in nine months, are a most effective method says Bunker, urging more courts and a State Dry Act."

As Sam read on Joe was quietly anticipating a response, then as Sam lowered the paper he looked up and shrugged.

"Just how long has this been going on for? I know it's been some years, but it seems to me that the authorities are fighting a lost cause."

"And what makes you say that?" Joe answered, surprised at the positive statement given by Sam.

"Well," Sam sighed, "those four hundred pubs, or speakeasies as they are called, surely they haven't been carrying on their business for all these years. It being illegal and all that. I think, what little I know about business, is that these places are popping up all the time and all over the place which suggests, that like at home, drinking is a social pastime even in America."

"Six years, the production, importation, transportation and the sale of alcohol beverage, in the United States has been illegal for six years."

Sam smiled, "Well, you being a newspaper reporter, you will know all that there is to know about prohibition."

"I wrote a column on the subject two years ago, but what I would like to know, is the consumer's perspective on the subject."

"Are you asking me for my views? With all due respect I am eighteen years of age, how on earth would I have an opinion on a law that is of another country."

"But you have an opinion?"

"Yes, I have an opinion, but my knowledge on the subject is that limited that my opinion would count for very little, I'm afraid." Neither spoke for a moment, then Joe raised a hand and with his forefinger stroked his moustache, reminding Sam again of the film stars he had seen at the picture house doing that sort of thing. Joe had that kind of face.

"So, you do have some knowledge on the subject, to be honest Sam and please don't be offended, I'm surprised that anyone of your age coming from Britain, would know anything about prohibition in America."

"It was my mother and Aunt Megan, who suggested that I should know a little about the country I was going to."

"Sound advice," said Joe, reaching into his coat pocket, he brought out a notepad and pencil.

"Would you mind if I made a few notes on your thoughts Sam, as I have just had a thought myself?" Sam looked out of the window as Joe talked about an idea he had thought of, to select three or four young people on board ship and write about their expectations and any preconceived ideas about the country that they had chosen to live. Maybe see them again in twelve months' time, to find if the reality was as expected. Although Sam was listening to Joe his thoughts were elsewhere and for a fleeting moment, he was again saying goodbye to Grace.

"So, what do you think?" Joe sounded enthusiastic.

"Think?" said Sam.

"Yes, to get some young people's thoughts about America, maybe I could do an article and present it at work when I meet my new boss. Then at least it would look as if I had work on my mind, which by the way isn't far from the truth."

"It sounds a good idea," Sam muttered. But he was more interested as to what Joe was scribbling down on his notepad, every time he stopped talking he would draw little lines and squiggles and sometimes while he was talking he would do the same. It wasn't words that he was writing down just squiggles and lines. Joe noticed him looking.

"It's shorthand," he said with a big smile. Sam gave Joe a curious look.

"Shorthand?" he queried, expecting an explanation.

"It's how we take statements from people, another way of writing, it enables us to write as fast as people can talk. From politicians to policemen, people on the street, there is always someone who will have witnessed things of public interest….and I talk too much." They both laughed.

"No, I find it all very interesting," said Sam eager to learn more "And you can understand from all those squiggles and lines, the words that people have spoken?"

"Pretty much, there is an element of poetic license, but that would usually apply to words that are irrelevant to the main thrust of a report."

Sam shook his head. Shorthand, poetic license, and the whole concept of what Joe had just been telling him seemed a little beyond him. Was this all about the new world that he had walked into. Yes, he had read newspapers at home, but he had never given a thought about how the reporter's stories got into print and the reporters themselves must have used shorthand, but he just never gave it a thought.

Joe suddenly looked at his watch, then slipped his notepad back inside his jacket pocket.

"I had better go, Pageant will be wondering where I am." He stood.

"Before you go, can I ask a question?" Sam rose from his seat. "Well, there are many questions I would like to ask, but this one in particular."

"Ask away."

"Why are speakeasies so called?"

"Good question," answered Joe, placing his newspaper under his arm, "A speakeasy, as you know, is a nickname for an illegal bar. They are usually situated in cellars, shady night clubs and sometimes not so shady, depending on who you are, but they all have one thing in common."

"And that is," said Sam smiling. Joe leaned forward and spoke softly.

"Patrons of these establishments… whisper certain passwords to gain entry."

After Joe had left, Sam picked up his book and walked out onto the deck. The sea had calmed some and what little rain there was, had stopped. As he walked, he noticed people huddled on deck chairs, most with blankets wrapped around themselves keeping out a cold wind blowing across the deck. A group of children playing hopscotch. A man with a flat cap and a blue scarf wrapped around his neck, wearing a brown overcoat, stood with his legs apart facing Sam. At waist height he held a box camera, taking photographs. He motioned with the palm of his hand for Sam to stop walking. Sam obliged, he pressed a button…, click, he asked Sam his name, his age and his reason for being on board the ship. He told him he was a freelance photographer selling where he could the many photographs he would take. Sam smiled and moved on.

People were playing cards, babies cried, lovers embraced, a group of girls chanted songs while skipping, sometimes tripping over the rope as it swung through the air. Old people looking out to sea, some no doubt wondering how many more sun rises they are likely to see. Then there was Sam, young, healthy, full of life and ambition and by his own admission willing to do almost anything to achieve his goals. The problem was, the goals to be realized were as yet ones he hadn't even thought of. He was not even aware of the rules of engagement, never mind learning how to bend them a little.

For the next two days, Sam tried to read his book but due to distractions did not get very far. Going early to the reading lounge he sat at the same table that he had shared with Joe. Sam settled in his seat and turned back the folded corner of the printed page that he had last read. Page after page, brought him closer to living the life of those men that had sailed the oceans and walked the shores of far off lands. The rolling of the ship, emphasized the atmosphere, the shouting and cursing that went on in the rigging. Men would unfurl sails that would catch the wind and blow them out like Sam's mother's sheets on a windy day. Every now and then he would look out to sea, checking, looking for fountains of water, as one day soon, the call of, "Thar she blows," would run the length of the ship.

Chapter Six. In New Bedford.

Chapter Eight. Captain Ahab, obsessed with the capture of Moby Dick and Queequeg, being measured for his coffin.

Sam had been told by a dock worker in The Admiral Rodney that it would be unusual not to sight a whale on the crossing to America, usually in the last two days of the journey that is when you would likely see them.

Chapter Twelve. Queequeg was a native of Rokovoko, an island far away to the west and south. It is not down in any map; true places never are.

6

An hour later he went for lunch. Eddie was already seated at their allocated table, along with two other couples, of who, from the time of their first meeting had become quite chatty. Simon and Brenda Smyth, an elderly couple, had been to England visiting relatives in Oxford, they had emigrated to America over thirty years before and their children had clubbed together to give them this trip of a lifetime. Simon had worked for an American railway company driving passenger and freight trains in the midwest for many years before retiring to New Orleans. Colin and Sybil, of a similar age as their table companions, were doing much the same thing, only the other way around. It would appear, some wealthy relatives in New York had discovered that part of Sybil's heritage on her mother's side lived in Cornwall, England. Sybil told the story of two brothers leaving Cornwall and joining the forty-niners in the California gold rush. As it turned out the descendants of these brothers, having found out that they had relatives in England, invited Colin and Sybil for an all-expenses paid trip across the water. The question that sprung to

Sam's mind, was, did these brothers make good in their quest for riches? Sam smiled and hoped they did.

After a delightful meal of beef stroganoff and roly-poly pudding, Sam and Eddie excused themselves from the dining table and headed off to one of the entertainment lounges where a jazz band would be playing. Eddie, a keen jazz follower, suggested Sam join him. Sam quite liked the music himself, as he would hear it being played a lot on the radio. The broadcasters would say that we were in the middle of the roaring twenties, it was the time of exhibitionism and you could see that on the dance floors all over Britain. Maybe not so much in the back waters of mid Wales, as everything that happened there was about two years after it had happened everywhere else. But in the big towns and affluent cities, the wave of American music culture swept over the country. Flappers in their shimmering dresses, bangles and beads, new hairstyles, shoes and handbags. The war had been over a long time ago. Ask any twenty year old of either sex? Their time was now. Smoking, drinking and flaunting themselves seemed to be a social pastime, having a good time was the key to it all.

Sam reflected on the lifestyle he had lived up until a few days ago, to the one he was witnessing now. He looked around the room, a clarinet played, its rich haunting sound had the dancing crowd move at a more leisurely and seductive pace. He detected the affluence of some of these people, by noticing how they were dressed. Their confident movements and gestures produced an air about them that shouted, "Hey look at me," a request that could not be ignored. But in the last six months Sam had noticed a change. There was a mood in the national newspapers that hard times were coming, whether it would affect any of those jitterbugging on the dance floor he wouldn't know? It depended on how wealthy they were he thought.

The clarinet instrumental was followed by a lady singing some of Sophie Tucker's songs. Sam had never heard of her or any of her songs. Next, came the piano player, doing Al Johnson's 'I'm in the mood for love' to which Eddie sang along, not missing a word. They were told that the sax player had done a stint with Duke Ellington's Jazz Band before joining the ship. The entertainment ended with a rendering of 'Ukulele Baby', sung by a lady impersonating Bessie Smith, who in all fairness did a fairly good job of it. As they walked out, Eddie asked Sam what he thought of the band,

"I enjoyed it very much," he said, adding that as he had never seen a live jazz band before, he really had not known what to expect.

"Individually the music played by the musicians seem all jumbled up, but when they come together, the sound made sense, a bit like a jigsaw if you know what I mean."

"I know exactly what you mean, fancy another drink?" Eddie asked.

Sam declined saying that he was three quarters through his book and he needed to finish it.

"Maybe after dinner tonight?"

"Sounds like a good idea, I think we should have a few beers together. We have two days left, before we get off this ship and God knows what will happen then. See you later." Eddie slapped Sam on the back and sauntered off. It had started to rain again and a choppy sea was upon them. Sam made his way to the reading room. Someone was sitting at his table, so he sat at another. Taking his book out of his pocket, he placed it on the table and eased himself into a more comfortable chair than the one he had previously been sitting on.

He opened his book.

Chapter One Hundred. The Pequod of Nantucket meets the Samuel Enderby of London.

At this point in the book, Sam was totally consumed by the writing of Herman Melville and like a locust, he devoured it. Page by page until there would be but a few pages left. But that is to come, there are many words that Sam is to overcome. He reads it like an uneducated fool, but understands it, as if it were a masterpiece that he had written himself. In the beginning he had found it difficult to read, the vocabulary was not of his understanding and now he relished the challenge.

Sam felt a sudden lurch of the ship, he looked out of the window, the rain had intensified and was bouncing off everything, a whirlwind of water spun across the deck disappearing into a mountainous sea. The ship started to role and sink into a deep trough where the waves seemingly rose above its railings. There was no one on deck, except a man in a black oilskin overcoat, one that dropped to his ankles. He held the ship's outer railings with both hands and didn't move. Sam studied him for a moment. He was on an open part of the deck and Sam had a feeling that something was not as it should be. The gentleman had long white hair that flayed in the wind and a beard as white as snow. He just stood there, looking out to sea. Sam followed his gaze, out there! There, upon broken waves Sam could make out a ship, then another, the man on deck was looking at these ships.

Again, he found it difficult to see through the window. He had a strange feeling, a feeling he couldn't explain. He put his book down and stood, not taking his eyes from the man in black. He walked unsteadily, with the ship moving beneath his feet. He got to the door and slid it open, the man hadn't moved. Other people in the reading room looked, then carried on doing what they were doing, uncertain as to stay, as chairs started to fall over, some muttering something about a silly old man standing out in the storm. The wind howled through the doorway blowing rain in with it. Sam slid the door shut. He stood under a canopy that was part of the deck above, again he looked out to sea. The two ships seemed to be nearer now, they were bobbing about, the sea being responsible for taking them into deep depression, then seemingly throw them in the air. Sam looked from the man to the ship and then back again. It was when one of the ships presented itself side on that Sam noticed it, on the bow of the ship was mounted, Sam couldn't believe it, a harpoon gun. He looked again at the man in black, who it seemed was frozen to the ships railing, he then raised an arm and pointed to the sea. Sam was gulping for air as he ran the twenty paces or so toward the man in black. Reaching him, the man was bellowing, his voice reaching a crescendo above the sound of the wind.

"Tharrr...she blows..., tharrr...she blows," Sam could see the whale breaking water and the fountain of warm air blowing through its blowhole. Sam looked at the man in black his arm still outstretched, his finger still pointing forward. On the back of his hand. Sam could make out a tattoo, it was of two crossed harpoons. And the rain still fell.

At this point, Sam was aware that he and the old man were not on their own. Two men and a woman were on deck, they stood a few yards away under a permanently fixed canopy. Their subdued muttering, hardly audible along with a lot of "oohs and aahs" seemed an interference that this spectacle could do without. Sam was mesmerized by the whole scene. He moved forward to see the face of the man in black. Reaching out with the rain lashing his face Sam clasped the ships uppermost rail for fear of falling over, at the same time taking a hurried look. The man's face was contorted, there was fire in his eyes, and his white hair blew like rat's tails about his head, with the rain running down his face and into his beard, and all the time shouting.

"Tharrr... she blows." Sam suddenly felt cold and was struck with fear, for this is how he imagined Captain Ahab to be. This was he and he was Ahab.... Ahab turned and looked deep into the eyes of Sam. Then they all heard the harpoon gun go off, they looked to see a rope snake out, low across the water. They all saw it strike the whale. Almost immediately a foaming red fountain left the blowhole of the whale. That was when the man in black stopped his crow's nest cry. He lowered his head, all four of them looked at him, the rain kept falling. He turned and with the eyes of a sad dog, he spoke.

"I'm a Nantucket man, I know about these things, we have just witnessed the living and the death of the greatest creature on earth. I am not a religious man, but may God forgive us all, because the whale won't." He turned and walked the deck, not saying another word, his shadowy black frame swaying through the rain that fell.

Sam was bewildered, never in his life had he experienced anything such as this. Ahab, as he couldn't think of a more fitting name, had walked away. He was a Nantucket man, or so he said, and before Sam had set foot on board this ship, he had never heard of the place. It was Herman Melville that had introduced him to its existence and now, he was standing on the deck of a ship bouncing along on the Atlantic Ocean, soaking wet from rain that persistently falls. He had just been in the presence of a man from the same place that even the Captain of the Pequod came from…. Nantucket. Sam looked at the three people that, like him had seen all that had taken place They were staring after a man that could no longer be seen. Simultaneously they turned their heads and looked at Sam, in a manner that suggested that he was maybe an acquaintance of the old man. He, the old man that had just played the last act, reminiscent of a Shakespearean play had gone. Sam still held tight to the ship's railing. The others hung onto some rope netting that was holding down a stack of deck chairs. They made a dash for it, running through rain that bounced off the mackintoshes they wore, but not off their heads, as none wore a hat of any description.

Sam stood for a few moments; he was getting cold. Running through the rain would not make any difference as to how wet he was, as the amount of water that ran from the bottom of his trousers equalled the amount that fell on his body. Against the wind he struggled to the reading room, slid open the door and walked in. People looked at him and one gent asked what was going on outside.

"Whale boats," Sam answered picking up his book, trying to keep it dry. He walked out leaving a trail of water on the carpet of the reading room, along with some puzzled looks that followed him through a different exit, out of the room. He descended staircases between decks and walked the long corridor. Outside his cabin he knocked and turned the door handle. Inside Eddie was lying on his bunk reading a magazine, he looked at Sam in disbelief.

"Jesus Christ! Have you fallen overboard? Where the hell have you been?"

"In answer to your first question," he said, throwing his book on his bed. "No, I haven't fallen overboard and to the second, I have been outside, and now I'm bloody freezing." In the following half hour, as Sam changed clothing, he told Eddie about his experience on deck. The man in a black oilskin overcoat, the whaling ships, the harpooning and the old man's comments before walking away.

"All this has happened, since I last saw you," he looked at his watch, "three and a half hours ago."

"Yes", said Sam combing his hair. Within the next two hours the rain had subsided, and with the ship sailing on an even keel, people started to relax, some telling of how they managed during the storm.

Apologies were said to their table companions. Sam and Eddie sat down fifteen minutes late for their dinner. There was a buzz about the dining room. People were talking about the whaling ships, although there was no mention of a white haired man in a black oilskin overcoat. At one point during their meal, Eddie leaned towards Sam.

"It was an apparition," he said with a big grin.

The following morning Sam was on deck early. Sleep didn't come easily. Even after having a few beers with Eddie and the friends he had arranged to meet. Yes, Eddie was a sociable person, he had the gift of being likeable. They laughed and joked all very amicably, music played and young ladies danced. Sam left early, he took Eddie to one side and apologized for his not feeling as jovial and as talkative as he might have. But he really didn't feel in the mood. Eddie placed an arm around Sam's shoulder.

"It's that book and that man in black isn't it," he said with some concern. Sam nodded.

"It's the man really," he shook his head. "Nothing has ever affected me like that man, the sadness and pain in his face was, I don't have words for it." Sam turned to go.

"Do yourself a favour Sam," Eddie said, "When you finish that book, leave it on the table."

Sam had been reading since eight o'clock, on the last full day of their voyage. It was midday when he turned to page five hundred and twenty and a short time later, he reached five hundred and fifty five. He did not want to stop, he could not stop, not far to go now and it would all be over.

Captain Ahab is dead and the ship is fathoms deep.

The epilogue. "And I only am escaped alone to tell thee" Job.

The dramas done; why then here does anyone step forth- because one did survive the wreck....

Sam read on, anticipating his own release.

Then with three lines to go.

On the second day as sale drew near, nearer and pick me up at last, it was the cruising ship Rachael that in her retracing search after her missing children only found another orphan.

Sam looked at the last word printed.... Orphan and closed the book. He calmly placed it on the table, touched it once more and walked away.

7

It was two o'clock in the afternoon, when Sam walked on deck. There was a deck reserved for first class passengers, but Sam had no complaints about anything the shipping company had to offer the people, in the way of looking after their second class passengers. The sea was calm and the sky was blue, not surprisingly there was a chill in the air, as it was still January. The time given for disembarkation was just after midday the following day. So, Sam decided to visit every bar and public room that was available to second class passengers. He was relieved that he had finished the accursed book as he had called it and maybe his description of it was not justified, but for now it fitted his thoughts. He stopped and chatted to his dining companions; he had spotted them in one of the large lounges. They were with a group of people that they had become friendly with over the course of the last few days. He was introduced by Sybil and in return the three couples introduced themselves back. A few minutes later he had forgotten every one of their names.

In the same room he spotted Joe and Pageant. They were looking all very regal, Pageant, sitting with a straight back with Billy on her lap. Joe sat, with a stern face, and perfectly still. They were posing for the cameraman that had already taken a picture of Sam. There was a flash from the camera, people looked with interest then carried on doing what they were doing. Billy having seen Sam slid from her mother's knee and ran towards Sam. She stopped and smiled. Hello, she said, then turned and ran back to her parent's.

Sam spent some time with Joe and Pageant. It was the first time they had visited this second class lounge.

"Hello Joe, and good afternoon Mrs. Fleming."

"Now Sam, there is absolutely no need to be so formal, please call me Pageant. I may come from the city, but I am a country girl at heart. In fact, I was born in Minsterly, Shropshire, your neck of the woods I believe."

Sam gave a broad smile.

"You correctly believe, Mrs. Fleming, Minsterly is, as you put it, in my neck of the woods, but with due respect, I would feel more comfortable in calling you Mrs. Fleming."

"As you wish Sam, but I repeat, there is absolutely no reason that you should do so. Joe has been telling me that you are reading the novel Moby Dick."

"Just finished it, about an hour ago."

"Well, I'm afraid I've seen enough of the sea to last me a number of years, than to start reading a book that has anything remotely to do with waves crashing about all over the place."

"Well, that's one way of putting it," said Sam, laughing.

"No! I much prefer a good romantic novel, a woman thing I suppose," she said, ironing out on her lap some imaginary creases on the satin dress she wore. They talked for an hour or so, Sam giving Joe all the answers to questions he had given him. Joe had also interviewed three other young people He didn't elaborate on who they were, just saying that there were two young women and two men, one of whom was Sam and that he would arrange for them all to meet up in twelve months' time. As Sam got up to leave, Pageant delved into a tote bag she was carrying and took out a card and handed it to him.

"This will be our new address in New York, Sam and if you are in the vicinity, we would like you to call." Sam stood and shook hands with Joe and as he held Pageant's gloved hand, he smiled.

"Thank you both for your company." Sam was pleased that he had seen Joe and Pageant and his assumption of Mrs. Fleming was not as he had first thought. Yes, she was elegant and sophisticated and had a regal way about her, but that was dependent on the company she happened to be in. She could, like Miss Mavis, cast off the elegance and sophistication of her upbringing and return to her roots, that of being someone who could accommodate without favour the common people that no doubt she was once a part of. He recalled Miss Mavis telling him not long before she died that being able to conduct oneself in the company of people of all classes was something that would be of benefit to him. Being polite and able to speak in the manner that is equal to the people you are conversing with, would one day be an asset. She mentioned that being an undertaker, he would no doubt, one day be invited into the homes of the gentry and people of that ilk. "And believe me," she had said. "It is up to you to impress them, more so than it is for them to impress you. They may not see it like that, but that's the way it is. As even...." and that was when she winked at Sam. "Even bad and not very nice people.... they also die."

Sam did the rounds of the ship and ended up in the ballroom, where lots of people were celebrating their last night on board. Many people were giving out contact addresses and telephone numbers. Sam didn't have a telephone number or a forwarding address but Eddie had a contact number that he gave to Sam. In total he had six contact numbers. Joe and Pageant, whose number and address was on the card she had given him, and Curtis, who Sam had met a couple of times in the company of Eddie. As it turned out Curtis was a banker, of what position, he didn't divulge, but he did like his Johnny Walker whisky. He was a fun guy. Then there was another Johnny. Everyone called this one, "Johnny Be Good", as he told them that was the last thing his mother had said to him before he left home. Johnny would be making his way to his uncle's place in Detroit, Michigan, which he told everyone, was a long way from New York. Sam shrugged.

"I wouldn't know if it was next bloody door," he said.

"So, it seems your contact number wouldn't be much good to any of us."

Johnny told everyone that he would be working at the Chrysler car plant. Dean Bocelli another member of the gang on board ship gave him a contact number too. Dean was Italian, a baker, Bocelli on his father's side with an English mother. He was going to America to pursue his career in the pastry trade and would be staying initially with friends of friends.

Sam was surprised at just how many people were going out to join relatives and every one of them, that he had met, had some sort of profession. Was this the American dream that he had heard so many people talk of? Apparently, there was plenty of work in the car manufacturing industry. Johnny had been an apprentice tool maker for Bentley Motors in London. When he had finished his time, his uncle asked if he would like to join him, go over and make some money. He said it hadn't been a difficult choice to make and anyway it would be a change for him.

"So maybe we had better hang on to his telephone number," interrupts Curtis, "You never know he may be able to get us a cheap car one day." At that moment Pat sided up to Sam and placed her drink, a gin and tonic, on the table beside his half empty pint of bitter. She sat on a spare seat opposite him.

"And you Sam," she said, running her index finger, seductively up and down the highball glass, containing her gin and tonic, "how easy will it be for you to get a job making coffins? I mean," she shrugged her shoulders, "will there be a lot of call for people in your profession?"

Sam turned to Pat. He wasn't sure if she was being sarcastic about how he earned his living. Most people were interested but there were others that would see his job as a joke and he had heard it all before. If she was, it would be a pity. This five feet something girl, with a lovely smile and a contagious laugh was pretty, he thought. She was a nurse and was emigrating with her best friend Sandy.

"You're a nurse Pat?"

"Yes," she replied, wondering what her being a nurse had to do with him being a man that makes coffins.

"Well, there is something that we have in common, that most people don't come across but rarely."

"Go on," she said, tilting her head, intrigued and thinking what was coming next. Sam could see her interest, he looked her in the eyes and for a moment held his tongue.

"Dead bodies."

"Shit," she said laughing, "but what has that got to do with you making coffins?"

"Everything, dead bodies equal coffins."

"Jesus Sam, you must think I'm thick. I should have figured that one out."

"Look, if I were to tell you that two thousand people die every month in New York. That's a lot of earth to move."

"And a lot of fires to light, that's if you don't want to be buried." Pat hesitated. "And a lot of coffins to make, I get the point you're making Sam," she smiled.

"I'll take my chances on finding a job," said Sam.

"I'm sure you will," Pat squeezed his hand and raising her eyebrows, quipped, "is there really that many people that die in New York every month?"

Sam gave Pat a false smile, "I don't know, I just thought there must be a lot…. and two thousand seemed a reasonable figure."

"You, bugger, bugger…." Pat said slapping him on the shoulder.

"And what about you Pat, what is your story? Everyone seems to have a story on this ship."

"You mean how did I come to be going to New York?"

"Yes," said Sam," as he raised his pint to take a mouthful of beer.

"Sister Ruth, it was Sister Ruth, she was a nurse in the hospital that Sandy and I worked in. She nursed an American soldier that got blown up in the last days of the war, he wasn't expected to live. She saw him every day for three months. Anyway, they fell in love, got married, stayed in England for four years, he talked her into going to America and she went. Sandy and I kept in touch. Two years later, she said she could get us a job in the Lenox Hill hospital, in Manhattan, if we fancied going. We fancied going, and she will be picking us up from the docks, end of story." She gave a little laugh, she looked teary as she placed her elbows on the table and looked over her gin and tonic.

"Would you mind Sam," she said hesitantly blinking her eyes, "If maybe…. maybe you could sometime call and see us at the hospital? It's on Park Avenue." Pat was rushing her speech, "Seventy Seventh Street. Or give us a telephone call, you have Sister Ruth's number." Sam was surprised in the sudden change in Pat. She had gone from a confident, seemingly self-assured young woman, then in the blink of an eye become someone who could burst out crying at any moment. She looked vulnerable and a little lost. Again, he wasn't sure how to handle the situation.

"How many gin and tonics have you had Pat...?"

"For fuck's sake Sam," he heard himself say, "that really wasn't the right thing to say." He reached for her hand and being a little more kind, asked her if she would like to go outside for some fresh air. Pat stood up, Sam told her he would tell Sandy, who was dancing with a blonde lad, that he was taking her outside for some air.

"Just make sure that's all you are taking her outside for," she said stumbling over her words. Before they went out, Sam called Eddie over, and told him to watch out for Sandy. Eddie looked over to see Sandy walk to the table carrying her shoes. Pat grabbed Sam's hand. He guided her through the cheering and laughing crowd, all celebrating their last night on board ship. Coloured streamers were flying through the air, as Sam feeling somewhat foolish with Pat's bag over his shoulder walked through the door. Out on deck, he gave her handbag back, she still clung to his hand. They walked as far as they could to the bow of the ship, then sat down on a bench facing the sea. Sam looked at the stars between the few clouds that slowly drifted across the sky. The moon was bright and only a few days from being a full one.

"Isn't this romantic?" she said interrupting Sam's line of thought. "Look at us. Two starry eyed young people, sitting on a bench, on a ship under a full moon. It's something you would read in a book isn't it." Sam didn't have the heart to tell her, that she was a little more starry-eyed than he was and it wasn't quite a full moon, although he could have been accused of being a bit picky on that one. As for it being romantic, well admittedly it could be in different circumstances, but as for the book thing! Sam didn't read that kind of book and there was nothing romantic going on in the book he had just read. For a moment they didn't speak, they just sat enjoying the cool evening breeze. Pat squeezed Sam's hand. He looked at her as she stared out to sea. As fireflies would attract, would be lovers with their glow, Sam was drawn to Pat's raven hair as it glistened in the moonlight.

"At one stage in there I got a bit upset but I'm alright now, drama over."

"Yes, l could see that you were upset about something." Sam said, looking again at the stars, "and I know it's none of my business, but I'd like to know what made you upset."

"Well, you are right Sam, it is none of your business, but I will tell you anyway. But first I would like to apologize for the way I came over, in asking you about your job, I was being flippant, I don't know why and I'm sorry, and your question about how many drinks I have had. Well, the answer is, probably not nearly enough." She looked at Sam and smiled, "Just kidding. You asked what made me upset? It's…. it's my mum, I'm going to miss my Mum Sam."

The party was in full swing when they re-joined their friends after their short absence on deck. Sam asked if he could get her a drink and to his surprise she just wanted an orange juice, he brought a beer for himself and on his return from the bar, he saw Pat beckon him. He pulled out a chair next to her and sat down. She wondered about him, just who was this boy. He was tall, good looking in a way that appealed to her and maybe if he was a few years older she might have pursued a relationship. He was polite, pretty sure of himself, but sometimes she felt that he lacked confidence, then, only to surprise her with words that would have been spoken by a person of more senior years. So, it didn't come as a surprise when he told her of the people in his life. He didn't really have many friends his own age, maybe he felt more comfortable in the company of older people, but that was alright she thought, and she could find worst friends than Sam Pryce. Sam walked her to her cabin and as he stood outside her door, he thanked her for her company.

"Will I see you before we leave in the morning Sam?"

"I'd like to think so," Sam said softly as he bent his head and kissed her on the cheek. "Goodnight Pat. I'll see you in the morning."

"Goodnight Sam," she said as she opened the door, then letting go of his hand, she walked in.

The Immigration Act of 1924 had made it more difficult for people of many countries to immigrate to America. But the new quota did include large numbers of people of British decent whose families had long resided in the United States and the percentage of visas available to individuals from the British Isles and Western Europe had increased.

Sam caught a glimpse of Pat amongst the crowd on Ellis Island shouting that he would give her a ring. Eddie and Sam went through the formalities of immigration, having had medical, legal, and financial checks, changing their British money for American dollars in the same complex. Soon after, they found themselves on the streets of Manhattan, looking through a list of addresses of boarding houses where they would most likely get accommodation. They found one on Sixth Avenue, a room with two beds. They had a shower and changed clothes, wasting no time in going outside to have a walk around. It was three thirty on a Friday afternoon when the boys, having found their land legs, walked around the block where they lived looking for the nearest landmarks to know where they were. They could see the tall buildings of New York in the distance, both agreeing that the following day they would walk there and have a look at this city of skyscrapers.

8

"Pat it's for you," Sandy's voice echoed up the stairs in Sister Ruth and Ray's condo. Pat stood outside the bedroom door of the room that she shared with Sandy. "Who is it?" she shouted back.

"It's that young lad we met on the ship, Sam, he wants to speak to you. She's coming now," Sandy said as Pat was halfway down the stairs.

"Hello, is that you Sam?" she said excitedly.

"Yes, I'm ringing you from a phone box outside the boarding house I'm sharing with Eddie. Just thought I'd ring to see how you have settled in and to see where you are living."

"That's nice of you Sam. Sister Ruth and Ray have been really kind and helpful. We have four days before we start work and then a month to find our own place. Have you got a pencil?"

"Yes," Sam said, "I have a pencil and paper, all right Pat, what's your address?"

"We are at 170E 81st Street, just off 3rd Avenue."

"Now I haven't got a clue where that is, but at least I have it. I don't know when I'll be over to see you, so I will give you a call first, probably in a few days' time."

"All right Sam, till then, look after yourself. Bye."

The image of the city of New York, that Sam would get to know, was one that could not have been visualized unless seen. For Sam, it was a scene of science fiction, as viewed from a Fifth Avenue coffee shop, where he sat with Eddie.

"And you want to work up there?" Sam said looking skywards,

"Can't wait."

"When do you start?"

"Monday morning."

"So, the interview went well? You were only in the site office a couple of minutes; did they ask you what work experience you have had?"

"Not in so many words," said Eddie smiling, "look, people just don't apply for those sorts of jobs unless they know they can do it, and it's not so much the job, it's being able to do it three hundred feet in the air."

"Yes of course," said Sam still looking at the skyscraper across the street, "I feel sick just thinking about it."

At twelve noon Sam caught a cab to 226 Hudson Street, walked a garden length of wrought iron fencing, opened a gate and trod a red brick garden path to the imposing entrance of a rather large house. The lawn and garden were reasonably well kept, but the dormer windows and the double front doors were in need of maintenance.

Sam noticed that the lime green paint had started to peel. He knocked and waited, the door opened and a black lady poked her head through an opening just wide enough to take her head. She looked at Sam with suspicion.

"Yes Sir, and what can I do for you?"

"Hello Ma'am," said Sam, "my name is Sam Pryce, I'm from England." Sam said England, to save any confusion over his explanation as to where Wales was. The lady then opened the door wider and stood outside, she was a little on the large side, stood about five feet four and had about herself a red and white chequered pinafore with a matching headscarf. Her suspicious look didn't change as she stood anticipating Sam's reason for knocking on the door.

"I know this may sound strange and the chances of the lady I am seeking is either dead or will have moved on years ago." The lady still didn't speak but Sam caught the hint of a smile. "The lady I am enquiring after is a Mrs. Doyle, Mrs. Margaret Doyle." Immediately the lady's facial expression changed.

"You are looking for Mrs. Margaret Doyle?" Sam shivered and could feel the hairs on his arms standing.

"Yes," said Sam excitedly, "you know of her?"

"Where are you from?" she asked.

"Actually, I'm from Wales but..."

"You from Wales," the lady raised her eyebrows, "how come you have this address and what is your reason for information about Mrs. Doyle?"

"It's a long story, but a man by the name of Michael Barry Gill knew Mr. and Mrs. Doyle many years ago."

"Michael Gill," the woman said clutching her hands to her chest, "I remember Mama saying something a long time ago about a man named Michael Gill, on account my Mama did house maid work for Mrs. Doyle, I've remembered his name since I've been a little 'un."

Sam couldn't contain himself, could Mrs. Doyle still be alive after all these years?

"Is she still alive?" he blurted out.

"Oh yes Sir, she is still alive, God only knows how come, why some days she like a young 'un and some days she says she wishes she was dead and I says, Mrs. Doyle, one day you will wake up and you will be dead. Now you follow me and when I say stop you stop and I will go and see if Mrs. Doyle wants to see you or not."

It was a large house and from the outside it looked as though most of the curtains were drawn. It looked and felt cold, there was a musty damp smell, one of age and of being abandoned. Sam followed this lady who hadn't given her name into a large room with high ceilings, a chandelier hung from an intricate ceiling rose, cobwebs could clearly be seen, their dusty, wispy strands were strung from one glass teardrop pendant to another.

"You stop here."

Sam did as he was instructed. He stood and looked around the large reception room, life sized portraits in gold picture frames hung on the walls, one he noticed was of a man with a dark beard sitting at a desk. His hands were spread out, holding down what looked like some architect's drawings. On the wall opposite, a portrait of a lady seated at a baby grand piano. She looked demure, straight faced but content. She wore a white blouse with frills around the cuffs and collar. She sat, with her hands together holding a fan. A choker of two rows of pearls were around her neck and her long hair was tied with a black ribbon. To Sam's right a staircase swept up to a landing where other portraits hung. The splendid oak balustrade with its wrought iron spindles contrasted with the discoloured and threadbare red carpet that climbed the treads and risers of the staircase. The black and white floor tiles were laid diagonally to the walls, in the center of the room where Sam stood was a circle of glazed mosaic tiles. In its centre, again in small mosaics was the image of an American bald eagle. For a moment Sam tried to imagine this room in its past glorious years. When the lady with the chequered pinafore reappeared through the door she had gone through some minutes before, she beckoned Sam. He entered a large drawing room, the curtains of this room were drawn back and although it was bright and airy, Sam still detected the same musty smell, although not as pronounced.

"Mrs. Doyle, this is Master Sam Pryce, the young gentleman that wishes to see you."

"Willena," Mrs. Doyle called, "I would like for you to stay and listen to what this young man has to say." Willena didn't answer, she just lowered her head.

"Mr. Pryce, please take a seat."

"Thank you, ma'am," said Sam as he sat in a chair opposite the rocking chair that Mrs. Doyle had risen from when Sam had entered the room. A fire lazily flickered in the hearth as Mrs. Doyle poked it with a poking iron. Sitting down Margaret looked at Sam, she studied him from head to foot, could this be true, she wondered? That this young man knew Michael? She smiled… a little smile.

"So, you know Michael Gill?" she said slowly.

"Knew him, yes I knew him, he died over seven years ago. I know this must be hard for you to believe, but I would like to show you something that will allay any doubt in your mind that what I say is true." Sam reached into his jacket pocket and brought out a faded white envelope. He rose from his seat and handed it to Mrs. Doyle, she opened it, taking out a folded piece of paper, she looked at Sam as she raised a monocle that hung on a thin black ribbon around her neck. Placing it to her right eye she started to read out loud the contents of the letter that she held, stopping after the fourth word, "I taste the liquor." On stopping she uttered the words "Good Lord," her monocle dropped from her eye and the envelope slipped from her lap onto the floor.

"How did you come to be in possession of this?" she said raising her hand with the letter firmly clasped in her hand. There was a slight tremor in her voice edged with a degree of accusation.

"It's a long story Mrs. Doyle but I can assure you that there is nothing sinister in my being here". For a moment Margaret said nothing, she remembered vividly the day she had placed the poem in an envelope and signed her name to the paper she now held, nearly sixty years earlier.

"Now Sam, if it's going to be a long story, I suggest you tell it over a cup of tea and a biscuit."

"Willena would you mind," Margaret asked glancing at Willena sitting with her hands on her lap, a couple of yards behind Sam. Willena got up and walked to the door, "and bring a cup for yourself," she added.

Sam told Margaret his life story, his relationship with his Aunt Megan and her relationship with Michael. He told her of Michael's respect for her and Mr. Doyle, saying that he himself had heard of the Doyle's from Michael when he was nine years of age. Sam spoke of his wanting to follow in Michael's footsteps, to visit the places he had visited, and his first call would be the Doyle's last known address, not thinking for a moment that either Mr. or Mrs. Doyle would still be alive, never mind the fact that they still lived at the same address. Willena placed a tray laden with a tea pot, sugar, milk and three cups and saucers and a plate full of biscuits on a small table between Mrs. Doyle and Sam. She poured a cup for Mrs. Doyle and handed it to her, then one for Sam who added his own sugar and milk, taking her own back to her seat.

Margaret didn't speak much, letting Sam explain things without her having to ask the questions. Now and again, she would close her eyes and think back to those times, the times that Sam spoke of. Sometimes his voice became a blur in the background, as she recalled the life she had lived with Gordon, of whose company she had been without for the past fifteen years. She longed to hear again the singing and the laughter that would echo throughout the house, she looked around the room, the pictures hanging on brass wire, some of which had hung there since the time Michael had given Gordon a hand to put them up, and the time they hung the imported William Morris wallpaper on the walls. She couldn't believe that the paper had stuck to the walls all these years.

"So, I hope you don't mind my calling, as it is, my Aunt Megan will be over the moon that I have actually met you." Margaret looked at Sam and smiled.

"Sam," she said wistfully, "until I heard your story, I felt that for the last fifteen years I have been stagnating and wallowing in my own self-pity. In front of you is a ninety three year old woman with a mind of half those years, I never intended to be the way I am, but after Gordon died the years slipped by, less people visited my home but I didn't care, as most of my friends had died. The rest, they had their families to worry about, after a while everything for me became a memory. Willena has tried her best to get me to do things, I have a brand new Roosevelt wheelchair that I have had for over two years," she paused, "it's never been used."

"Maybe I could take you for a walk one day." Margaret glanced at Sam and then at Willena who nodded her approval.

"We will see," uttered Margaret, "now Sam," her face lighting up, "I want you to do something for me."

"You only have to ask Mrs. Doyle."

"As it's Sunday tomorrow I would like it if you would share lunch with me, if you have already made plans then maybe we could meet again soon."

"I have no plans for tomorrow Mrs. Doyle and it would be a pleasure to accept your invitation."

"Very well," she said, "Twelve thirty."

"Twelve-thirty," replied Sam, as he stood up, Margaret stood to acknowledge Sam's departure. Willena opened the door and as Sam reached it, he turned. "Mrs. Doyle, can I ask is that a portrait of you in the hallway?" Margaret looked surprised and answered with a smile.

"Yes, yes, it is, it was painted a long time ago Sam, a long time ago."

"I hope you don't mind me saying Mrs. Doyle, but I think it has been too long in the dark, and in my opinion, it needs the sun to shine on it. A beautiful painting needs light Mrs. Doyle so that it can be seen. Till tomorrow Mrs. Doyle till tomorrow."

With mixed emotions Margaret sat and stared at the door that Willena had closed. Her thoughts shifted from the past to the present, her home was littered with memories and the future held nothing. She thought of Sam's words on leaving, about her portrait being too long in the dark, could this be herself, herself being too long in the dark. Maybe she should walk in the sun again and this was one of those moments, a serendipity moment to coin a phrase. "Willena," she shouted, "Willena," she repeated her call, Willena came running into the entrance hall as Margaret opened the door.

"Mrs. Doyle whatever is the matter."

"Sam is right, it's been dark in here for too long. Draw the curtains Willena and let the sunshine in."

Willena squealed with delight as she ran up the stairs to draw the heavy jade green curtains.

Margaret stood at the foot of the stairs looking at the portrait that Sam had mentioned when a beam of light cast its magic on a sixty four year old painting. Margaret gazed upon the portrait as more light cascaded into the room. She slowly walked around the hall, looking at it from different angles. The portrait of someone she once knew.

Willena was running around shrieking with joy, but Margaret did not hear her, she was losing herself in the picture. She tilted her head, the brush strokes on the lady's dress, its crimson shades depicting its folds. The soft shadow of the candelabra lay across the shining surface of the baby grand. She looked at the lady's face, how young she thought the lady was, twenty nine years of age, and Margaret was told at the time it was a good likeness. She looked happy, she was happy, Margaret said to herself. She turned and looked into the eyes of a man in another portrait, "Gordon," she sighed then she smiled, "it seems I have neglected us both, Sam has told me," she stopped, "I'll tell you about him later, anyway I have decided that whatever time I have left on this earth the sun will shine on all of us."

9

Sam could not believe that Mrs. Doyle was still alive, and the fact that at the age of ninety three she was lucid, sharp in thought, and seemingly to be a nice lady was a bonus. To think, she handed Michael Gill that poem to read on board a ship all those years ago, and it was he, Sam Pryce who had brought it back and placed it in the hands of its original owner.

On closing the iron gate to Mrs. Doyle's property, Sam looked up, he could see curtains moving through a ground floor window. When thrown open, he saw Willena, she was waving to him, he raised his hand as more curtains were drawn back. Was he responsible for that, Sam wondered as he walked away?

When Eddie got home, Sam was looking through the Manhattan Gazette.

"Anything of interest?" he asked.

"I don't recognize any of it," Sam said throwing it onto the seat he had just got up from, "and you Eddie, how was your day?"

"I had done a lot of walking and got rather thirsty, I know the sun is shining but it's still cold, I heard people say that we could have some snow next week. Anyway, I had forgotten about not being able to get a beer so I asked a rather fashionable gentleman on the street if he knew of a bar where I could get a drink. He looked surprised at my question then he looked over my shoulder and then over his shoulder before smiling and asking how long I had been in America. Of course, by then I had realised my mistake. I apologised, telling him that I had only been here a couple of days, "Come with me," he said. He took me down a side street and then an ally, he knocked on a door, spoke through a metal grill and the door opened. We went inside; a black man was playing a piano as a black lady sang. Several ladies accompanied by their menfolk sat at tables, with a lot more men standing at the bar, it seemed all very well run, I mean it being illegal and all that. I was asked a few questions by a couple of well-dressed men, black shirts, white tie, bracers, the type you can't buy in shops, and fedora hats. I noticed one of them wore a brass knuckle duster on his right hand. My new friend, who by now had introduced himself as Horace, muttered something about not wanting to get on the wrong side of these guys."

"Horace?" said Sam.

"Yes, it's the first Horace I've ever met, anyway, he stood me a few drinks, hardly put my hand in my pocket. He could have been part of the operation," said Eddie as he poured some boiling water into a green teapot.

"Operation?"

"Yes, maybe he was on the street touting for customers to take back to the bar."

"Honky Tonk," said Sam.

"Whatever," Eddie replied shrugging his shoulders, "and you Sam how did you get on with your quest to find the mysterious Mr. and Mrs., was it Doyle?"

"Yes, Mr. and Mrs. Doyle, well surprise, surprise, Mrs. Doyle is still alive. She is ninety three years old and in good health as far as I could make out. She lives on her own with Willena, her house maid, in a big house on Hudson Street and she has invited me to dinner tomorrow."

"You must have made an impression on the lady to be invited to dinner."

"Not necessarily me Eddie, more likely my connection with Michael Gill. Still, it will be nice to see her as there are a lot of questions I would like to ask, and no doubt she will have a lot of questions to ask me."

The following morning Sam awoke to the sound of rain on the roof of their lodgings. He looked out of the bedroom window and on a balcony across the road a woman was hanging out her washing. Her washing line was strung back and forth the full length of her balcony being fixed at both ends to partition walls. Her washing being protected from the elements by the balcony above. Below, and in the street, a motor car passed, it went through puddles of water spraying the footpaths. Some people were out walking with umbrellas. There were people on push bikes, some wore raincoats some didn't. A dog, a little black one, unconcerned as to its surroundings, walked down the road with a stick in its mouth. So, this is a street in Manhattan on a wet Sunday morning in February, thought Sam.

He dressed and went into the kitchen, the kettle was boiling, he noticed two cups on the table. Eddie was putting on his boots as Sam switched on the radio, he played around with the dial trying to find a station that played music, finally landing on WJY, a station that played Honky Tonk music.

Sam had discovered that New York had five boroughs. The Bronx, Brooklyn, Manhattan, Queens, and Staten Island. How much they differed from each other in any aspect he didn't know, but there seemed to be a mixed bunch of people that he had already seen in Manhattan. The diversity of people was many, ranging from nationality, languages spoken, colour of skin, to the way they were dressed. And judging from what he had seen New York was going to be an interesting place to live.

"I'm meeting some of the lads I'll be working with this morning," Eddie stood and reached for a cup of tea that Sam had just made.

"And how do you feel about being the new kid on the site?" Sam asked as he placed a teaspoon on the table.

"I'm alright with it," Eddie answered. "People come and go all the time on those sites, if they are anything like the ones back home I'm sure everything will be alright. I will be looking for accommodation in the city later, so you will be here on your own unless you fancy coming with me."

"No, you do what you must do, I will be looking for work myself tomorrow. In any case our rent is paid up until the end of next week so we have till then."

It was an hour's walk to Mrs. Doyle's home during which Sam cast aside thoughts of the future and concentrated on the here and now. His friendship with Eddie was, he believed to be, genuine, and his contact with Mrs. Doyle in itself was exciting, maybe they could become friends for whatever time Mrs. Doyle had left. Willena met him at the door, she seemed excited to see him, a beaming smile lit her face, as she ushered him into the entrance hall.

"You have no idea the change in Mrs. Doyle," she said, "it's like she's woken up from a long sleep." Incidentally, Sam noticed Mrs. Doyle's portrait. The rain had stopped before Sam had left home and now beams of sunlight shone through the windows onto walls that had been denied them for so long. The sunlight had changed the very essence of the room, the cobwebs and accumulated dust was still there but behind the dust and cobwebs was a room that wanted to echo the sounds of the past. And at that very moment as he gazed from wall to wall from painting to painting Sam wanted to be part of its restoration.

"You like this room, Sam?" Sam turned to see Mrs. Doyle standing in the doorway of the lounge.

"Yes, Mrs. Doyle I do, very much so."

"May I ask as to your thoughts at this very moment?"

"My thoughts?" Sam said surprised at the question.

"Yes Sam, your thoughts as you entered this room?"

"The truth?"

"Is there any other?" Margaret said warmly.

"Do you have a mop, bucket and a feather duster," he answered with a laugh.

"All in good time Sam, all in good time, now come and join me at the table we have a lot to discuss." Nervously, Sam followed Mrs. Doyle into the lounge, her black velvet dress swayed as she walked on legs that had been accustomed to more sitting down than standing up.

"Sit here Sam," she said pointing to a set place on the large oak dining table that stood in the same room that he had met Mrs. Doyle the previous day. As he sat Margaret called Willena saying that they would be ready for their meal in fifteen minutes.

"Now Sam," said Margaret sitting opposite, "after you left yesterday, I did a lot of thinking. To say your visit was a revelation would be an understatement. I went to bed thinking of how my life would end, and before you came knocking on my door, I had it all planned, in fact I've had it planned for many years but now," Margaret paused, "Now I see my life, as old as it is, in a different light. Look at me Sam," she said with a little chuckle. Sam looked up from the cutlery in front of him, "What I am going to say could well be a turning point in your life as I hope it will be for mine." Sam listened intently as Margaret carried on, "It's funny how just one word can change one's life."

"I don't understand," Sam said in a whisper.

"Light, Sam," you said the word light just before you left yesterday did you not?"

"Did I?"

"Yes, you did, and I knew immediately what I must do. I had Willena draw back the curtains before you opened the garden gate." Sam smiled, now he understood what Mrs. Doyle was talking about. Willena walked in carrying two plates, one she placed in front of Mrs. Doyle, the other in front of Sam.

"I'll never eat it all," Sam said looking at Willena.

"Yes, you will Sam," then correcting herself said, "Mr Pryce."

"No, please call me Sam," Willena looked at Mrs. Doyle, Margaret smiled at the same time, nodding. As Willena walked out of the door Margaret looked at Sam, "See even Willena likes you." Sam again looked confused.

"It is customary for servants to address visiting guests by their surname Sam, obviously Willena doesn't regard you as a visiting guest.

"You won't scold her will you, Mrs. Doyle?"

"No Sam, in fact I'm pleased that on the two occasions that you have met, she already regards you as something more than a guest. Now eat your food as I have a lot more to tell you." Sam ate his food, roast rib beef with potatoes, peas, carrots and cauliflower with gravy, followed by apple pie and custard.

"Thank you Mrs. Doyle that was the best meal I've had since arriving on these shores."

"I'm glad you enjoyed it Sam," she said as she rose. Sam followed as he was directed to the chair that he occupied the day before. He was in a quandary as to what Mrs. Doyle was about to say when she asked him his plans for the forthcoming week. He informed her that he intended to look for work and as he and his living companion had accommodation until the following weekend, he was confident in finding a job that would tide him over until he could find something more permanent in doing what he did best, that of making coffins.

"Well maybe I can be of help in that department," said Mrs. Doyle. "How would you like to live here? I have a big house and you would be welcome to stay. There are conditions of course."

"Mrs Doyle," Sam said sitting upright in his chair, "with due respect you don't really know me, I came to America to pursue a dream to find work without favours, and to… to…"

"To what Sam, do you think I haven't thought of these things? I have told you there are conditions, let me finish what I have to say before you decide. The mop, bucket and duster I can provide," she smiled as she mentioned the mop and bucket, "I want you to do some maintenance on my home. I will pay you but I insist that you will not be paying me rent, I have had a word with Willena and she would be happy if you were to accept my offer. As for making coffins I have contacts, the funeral company that I employed to take care of Gordon's internment, I'm sure, would help you find employment, but for the moment I would very much appreciate your being available for a short while, if not for the term of my natural life." Sam saw her smile.

"Mrs Doyle," he said, "how could I possibly refuse your offer, but may I ask a question, who do you normally get when you want things done?"

"Look around you Sam, nothing has been done around here for years, I've been waiting for you," she said with a laugh.

"When would you like me to move in Mrs. Doyle?" Sam asked.

"Well, it will take Willena all day tomorrow to get your room ready so I suggest you take a day off to sort out what you have to sort out, and I will see you on Tuesday morning. I don't get up until nine thirty so if you are here before then, Willena will show you to your room. She can take you around the place so you can take a note of the things that need repairing, make a list so then we can go through it and you can get to work."

Sam stood and thanked Mrs. Doyle for the invitation to stay. "I am to be," he thought with a grin, "her handyman and she will be his first employer in America."

"I don't know whether to shake your hand or give you a kiss," Sam said without thinking. Mrs. Doyle laughed.

"I think we'll get on just fine, see yourself out Sam and I'll see you Tuesday."

As Sam closed the garden gate, he looked back at the big house he was about to move into. "Who would have believed it," he said to himself, "I must write and tell Aunt Megan."

10

As Megan turned the pages of Sam's letter, she couldn't help but feel that she was there with him. He told of his night at The Admiral Rodney, briefly mentioning a young lady who came to the dock to see him off and his promise to pay her father the debt he owed. He thanked her for the book she had given him, also telling her about the man from Nantucket. He told her of the people he had met, the newspaper reporter and his wife, Eddie who wanted to work on the skyscrapers, the banker, the toolmaker going to a car factory in Michigan, of the two nurses who were to work in a hospital in New York. He kept the best till last when he told her of meeting Mrs. Margaret Doyle, a tear fell from Megan's eye as he told of a lonely lady who had lost her husband Gordon fifteen years earlier, himself having lived to a grand old age. He told her about the poem that she had given him to give to Mrs. Doyle, if she was still alive. About the opportunity Mrs. Doyle had given him to live rent free in the big house that she lived in, along with her house maid, a black lady called Willena who was, as Mrs. Doyle put it, over the moon that

Sam was moving in. Sam mentioned that his living there was on condition that he did paid maintenance work for as long as it took. A half hour later Sam's mother called round with a letter of her own. There were tears in Violet's eyes as she held Megan,

"He'll be fine," said Megan, "He'll be fine."

On the same day another letter popped through the letterbox of a pub in Liverpool, it was addressed to: The family, The Admiral Rodney, Liverpool Docks, Liverpool. Mary picked it up off the coconut mat it had dropped on, and handed it to Grace, she opened it with all the excitement of opening a Christmas present, she shouted her father as she wanted to read it out loud with both her parents sitting at the kitchen table. Grace started to read with trembling hands, the words Sam had written.

"Dear George, Mary and Grace," Sam firstly thanked them again for the kindness they had shown him during his overnight stay. Then went on to tell them about his voyage and the people he had met. His visits to the city of New York and a little about Mrs. Doyle. He told them of her invitation to stay, and the loyalty she still held for Michael Gill from all those years ago.

He ended his letter with the words. The word is full of wonderful people.

Regards to you all, Sam.

PS. Thank you Grace and Mary for coming to see me off it meant a lot to me. And to you Grace for being who you are.

Grace folded the letter and placed it back in the envelope.

By the time Sam's letters had arrived at the homes they were bound, Sam had settled into his new lodgings. His bedroom was huge, and the bed where he slept, as he told Mrs. Doyle, was a bed to dream in.

"Well let's hope you have some pleasant ones."

His relationship with Willena was friendly and respectful. She showed an interest in the place from where he came, insisting he tell her stories of the life he had left behind. Likewise, Sam asked Willena about her life. Willena's stories began with her mother being sold into slavery along with her parents when she was one year old. Her mother was pregnant with Willena when she was taken in by the Doyle's, on account of her being destitute. Willena was born in 1867 two years after the Civil War and was one year old when Michael Gill left for England.

"My mother remembered him well," She smiled as she spoke of her mother. "Then she ups and dies of the pox. From the beginning Mr. and Mrs. Doyle were our saviors. Them being hard times, as us niggers had nothing. When my Mama died, I cried for a long time but on her death bed she makes me swears to God that I will look after the Doyle's when they get old and as God is my witness Master Sam, I have done just that. Then the good Lord himself called on Mr. Doyle. Mrs. Doyle is fond of you Sam and as I swore on my Mama's death, I want you to swear to me that you will not give Mrs. Doyle reason to grieve. When you come along, I swear that I ain't seen Mrs. Doyle smile so much in years."

Sam listened to Willena's life and was suddenly struck with the thought that the world could be a cruel place. As a child growing up, he realised that he and his family had very little, but less than very little was nothing and it seemed that was what a lot of unfortunate people had.

"I have been very lucky," said Willena, "the Doyle's have been very good to me and my family, although I don't get to see them often, they live in Detroit, you heard of that place?"

"Yes, I've heard of the place."

It was during Sam's tour of the house six weeks earlier while making notes of work to be done that Mrs. Doyle had Sam open the garage door. Inside to Sam's amazement was an automobile, one to him that looked brand new.

"How long has this been here?" he asked, standing back admiring its sleek but very dusty lines.

"It's been in here ever since Gordon passed away," she said placing her hand on one of the cars brass headlights. "Gordon liked his automobiles so I bought him this one six months before he died. It's a Packard, model thirty, not that I know anything about them but it was one that he fancied and our chauffeur agreed with him. We had a chauffeur for a number of years but after Gordon died, I didn't want to go in it anymore."

"And now Mrs. Doyle, wouldn't you like to have a ride in it once more? You could make believe Gordon is with you, would that be so wrong Mrs. Doyle?" Margaret looked from the car to Sam, she smiled.

"You say the nicest of things. Can you drive Sam?" she asked.

"No, I've never had the opportunity, not many people have cars where I come from."

"Well, you must learn to drive this one." Dust rose from the mudguard as she tapped it, "but in the meantime I will hire a chauffeur to take us all, you, me and Willena for a ride into the city. I can't remember the last time I was there, so your first job Sam is to clean and shine it. I will ring a man to come over and get it going, then New York City here we come."

In a matter of weeks Sam was learning to drive the prestigious luxury Packard. The manufacturers advertising slogan was something Sam would have to get used to. "Ask the man who owns one." Sam didn't own the car, but felt responsible for it. On the Sunday morning following Sam opening the garage door the chauffeur called. The car was parked on the forecourt, its red exterior paint shone in the cool morning sunlight. Sam helped Mrs. Doyle onto the cream leather upholstery.

"You sit in the front Sam, next to the driver, Willena you sit next to me."

That first drive into the city of New York was a treat for them all, they drove past Lenox Hill Hospital where Pat and Sandy worked.

"You must ask them to come for Sunday dinner one day" said Mrs. Doyle, "It's a long time since we've had young people in the house. 259 Broadway that's Tiffany, Gordon bought my engagement ring from there when I was twenty one. My pearls and other stuff came from Tiffany too."

"The pearls in your portrait?" asked Sam.

"Yes," answered Mrs. Doyle, "I was twenty nine when that was painted, and only a child when Tiffany was first opened. Charles Lewis Tiffany and his partner, I think his name was J B Young opened it as a fancy goods store, and it's still going." They drove all over New York city passing Macys and Bloomingdales, the latter, Mrs Doyle informed Sam and Willena that she went through its doors on the very day it opened, adding that she was a young woman at the time. Times Square passed by. The Apollo theatre on 42nd street and Central Park. The Onyx Jazz club on 52nd street, the Roseland Ballroom in the theatre district and the Cotton Club in Harlem. Willena mentioned that the Cotton Club had only been open a few years and was a place where black people couldn't go. But the venue, she said featured many black entertainers, some of whom she had met through friends at a gospel singing event. Ethel Walters, Adelaide Hall, Fats Waller, and Count Basie. She had also seen Lewis Armstrong play his cornet.

"Doesn't he play a trumpet?" asked Sam.

"He didn't when I saw Him," answered Willena. Apart from Lewis Armstrong, Sam hadn't heard of the people Willena had mentioned, but she assured him that in time he would. On arriving home Willena paid the chauffeur and Sam drove the car into the garage.

It was later that night after Mrs. Doyle had retired for the evening that Willena called Sam into the kitchen. She was to explain to Sam how the household finances were arranged. Willena it seemed was instrumental in the distribution of Mrs. Doyle's monthly home accounts. Sam was surprised to learn of Willena's financial responsibilities, she may have appeared uneducated but her approach regarding matters of money was second to none. Mrs. Doyle, she explained was a wealthy woman, Mr. Doyle making his fortune from the construction industry and up until his death moved in circles of the upper class, high society families with old money. As a child Willena's interest was numbers, she would run round the house counting how many panes of glass were in all the windows, then take away from that number the number of panes in the first window that she counted. Sam remembered someone else who was very good at figures and for a moment he thought of Grace at the kitchen table counting the takings at The Admiral Rodney.

Sam was earning one hundred dollars a month and up until this point was paid by Mrs. Doyle herself. But as Willena was the administrator for overseeing the expenses for the house she would be giving Sam a cheque every month for his labours. This would be signed by Mrs. Doyle and countersigned by Willena. There was another person involved in the running of Mrs. Doyle's investments and that was a Mr. Warburton, Mrs. Doyle's banker, whom Willena didn't like. She didn't trust him, he had shifty eyes she said.

For eight weeks Sam worked on Mrs. Doyle's property, replacing rotten windowsills, fixing guttering and facia boards. All walls external and internal painted. The chandelier in the entrance hall was taken down with each crystal unhooked from its frame and washed. The portraits and landscape paintings were cleaned, and ceilings painted. There was a general clean-up all round and when it was finished Mrs. Doyle suggested they had a party, she asked Sam to invite all the friends that he had met on board ship to attend.

During his time working for Mrs. Doyle he had been in touch with all that had given him a contact number on board ship. Several of them he had already been to see. Joe and Pageant lived in the city where Joe had settled into his new job. Pageant seemed to love the city life with all the different shops to wander through, it was a new experience for her. Sam had told them, as he did everyone else, about Mrs. Doyle and his good fortune in meeting her and Willena. Everyone seemed to have settled into their respective jobs and careers. Eddie was swinging from steel girders five hundred feet above the New York skyline. Curtis was pleasantly surprised when Sam gave him a ring, he had in a matter of weeks been promoted, as the McFadden Banking Act came into being on the 27th of February. Curtis tried to explain to Sam that the new legislation gave individual states the authority to govern bank branches located within state lines. All of which meant absolutely nothing to Sam but whatever it was, it would keep the banking business busy for a little while.

Sam rang him some weeks later inviting him to the get together at Mrs. Doyle's, his reaction, "I love parties," and thanked Sam for the invitation. Pat and Sandy of whom he had seen on a couple of occasions also accepted the invitation, and Dean offered to bring along some cakes.

Sam had managed to speak to Johnny Be Good, but he would be unable to attend due to the distance and his work but thanked him anyway. They spoke for some time, mostly about cars, Sam telling Johnny about the car he was learning to drive.

"You're driving a Packard thirty," said Johnny excitedly, "do you have a rich lady looking after you Sam?" Sam confirmed Johnny's question. They said their goodbyes, with Sam promising he would go to Detroit to see him when he could.

Mrs. Doyle invited three couples and two long standing lady friends, all elderly, Sam being introduced to them as a friend who would be staying for the foreseeable future. They in turn looked at Sam with suspicion and some misgivings and were somewhat taken aback when they were introduced to Sam's friends. The banker and the newspaper reporter would maybe just fit into their circle of friends and Curtis' standing went up a couple of points when it was disclosed that he was an investment banker.

Dean the baker impressed everyone with his cakes, these were uncovered by Willena along with sandwiches and other goodies that she had prepared. Dean's cakes gave rise to an exclamation by one of Mrs. Doyle's guests, a Mr. Antonio Archelli praising in Italian, Dean's expertise in his creation and display of Italian cakes. Dean not being a shy person responded likewise, suggesting in Italian, that Mr. Archelli sample his cakes, saying that food connoisseurs have got it all wrong, one should eat cake before anything else, as a pork chop, or a cucumber sandwich would spoil the delicate taste of a cake. Mr. Archelli burst out laughing, but he wasn't sure if Dean was serious or not.

Mrs. Doyle was responsible for the array of drinks available as weeks before the party Sam was taken by Willena into the cellar. She explained that Mr. Doyle had a substantial amount of alcoholic drink which he kept stocked up. Mr. and Mrs. Doyle were very sociable having small dinner parties at least once a month, the other weekends would be spent at other people's residencies.

"This rack here," she said pointing, "is gin of various distillers. This one bourbon, this one whiskey and this rack is vodka. Over there is red wine, underneath is white wine and in those crates are magnums of French champagne." Mrs. Doyle had the cellar restocked seven years ago before prohibition came into force, she had some people around eight years ago and that sadly was the last time laughter was heard in the house.

Sam was waiting to see Curtis' face when presented with Mrs. Doyle's array of spirits. Encouraged by Mrs. Doyle to sample her variety of whiskey, both bourbon and malt. They both spent a few moments discussing the merits of the malt variety before Mrs. Doyle handed him a sample of specially distilled Jack Daniels of which he approved.

Pageant found a companion in one of Mrs. Doyle's longstanding friends, discussing the changes in the old lady's lifetime, as opposed to life today as she saw it. Eddie saw himself at one time in the unfortunate position of being in the company of three of Mrs. Doyle's male guests, they were discussing New York in general terms when one asked Eddie what he did for a living, he didn't answer but instead asked as to how these people acquired their own wealth as to him it amounted to the same thing. As it turned out one was in stocks and shares another in property development and the third said his family had made their money some time ago in shipping.

"And how important has the city of New York been in the creation of your wealth?" Eddie asked looking at all three one after the other, there was a puzzled look amongst the men.

"I'm not sure as to your question?" said one.

"The City of New York, your businesses, has New York as its address has it not? This city that is known throughout the world. People come from all over to invest their lives and their family's lives to accomplish their dreams. This city, gentlemen…. where your families invested their money and their lives a long time ago, they had those same dreams as those having just set foot on these shores." Eddie's voice was calm and sounding almost rehearsed. "The city, how important is this majestic metropolis to your business?" After a slight pause one of the men answered Eddie's question.

"The City of New York has been everything to our businesses, no matter what business. For years it has brought in the investment needed to grow, the money men, men with ideas, and the logistics of how to use the capital raised. The City of New York is a byword for success."

Everyone had stopped talking and were now listening to the conversation that was going on between Eddie and the three elderly gentleman. "The Big Apple is not as it was, today there seems to be more urgency about growth and since the end of the war more people are coming." He turned to Eddie, "And I think what you are trying to say is that this country Eddie, would not be where it is without people like yourself. Since the end of the war. It seems more people are coming, this is not a criticism of those people, on the contrary this country needs people like you Eddie, as I believe you work on the skyscrapers that dominate our skyline. Dean, I have no doubt you will one day have your own confectionery business and maybe you Curtis being in banking will be able to help us all out, or at least be there to advise."

He turned to Sam smiling, "And one day we will all need your service. But before people need the services of Sam, we all, at some time or other be seeking the care and attention of," he raised his glass, "Those two young ladies, namely Patricia and Sandy." Both of whom at the mention of their names looked slightly embarrassed, "And last but not least to the person that who may be present at all events in the state of New York reporting on events such as the opening of new buildings, the meetings of heads of state, from sporting events to births, deaths and marriages, Joe and Pageant. To you all I toast the adventurous spirit, that you, the ones before you and the ones that will come after you." Everyone raised their glass and made a toast to the future.

The rest of the afternoon was spent with Mrs. Doyle's acquaintances, listening to the stories that Sam's friends had to tell, and in return, their stories about the lives that they had led. Frank Trevor, the gentleman that had everyone raise their glasses to toast the future, came over to Sam, he was a short thick-set man probably in his mid-seventies with whiskers and a well-manicured beard.

"I have heard the story of Michael Gill many times over the years," he said, "but I find it difficult to understand how a young man like yourself feels the need to walk the streets of Manhattan like he did. To follow a man like Michael who had pulled the trigger on a rifle in a conflict that he had no political grievance with, and would have had no, or little, understanding of the complexities in the war he fought."

"From my understanding of it," answered Sam, "Michael was not the only one with no political grievance who fought and died in the Civil War. Look at the last war, ten years ago how many Americans understood the complexities of that one, yet they fought and died to the wishes of their government."

"Point taken Sam, point taken. Now the matter of Mrs. Doyle and your relationship with her, my wife and I, and our friends here this afternoon, have known Gordon and Margaret for many years."

"Yes, I know Mrs. Doyle has told me."

"Well, you can understand our concern for her, and to put your mind at rest I am not for one moment questioning your loyalty to her, on the contrary we are all happy that Margaret has found a reason to get up in the mornings. For a long time after Gordon's death, we tried to get her back from the grief that had made her housebound, but there was nothing we could say or do that would bring her out of the darkness that she had found herself in. In those years she has lost a lot of her old friends and it is only now since you came along that she has become the person she used to be, in fact it is many years since I have heard her laugh. Incidentally did you know that Gordon and Margaret mixed with the high society of New York and whose names were included on the official list of the Four Hundred, the cream of New York Society, it was led by Caroline Astor of the Astor family?"

"Was your name on the list?"

Frank smiled as he looked around the room, "That's where we all met, but that was a long time ago, the society has been dissolved thirty years ago due to a lack of interest."

"They sounded like good times Sir."

"They were Sam, they certainly were." Sam looked at Frank, he had a friendly face and a friendly manner to go with it, a likeable man. Sam didn't take offence at the curiosity Frank showed in his relationship with Mrs. Doyle, in fact he welcomed it, he wanted all that knew her to know that there was no inference or anything untoward in his friendship with her. He told Frank this and felt that he just wanted to hear it from Sam himself. With that said Frank reached out and shook Sam's hand.

"I will look forward to seeing you again Sam, and we will be following your career with interest."

11

By seven thirty all the guests had left and Mrs. Doyle commended Sam for his choice of friends saying that she felt better knowing that he would be around people of sound morals. Sam smiled to himself, sound morals, he didn't know them well enough himself to assess if they were of sound morals, still, it was nice of her to think they were.

"And my friends," Mrs. Doyle asked, "I don't see them often but of the people I know I thought these would be more to your liking."

"Thank you, Mrs. Doyle, I think your friends were very…. very."

"American," answered Mrs. Doyle.

"Yes, they are very proud of their country and not without reason, but there is a brashness that to a newcomer would seem as," Sam hesitated.

"Showing off, yes I know," answered Mrs. Doyle, "but it's the way they are and to all New Yorkers it's normal."

While Sam was helping Willena clear up, he asked Mrs. Doyle about the phrase The Big Apple. The term was mentioned by Richard Holmes one of Mrs. Doyle's guests when he spoke of New York.

"Are you a betting person Sam?" Mrs Doyle asked.

"No."

"Well, probably you have not heard of a gentleman by the name of John J Fitzgerald, he's a sportswriter for the New York Morning Telegraph. Anyway, he was in New Orleans when he overheard some African American stable hands refer to New York's racecourses as the Big Apple Where they got that from God knows, anyway John liked the term that much that he named his racing column The Big Apple. When Gordon was alive we used to go to the races a lot, it was an exciting day out especially at the big races, like the Belmont Stakes and the Jockey Club Gold Cup, yes, we had some good days at the races, but it's all in the past Sam."

A week later Sam started work making coffins. A funeral director that had just opened a branch on 180 West 76th Street Manhattan. The workshop was situated in a building next door. The circumstance of Sam's employment came about when one of Mrs. Doyle's guests at the party, the Italian Mr. Archelli, learned of the impending opening. He suggested to the owner, who was an acquaintance of his that he take on Sam, an experienced carpenter who specialised in the making of coffins. Sam went to see the owner on the Saturday and was asked to start work on the following Monday where he would meet the man who would be running the workshop. Sam got to work early, he had allowed himself a half hour to walk the one mile distance from his home to his place of work, arriving five minutes before the gentleman who was to look after that side of the business.

"You must be Sam," he said as he held out his hand, "I'm Ian." The man, in his mid-fifties shook Sam's hand, he had a rough and calloused hand whose firm grip took Sam by surprise, "You look young, how long have you been in this business?"

"Four years," answered Sam.

"Same as me, I've spent most of my working life as a cabinetmaker and fell into this by accident. Yosef Acker the man you met on Saturday had asked my last employer if I could help him out for six months, knowing that we weren't that busy. That was four years ago." Ian unlocked the workshop door and walked in. Sam looked around, opposite the workshop door were racks of coffin boards both hardwood and softwood, there were two saw benches, a thickness planer and all manner of hand tools hanging on the walls. As he looked around Ian showed him the work benches and drawers that held coffin handles and all the furniture packs needed.

"From the plain standard pine to the more elaborate and expensive polished oak our turnover of coffins varies from around twenty per month, to as many as forty. So, we just make them and stack them over there," he said, pointing to the back of the workshop. "We make just two types, the cheap and the expensive, sixty percent of what goes go out of here are the cheap pine ones, the rest are the oak. There are three different types of lids, the fancy

one with the beading is again the most expensive. Don't
be too worried about getting your own hand tools as Mr.
Acker wants your expertise and nothing more. No doubt
you have discussed your terms of employment, so let us
get started. It will take a couple of days for you to get into
the swing of things, so don't go thinking that you have to
prove yourself on your first day, you will have plenty of
time to do that."

Unlike the village workshop back home where a
coffin order would come in maybe three times a month,
in the grand scheme of things little time was spent making
coffins, here it was vastly different. The average in the
three months that Sam had been there the orders were
coming in at around thirty five to forty a month. Of
course, they were not all for the undertaker that Sam and
Ian worked for, some were for other funeral parlours, some
for private burials and now and then they would get one
for a birthday party, one came through from a theatre
company on Broadway and another order was for one to
go to a bordello in Lower Manhattan... the mind wanders.

12

Sam opened the letter on his way to work, he didn't recognize the handwriting on the envelope but it was from Grace. She had replied to his first letter by return of ship, or so it seemed.

"Dear Sam, how thoughtful of you to write. It was a lovely surprise, mum and dad are well. I have just got over a cold that has kept me off work for a few days."

Sam looked at her handwriting how the stroke of her letters leant slightly off perpendicular and the calligraphic flow of her capital letters was, Sam thought, poetic in their application. Her news from home was mundane, nothing had changed, the drunks were still distasteful, ships still sailed away, her work she found boring and the rain still fell on The Admiral Rodney. He did notice however a change in her approach when it came to asking him about his life. There wasn't an instance where a capital letter started and a full stop ended that in between bore the excitement of her wanting to know everything, and at that very moment Sam wished she was with him. He would love to take her into the city and to meet his friends.

Then without finishing it he folded the letter and placed it in his back pocket. At lu nchtime he sat on a stool amongst the sawdust and wood shavings of the workshop. The permanent smell of piranha pine and wood glue hung in the air as he again opened the letter from Grace. Not once did she mention any romantic involvement that she had entered upon. But Sam knew that one day it would happen. Grace was some months older, so the time to find a suiter was going to be more pressing for her than it was for him, but maybe not just yet.

The summer months were spent working. Sam was saving his money; he didn't know what for but he was saving. Mrs. Doyle seemed to have more people calling, Sam's friends would drop by and Willena said that the place seemed to have awoken with a passion for the sound of voices.

Every two weeks Mrs. Doyle insisted that they go for a ride in the automobile. Sam had learned to drive and acquired his driving license but didn't feel confident enough to go on long drives or even to go into the city, so a chauffeur was hired. They didn't go if it rained, so they would stay indoors and talk. Sam once asked Mrs. Doyle to tell him about her husband, Gordon, and how things had changed in her life since his passing.

"Gordon," she said, "changed a lot after meeting Michael, I remember it well. Gordon was looking as he always did for good men to hire and being on a ship made no difference. He got hold of the ship's passenger list and noticed that there were two stone masons on board and he wanted them. One was Michael and I can't remember the other, anyway, I left Gordon talking to Michael on deck." Mrs. Doyle stopped talking and reached for her glass of port, she looked at Sam and smiled, "He was your age was he not?"

Sam smiled back, "I believe so."

"I went back to the cabin and sometime later he came through the door and poured himself a brandy, he never said a word but I noticed a concerned look on his face." Mrs. Doyle looked up from the glass of port she cradled. "You see Sam, Gordon was a successful businessman and to put it mildly he was ruthless in his dealings with people. He could be pleasant, charming and persuasive, but there was a side to him that I wasn't proud of. He thought that being cunning, shrewd and manipulative was being smart and in a way it was, but he was a bully, he didn't care if he sent people bankrupt, he did things Sam to achieve his ends."

Mrs. Doyle was silent for a moment. "I was young then Sam, young and impressionable and my God Gordon Doyle impressed me. I was twenty and married him twelve months later. He treated me like a Queen and always did, he had gained a reputation for being, as many called him, a bastard, long before I knew him. Thankfully, I knew the not very nice Mr. Doyle for a period of two years before he walked into our cabin on that ship," she paused, "I forget what it was called now." Mrs. Doyle had a blank look on her face, "Now, where was I?"

"On the ship, Gordon, in your cabin," Sam said, sitting on the edge of his seat absorbing every word Margaret uttered.

"Ah yes I remember, he took a sip of his brandy and looked at me, it was a distant look, you know the look Sam when someone seems to see through you. "Margaret," Gordon said, "Do you think I am a man of my word?" I thought then that it was a strange thing for him to say. I looked at him and asked him did he think he was? He didn't answer, "An eighteen year old kid has just asked me if I was a man of my word." And what did you tell him Gordon?"

Sam noticed Mrs. Doyle close her eyes, she seemed detached from the words she spoke as if she was reading from a book. "I told him I believed I was," he chuckled, but it was a false chuckle and Gordon bloody well knew it. Gordon sat down, "I have a problem Margaret, that kid Michael Barry Gill, I like him." Then you had better not disappoint him, I said sarcastically. "No, I won't," he said. He got up and went out saying he was going for a walk on deck. *The Lady Russell.*"

"I beg your pardon."

"*The Lady Russell*, the name of the ship, I remember it now. Pour me another port Sam, I'm getting rather comfortable sitting here talking to you. Why don't you pour yourself one?" Sam got himself a glass and from the drink's cabinet brought over a bottle of Portuguese port wine that Willena had opened sometime before. He topped up Mrs. Doyle's glass and handed it to her, then pouring himself a generous amount he sat back in his chair.

"Gordon went on deck for a walk," Sam said, reminding Margaret where she had left off in her story of their first meeting with Michael Gill.

"Yes, when Gordon came back, he was quiet and deep in thought, and from that moment on Gordon Doyle changed. Maybe he didn't like the way he was, maybe he saw Michael as a greenhorn, someone he could take advantage of, but he couldn't do it. And when he told Gordon that he was a man of his word, it struck Gordon that his word was not like that of Michael Gills. Imagine Gordon Doyle taking notice of a young Irish immigrant! Gordon Doyle had sat in boardrooms discussing multi-million dollar projects with the finest minds in the state, a man who has wined, dined and mingled with The Four Hundred."

Margaret paused and smiled at Sam, "Have you any idea what I'm talking about Sam?" Sam shrugged.

"And how did Gordon's change of character affect his relationship with his friends, especially his business friends?" Mrs. Doyle raised a white tatted cotton handkerchief and dubbed the corner of her mouth blotting up a little port wine that had seeped from her mouth. Lowering her hand Sam noticed a little red stain on the dainty white handkerchief as she rested her hand on her lap.

"Gordon's character didn't change overnight Sam, but he was a different man after twelve months, a better man. Some of his friends thought he had gone soft in losing the hard and selfish exterior that he could portray and to a few their respect for him diminished. But they were shallow people Sam, and Gordon's prize was the respect of many more people and it wasn't respect that was falsely earned. We owed a lot to Michael and from what you have told me about him he didn't change."

Margaret sighed, "So, it has come full circle, I used to pray that he would come back and, in a way, he has, he has come back in you Sam and if you are half the man, he was, you will do well. You remind me so much of him, and please don't think I'm being patronising because I am not, I am just telling you how it is. Now Sam Pryce I think I'll go for my afternoon nap if you wouldn't't mind helping me to my bed."

Sam rose, drank the last of his port and placed his glass on the table. He took Mrs. Doyle's glass from her hand and placed it next to his. He walked her to her bedroom door and opened it, the room adjoined the room where for many years she had rarely left.

On Saturday 17th of December Sam had his nineteenth birthday party. Although his birthday was on the following Thursday Mrs. Doyle suggested that Sam have his friends around. He was aware that at this time of year most young people would be out celebrating the Christmas holiday in places other than their homes. The speakeasies although illegal would be full, as would the dance halls and jazz clubs. There was always somewhere to go.

Sam arranged for his party to be in the afternoon so that people could leave early evening to party elsewhere. He was surprised that everyone invited could call at some time during the afternoon. He didn't see Eddie as often as he would have liked but he was eager to come, as was Curtis. It was lovely to see Joe and Pageant who also brought along Billie. Billie was given, by Mrs. Doyle, free reign to explore the house, then she wanted to play hide and seek with whoever was willing to satisfy the wishes of an energetic seven year old. Curtis brought along a bottle of port wine as he always did when calling, to which Mrs. Doyle was most grateful. Everyone that called had brought Mrs. Doyle a little present. You are all so kind, she told Sam. But it wasn't just Mrs. Doyle that received presents. Sam, on one occasion went into the kitchen to help Willena and found her weeping she held her pinny, wiping her eyes.

"We haven't had a Christmas like this for years," she said, "and people shouldn't be giving me presents as I can't do the same for them."

"It isn't about giving back Willena," he told her as he picked up a tray, "now I'll give you a hand, shall I carry in some of Dean's fancy cakes?"

As Willena placed the cakes on the tray Sam was surprised when she gave the Italian name to the cakes on each plate, "Those are called Zeppole, then we have some Bambolo Crostata and my favorites Focal Latele."

Pat and Sandy could only stay for a couple of hours before going back to the hospital to start another shift.

Eddie left early as he was expected to join some of his work mates in a speakeasy in the city. His last visit to one, he tells Sam, was raided and a lot of the booze was taken and emptied down the drain, but not before most of it was spirited away by the management.

Sam did his rounds, with everyone wanting to know how his job was going. Mrs. Doyle's old friends called having visited on a few occasions since the last party. Willena brought out a birthday cake and lit some candles. Joe started off singing Happy Birthday as he had done for Mrs. Doyle's 94th birthday party two months earlier, with everyone joining in. Curtis' baritone voice stood out above everyone else, everyone then demanded that he sing a solo. He obliged by singing a song that no one had ever heard of before, saying that an acquaintance of an acquaintance of his had written it only that year, he had acquired the words and music and so he sang it. The song, 'Bless the House' was liked by everyone, especially by Mrs. Doyle who insisted that the next time he was to call he was to bring the music so that she herself would accompany him on her baby grand.

It was when everyone had left and Mrs. Doyle had retired to her room that Willena called Sam into the kitchen. He could tell that there was something on her mind and had been for a few days, ever since Mrs. Doyle's banker, Mr. Warburton, had called. Sam was at work at the time of his calling and only knew that he had been as Willena had mentioned it.

"Is there something bothering you Willena?" Sam asked.

"Master Sam, I think you've been here long enough for me to tell you things." Willena had her hands in the sink with her back to Sam as she spoke. "You remember me telling you about my not liking that banker man."

"Yes," Sam answered, not having the slightest idea of what was to come next.

"Well, I wasn't going to tell you, but I must. Ever since Mr. Doyle's death I have had suspicions of some skullduggery going on regarding that man and Mrs. Doyle's finances."

"You mean he is doing something illegal."

"Is doing and has been for the last fifteen years, of course I couldn't say anything to Mrs. Doyle as she won't have anything said against him. He's been their banker for donkeys' years and she trusts him implicitly. He won't have me in the room when he is here. He has Mrs. Doyle put her signature to anything he puts in front of her. I've seen him do it through the window. There was supposedly some misunderstanding involving a sum of over twenty thousand dollars two months before Mr. Doyle passed away, apparently this was sorted out, but the day before Mr. Doyle died forty four thousand dollars was transferred out of Mr. Doyle's account into an account held jointly by Mr. Warburton and Mr. Doyle. I distinctly member Mr. Warburton calling on the Friday morning, there were two men in his company, one a Police Sergeant Charles Mahoney, and the other was Mr. Doyle's new doctor by the name of John Danton."

"A new doctor?" Sam queried, sounding concerned.

"Yes, his own doctor, the one he had for many years, had retired and moved away to live with his daughter after his wife died, anyways from what I gather Mr. Warburton had Gordon, who was a very sick man, sign a money transfer into an account at the Federal Reserve Bank Of New York, this transfer was witnessed by Charles Mahoney and Doctor John Danton. I didn't ask too much as I would be accused of prying into Mrs. Doyle's finances. I also think there is something going on regarding the interest on Mrs. Doyle's private account." Willena stopped to dry her hands.

"Sam, you have been in this house for nearly twelve months and I believe, you like me, are concerned for the welfare of Mrs. Doyle, who is a very wealthy lady. Maybe everything is on the level, but if there is anything going on, I would like to see him punished."

"Could I have a cup of coffee?" Sam said not knowing how to respond to Willena's revelations.

"I'll make us one each," she says as she goes into the cupboard for some cups.

"Willena, I have known you for as long as you have known me, and I can't see why you should make things up just for the reason you don't like the man. You have seen and heard things in this house that no doubt has led you to form opinions of people. I have no doubt that your suspicions of this man are well founded." Sam paused, "So what are we going to do about it?" Willena placed Sam's coffee in front of him. She raised her eyebrows.

"We!" she exclaimed.

"Yes we," Sam answered back, "firstly, Mrs. Doyle, she must not know anything about our looking into this man's dealings regarding her accounts. Secondly it seems that you suspect Mr. Warburton's accomplices, because that's what they are, Mr. Charles Mahoney and Doctor John Danton. We're going to find out a little about them."

"Well," said Willena, "the Doctor John Danton was struck off the medical board and not allowed to practice anymore."

"How do you know about that?"

"It was in the papers, that was ten years ago."

"Can you remember why he was struck off?" A broad smile began to spread across Willena's face.

"The misappropriation… is that the word… of one of his patient's money." Sam stood up.

"My God Willena, if Mr. Warburton was associated with people like that, and… and the policeman Sergeant Mahoney do you know anything about him?"

"Sorry Sam, I have never seen, or heard of him since that day he came here."

"No matter, I have an idea. Finding him will be no problem, Joe will find him. As for our banker friend, well I have a banker friend who enjoys the company of the lady whose finances are being abused by a man she has placed in a position of trust. Curtis will find out all that there is to know about him. It is Christmas Day in three days' time, so tomorrow morning I will make some phone calls and with a bit of luck we will get some information back before the New Year."

"Do you think we are doing the right thing Sam, you know I wouldn't do anything to upset Mrs. Doyle, and maybe I am wrong about everything."

"Willena, you know in your heart that this man has wronged Mrs. Doyle and I'm sure Mr. Doyle would be very proud of you."

"Yes, I know, but is it my place to even think about questioning the doings of a man in Mr. Warburton's position. I'm just a housemaid and a black one at that, my word counts for nothing."

"Willena," Sam raised his voice "Don't talk like that, your word is as good as anyone's, and better than most, so either we do this together or we don't do it at all, then he wins and he gets away with it, do you want to see that happen."

"No," she said, "no I don't."

The following day Sam made two morning calls from his workplace, one to Curtis and one to Joe. He got Curtis on his first call. He didn't tell him anything other than his need to see him about a financial matter and arranged for him to drop by at one thirty. He caught Joe on the second attempt, again he didn't elaborate on the main reason for his call but he did ask a favour of him saying that it was important that he knows the whereabouts of a policeman by the name of Charles Mahoney, Sergeant Charles Mahony. Joe asked if Sam would be at home between three and four o'clock, as he should know something by then. At twelve noon Sam walked home. At one o'clock he was washed, changed, and anxiously waiting for Curtis to call by. At one thirty five Sam opened the front door and Curtis walked in, he looked flustered.

"I came as soon as I could, is everything alright? You sounded, I don't know, bloody worried about something."

"Come in out of the cold," Sam closed the door behind him. He stamped his feet on the welcome mat. Sam led him upstairs and into his room, "Take a seat Curtis, I appreciate you calling at such short notice."

"Hello Willena," Curtis said on seeing her sat at Sam's table.

"I'm very well Curtis, I'm afraid this is all my doing, as Sam will explain." With the three of them sat at the table Sam repeated everything that Willena had told him. Curtis sat with a solemn face, glancing from Willena to Sam and back again. For a moment he sat quietly thinking, then with a professional approach, he looked at Willena.

"Willena, I commend you for bringing this to the attention of Sam, and firstly I will put your mind at ease and say that I believe every word of your observations in this matter, of course an accusation of malpractice is a very serious matter, but nonetheless if proven this person will be in serious trouble." From out of his breast pocket Curtis brought out a notebook and fountain pen, "Willena I need to ask you a few questions. This figure of forty four thousand dollars, how did you know about it?"

"Mr. Warburton didn't try to hide it; it was a sum he said, that was to be an investment for Mr. Doyle. This talk about a joint investment with Mr. Doyle had been going on for some months but I know for a fact that Mr. Doyle didn't want anything to do with it, he told me himself I swear to God."

"But if Mr. Doyle had signed the transfer, he has done nothing illegal."

"He couldn't have signed it."

"Why not?" interrupted Curtis.

"Because he was unconscious," answered Willena sounding somewhat bemused.

"Unconscious?" Curtis rose from his seat, "He was unconscious?"

"Put it like this, he wasn't of sound mind to sign away forty four thousand dollars. Yes, he was unconscious when the men entered the room and he was still unconscious when they left. They told me that he was awake and was eager to sign the transfer. Curtis, there was a policeman, a doctor and a banker in that room who would believe me."

"Do you think they forged his signature?" Sam interrupted.

"That, or he had unknowingly put his signature to it sometime before and they inserted the date to suit their timing. Now about Mrs. Doyle's personal account. What do you know of that Willena? But before you answer we mustn't lose sight of the fact that we are discussing someone's private finances and only for the fact that I have become quite fond of the lady in question and that the two of you only have her interests in mind, I will, with your permission, pursue any misdemeanors that Mr. Warburton may or may not be involved in. You must realise that there is only so much that I can do before I too would be pushing the boundaries of legitimate inquiries."

"Well, I do know that Mrs. Doyle gives money to two chosen charities, this money comes from the interest given on money deposited with the bank Mr. Warburton works for."

"Do you think he is manipulating that interest in some way or another?"

"Yes, I do."

"Do you know what charities she supports?"

"The New York Foundation and the Children's Aid Society." Curtis jotted down the charities mentioned and closed his book.

"Now you say Sam that Joe is looking into the whereabouts of, what was his name?"

"Sergeant Charles Mahoney, yes, he said he would be giving me a ring between three and four."

"Could you ring me around five?" asked Curtis as he rose from his seat, "as I would like to be kept informed of everything that happens. As it stands, I think you have reasons to be suspicious of this man Willena."

Sam saw Curtis to the door, they wished each other a Merry Christmas as Curtis buttoned up his coat and wrapped a grey scarf around his neck. Sam asked if he had done the right thing by ringing him.

"You did the right thing Sam, whether we will be able to prove anything is another matter, but yes you did the right thing. I will give you a ring when I have something".

They shook hands and as Sam watched him walk to his car, a gust of cold wind blew against the door. It started to snow as Curtis' car turned right out of Mrs. Doyle's drive and disappeared. Sam closed the door and wondered what would happen if nothing came of Willena's wanting to right a wrong that was being done to Mrs. Doyle.

13

Sam opened his post. He didn't have a lot and only for Christmas cards that had arrived in the last two weeks he would have had nothing at all. On the mantelpiece above the fireplace he had arranged all his cards, there were nine, plus the three he had just opened, one from his workmate, one from Pat and Sandy, and the other from Grace. He had sent one to her along with cards to his parents and all his loved ones back home. He took down and re-read the cards he had received from his parents, Aunt Megan and Bill, he felt alone. Mrs. Doyle had gone away for a few days that very morning to stay with one of the ladies that had been to his party on the Saturday. Willena would be leaving the following morning to stay with a relation of hers in the Bronx. So, he would be on his own. He was wondering what he would do with himself when the phone rang.

"Sam," Joe said excitedly, "you'll never guess where our Sergeant Charles Mahoney is… he's in Sing-Sing."

"Sing-Sing?" answered Sam, sounding confused.

"Yes, he's in prison."

"He's in prison!"

"Yes, and has been for the last six years, he's got another year to do before he comes out."

"And what did he do to end up in prison?"

"A number of things, conspiracy to defraud, bribery, theft and perjury amongst other things. Not a nice man, now could you tell me what this is all about," Sam paused for a moment.

"I think you had better ring Curtis, he has been here and left about an hour ago with everything you need to know, and he will be interested in the information that you have just given me."

"You have Curtis involved in this?"

"Yes, and you will be surprised at what has been going on in the Doyle household."

"I can't wait to hear; it sounds all very exciting."

"It is," says Sam.

"Just out of curiosity what are you doing Christmas Day, I believe you will be on your own and if that is the case would you like to come around for Christmas dinner, Pageant mentioned it to me this morning?"

"Thank you Joe I had nothing planned, so yes I would love to come. Is there anything you would like me to bring?"

"No just yourself, if you come at around midday that would be great, we'll see you then. Bye Sam."

"Bye Joe."

Sam put the phone down and looked around. Outside through the window he saw it was snowing. He had mixed emotions, elation would give way to sadness and sadness could usually be found in memories. So, Sam thought of home and Christmas. He could hear Willena calling from the kitchen, he popped his head around the door. "Joe has just rung with some information on Sergeant Mahoney, he's in prison." Sam was smiling, Willena stood with her mouth open.

"You don't say," she answered, returning Sam's smile, "well that doesn't surprise me, come and sit down Sam I've made a chicken sandwich and fried you up some potatoes."

"I have been invited to Joe and Pageant's home for Christmas dinner."

"I was hoping you had somewhere to go," Willena said, as she scooped out more fried potatoes from the frying pan. "I wouldn't like to think of you on your own, especially Christmas Day."

"Do you think I could take a bottle of something from the cellar to take over?"

"You take whatever you like, just tell me what it is and I'll tell Mrs. Doyle when she gets back."

On the Thursday after Curtis had left Sam, it snowed quite heavy but during late evening it had stopped and the temperature had risen. In the morning on Christmas Eve what snow there was had gone. From his room, he heard Willena calling from the bottom of the stairs, saying that she was leaving and wished him a happy Christmas. Then the sound of the door closing and then the sound of silence. In the ten months Sam had been in Mrs. Doyle's house he had never been alone in it. It seemed strange to be on his own. He got up and dressed, he stood at the bottom of the stairs and shouted, the entrance hall echoed, then he wondered why he did it. He looked around the kitchen, Willena had placed what was left of yesterday's potatoes in a bowl for him to fry up along with two eggs and two rashers of bacon.

Having eaten Sam went back to his room, he was bored, it was cold, it was ten thirty and it was Christmas Eve. He started to write a letter to Grace but gave up. He opened the drawer to his bedside table, he thumbed through a diary his mother had given him, there was little in it. He had given up writing in it a couple of months after he had arrived in America.

On closing it he noticed on the second page where it said notes, three addresses that he had completely forgotten about, they were, as his mother had said, addresses of local people, all of whom he didn't know, that had emigrated to America years ago. He looked at the addresses and not one of them was a New York address. There was one in Florida, one in Washington, and one in Chicago. The people in Chicago, a Mr. Bryan Humphreys and his wife Ann were from Carno, a little village nine or so miles from Sam's home. They had emigrated many years before. Apparently, a relation of Bryan Humphreys gave Sam's dad the address just in case Sam happened to go to Chicago, sometime, maybe, very unlikely thought Sam as he put the diary back in the drawer.

Before he closed it, he looked at the dollar bills beside his diary, they were neatly stacked, one on top of the other, there must be five hundred dollars in there he thought.

When Sam got his wages, he would put a few dollars in his pocket, give Willena a few dollars for food, not that Mrs. Doyle wanted him to but Sam thought it only right. The rest he placed in the drawer. I must buy some new clothes he thought. He was going to buy some new hand tools but his employer said that they had everything they needed, so he didn't bother. There was talk about getting a young lad in to help, but that was put on hold until after Christmas. Did they need a lad? Sam thought they did, and his workmate did, as they were hard pressed to keep up with the orders coming in. In winter the number of coffins needed went up five percent, so the likelihood of them needing an extra hand was probable.

For the rest of the day Sam moped about exploring the house in more detail going into every room looking at the paintings that hung on the walls. In the afternoon he finished his letter to Grace, then threw it into the fire, he had read it several times and concluded that it was neither interesting nor what he really wanted to say, plus the fact he wasn't really in the mood for writing.

He went into the garage and started the car. He was not really a competent driver; he should do more of it he thought. Siting in the driver's seat he listened to the sound of the engine and felt the vibration of the car, if Grace could see me now, he thought, then he stopped the car and got out. In the cellar Sam looked around, in a corner he saw three crates of wine, he picked up a bottle of red wine and looked at the label, Cribari Alter Wines, interesting he thought as he climbed the stone steps to the parlour.

He placed it on the kitchen table ready to pick up in the morning. Sam looked at his watch, it was four thirty and day light was fading.

In the library Sam ran his finger across the countless book ends that stood on rows of shelves on every wall. There were quite a few on the American Civil War, but Sam was looking for something a little less serious. He picked out one, a book about American birds, he put it back, another about the American Indian Wars, he put that back, in fact he didn't know if he even wanted to read.

So, he locked up the house and went to his room, he lay on his bed, after ten minutes he got into it, it was five thirty, at five fifty five, he was asleep. At three o'clock he awoke to the sound of voices in the street he looked out of the window and saw torch lights and people, six of them, singing Christmas carols, not very well, but who's going to listen at three o'clock in the morning. A car passed going in the same direction its headlights picking them out, there were three men and three women. Their behaviour and manner in which they walked suggested that for a country whose government opposed the drinking of alcohol were failing miserably. It will never last, Sam thought.

He got back into bed and closed his eyes; the carol singing grew fainter, he thought of the man who Willena was adamant had wronged Mrs. Doyle. He thought of Joe and Curtis and the help they would hopefully give in righting this wrong.

On Christmas Day Sam got out of bed and dressed, it was eight thirty. He put on a thick jumper and a new overcoat that he had treated himself to, wrapped a scarf around his neck and stepped outside. It was cold but there was no frost. His street was empty of people the only living thing walking was a greyhound dog and he seemed to know where he was going. There was an avenue of lime trees off Hudson Street that he walked, he heard a baby crying in one dwelling and raised voices in another. Birds were eating from bird tables in gardens, some he recognised and others he did not. A grey squirrel scurried in front of him and scampered up one of the lime trees. He had heard that these grey squirrels were a threat to the red ones at home, he passed that off as a scare story. After walking a couple of blocks, he turned and headed back home.

Sam pulled up outside the apartments where Joe and Pageant lived, he parked on the side of the road after an uneventful fifteen minute drive, the roads were quiet and the day was dull and cold. He clutched his bottle of Cribari and a box of chocolates he had bought one evening after leaving work, anticipating that they would come in handy. In a small carry bag, he had placed some crayons and a child's colouring book along with other Christmas bits and pieces. Sam checked his watch; he was a quarter of an hour early but he knocked on apartment twelve's door anyway. Billie opened the door and shouted her mother and father.

"Mum, Dad, it's Sam."

"Come on in," he heard Joe call.

"Sorry I'm a little early," Sam said, "but I was bored at home and got fed up pacing the floor." He followed

Billie into the lounge. "Brought a little something," he said placing the bottle on a table and his little something on a dresser that stood against a wall on the left as he entered the room.

"You shouldn't have bothered Sam," Joe said as he shook Sam's hand. "Pageant is in the kitchen basting the turkey," he paused, "I'm assuming you like turkey Sam."

Sam smiled,"I've never had turkey."

"It's just like a big chicken, it tastes a little different, but I'm sure you'll like it."

"I'm sure I will," said Sam. "At Christmas we usually had, have….…."

"Don't tell me," interrupted Joe, "you usually have goose."

"My Dad wouldn't have anything else, he reckons that the grease from a goose cures ailments. He uses it for dubbing his leather boots, keeping them waterproof and of course it makes the best roasties," Sam laughed.

"Will turkey grease do the same?" Joe wondered.

"I have no idea," answered Sam.

"Hello Sam, I hope you're hungry?" shouted Pageant through the clamour in the kitchen.

"Yes, I am and thank you again for inviting me," he shouted back.

"Not at all, it's nice having your company, dinner will be ready in fifteen minutes."

As they sat down for dinner Joe commented on the bottle of Sam's wine. "There isn't a better time to drink this wine," he poured the contents into three wine glasses on the table. Pageant looked up from her Christmas dinner a little confused at Joe's comment.

"Isn't anytime a good time to have a glass of red?" she asked.

"But this wine is special, it's been blessed and there is good reason for this," Sam smiled as he stuck his fork into a large piece of turkey breast. "Do you know the relevance of the wine you have brought to our table Sam?"

"Something to do with the church?" replied Sam.

"Predominantly the Roman Catholic faith," Joe said, taking a sip, he raised his head and closed his eyes savouring the taste, "and very nice too," he declared on opening them. "It seems the ban on sacramental wine was removed five years ago, thankfully, depending on your point of view, the lifting of the ban was a Godsend to the winemakers in California. Religious permits began to operate as a loophole and although it was for religious purposes only, many priests knowingly or unintentionally became bootleggers. The increase in grape production in California during this time increased hundreds of percent and it is still rising. So, I propose a toast, to all the priests that have increased their flock due to the bottle. Merry Christmas everyone."

Glasses were raised and chinked, and the wine was drunk. Christmas pudding followed a memorable turkey dinner and after the washing up was done, they retired to the lounge. On the radio Christmas songs were being played, Bessie Smith a popular singer, along with others, sang Christmas Blues songs and Pageant got up to do the

Charleston when Victoria Spivey sang the Black Snake Blues. A few songs and several drinks later Joe mentioned that Curtis had rang him and told him about Mrs. Doyle's banker.

"What do you think Joe, do you think Mrs. Doyle has any chance of getting her money back?"

"Well," said Joe, reaching for a box of Havana cigars, he opened it and offered one to Sam, who declined saying he didn't smoke, "I think the chance of getting satisfaction from Mr. Warburton is very good providing he has the money to pay it back. More importantly if we can get Sergeant Mahoney to sign an affidavit."

"Affidavit?" Sam interrupted.

"A piece of paper explaining his guilt by association, regarding the fraud."

"He would never do that!" exclaimed Sam.

"I'm not so sure Sam," Joe purses his lips, "I'm not so sure, he has one more year left in Sing Sing and if he doesn't sign one and it were to go to court, he could go back in for another five years, and I don't think he would want to do that."

"Could you draw up an affidavit Joe?"

"I have started to write one," Joe smiled.

"Have you got enough facts Joe, I mean if it's a legal paper."

"It won't be a legal paper Sam, but it will be sufficient for the purpose I intend it for."

"He won't sign it Joe."

"He will if we give him a reason to sign it," Joe drew on his cigar and exhaled, the smoke formed a circle, as it did so, the circle spiraled within itself as it rose, disappearing on its way to the ceiling.

"What reason, would you give him to sign?"

Joe flicked the ash from his cigar into an ashtray.

"It isn't him we want Sam and if we can convince him of this we will be almost there."

"And how do we do that Joe?"

"We tell him that it won't go to court if he signs. The ball will be in his court Sam, he either trusts us on that one, or he does another stretch in prison."

"And if he still won't sign?"

"We'll cross that bridge when we come to it. Now will you have another glass of wine?" Sam thought for a moment, maybe one more, he wished he had walked now as then he could have had a few more and maybe on his walk home the singers from last night would have had some competition. Pageant had opened the box of chocolates that Sam had brought and handed them around and Billie was engrossed with her colouring book.

"So how has this year been for you Joe?"

"Can't complain really, I've covered a few interesting stories, but most of it is pretty mundane stuff. I like to keep away from sports reporting, I'm afraid I don't have the enthusiasm for it, apart from my limited knowledge of the rules on some of the sports. It's been a busy year though, the Charles Lindberg thing, I think I told you about that. The Mississippi flood, then there was Mount Rushmore on the 4th of October. And the big one in the movie world, The Jazz Singer opened marking the end of the silent film era."

"Then there is the organised crime, they are dangerous people Sam, bootleggers, drug traffickers, racketeers, you name it and if it's illegal they are into it. I was one of the first on the scene when Jacob Orgen was gunned down on Norfolk Street in Manhattan, on the Lower East Side. We usually work on our own but I happened to be with a fellow reporter a street away when we heard the gunfire. When we got there Jacob a New York gangster was spread eagled on the pavement, his bodyguard Jack Diamond was seriously wounded, it was a drive by shooting. That sort of stuff happens all the time Sam. Al Capone's outfit from Chicago will be down after Christmas, I think a lot may happen next year. Of course, we get bits of information all the time, sometimes it's true sometimes it's not, it just depends on where the information comes from. One thing is for sure though, Ruth Schneider in twenty eight days' time will be no more."

Sam looked bewildered, "Ruth Schneider is she the lady that murdered her husband?"

"The very same Sam, and her lover, her accomplice will follow her in the chair soon after. Still look on the bright side they will have had Christmas."

"Joe that's not a very nice thing to say," Pageant lifted her head from a book she was reading.

"Well," answered Joe, "maybe not but that's how it is. You back in work next week Sam?"

"Yes, our stock has run down a bit, more people die in winter, so we have to make allowances. New Year's Eve I'll be going to Times Square isn't that where everybody goes?"

"Mostly the young people, but if you go, keep an eye on your money as the pickpockets have a field day."

Soon after, Sam bid his farewells and drove home, he left in the knowledge that Joe and Curtis would pursue the fraud perpetrated on Mrs. Doyle and he was happy about that. Pageant gave him a hug and some slices of turkey to take home along with some roast potatoes. He looked at his watch, it was five thirty, he sat on a chair in Willena's kitchen. So just how do the rich live, he pondered, I have just driven home in a rich man's car, I live in a bloody big house and have someone to wash and iron my clothes, my food is cooked for me and it all costs me next to nothing.

Sam thought of the friends he had made since leaving home, he didn't know what category to put Mrs. Doyle in, everyone else he could, even Willena, she had a protective instinct about her, she was the kind of friend who would listen and be sympathetic to your worries and concerns but she would never ever voice an opinion until asked and then she would tell it in an apologetic way so as not to hurt your feelings even if it wasn't what you wanted to hear.

Mrs. Doyle was something different altogether, if she was not to do anymore for him from this moment on, he would be forever grateful. For the want of a better word, he had become her prodigy always enquiring as to his work even asking that if it was his business what would he do to make it more successful? She was like Miss Mavis in her appreciation of men being gentlemen, "Good manners," Mrs. Doyle would say, "Is something all people should have, sadly some people never aspire to this basic principle of behaviour, men can work at desks or in ditches or they can live in mansions or mud huts, but it's manners that will ultimately set them apart. Don't you agree she would ask?" "Most certainly Mrs. Doyle, most certainly", Sam would reply. "Manners were the first thing I noticed about Michael Gill," she added.

Sam often wondered about the relationship between Michael Gill and Mrs. Doyle. Although she was five years older than Michael and Gordon was fifteen years her senior was there something that Mrs. Doyle had seen in Michael that wasn't in her relationship with Gordon. Mrs. Doyle admitted that after the meeting with Michael on board the Lady Russell, and his subsequent employment, Gordon had become a different person, thereby putting Mrs. Doyle's love for Gordon on a more stable course.

Sam pondered on the possibility that maybe, just maybe, there was some chemistry, something of a romantic nature that Mrs. Doyle held for Michael. It would be undeniable that Mrs. Doyle loved Gordon even more so after the influence Michael unknowingly had on him. But that for Sam, did not explain her undying memory of Michael. It also brought into question, why she was so taken with him, yes, he had connections with Michael but did it warrant the attention that she gave him? Did he and Michael really have similar characteristics? Was it her way of saying thank you to Michael? He wasn't complaining, on the contrary, his having met Mrs. Doyle may prove to be a gift that would be unparalleled. He knew she was a wealthy lady; just how wealthy he didn't know and in reality, it didn't bother him and it had no bearing on his liking the lady for who she was. One day she would be gone and when that happened, he would move on.

It was too early to go to bed, so Sam found himself going into the cellar and picking up another bottle of the red wine he had taken to Joe and Pageants. His thoughts were, should I really be taking a bottle, he had no intensions of not telling Willena on her return so it should be all right. He poured himself a glass and took a sip and then another, then he thought of Grace, what would she be doing at this moment. Her letters didn't mention any romantic involvement but he knew one day it would come. Then he thought of Pat and Sandy. He had kept in regular contact with them but had not socialised to the extent that he would have liked. He had arranged to see them on New Year's Eve, a walk of three and a quarter mile to Times Square. I hope it stays dry Sam thought.

He got up at eight o'clock the following morning, he didn't feel the best but he didn't have a headache. He dressed and went in the kitchen, made himself a cup of tea and looked at the empty bottle of wine on the table then shrugged.

14

"Hurry up," shouted Pat as she wrapped a scarf around her neck, "we're meeting the others at eight o'clock and it's a twenty minute walk to that place off Times Square. And don't put those strappy shoes on it'll seem a long walk home at twelve thirty."

New York on New Year's Eve to those that had never been to Times Square before was unlike anything newcomers had ever seen. The city was buzzing with people spilling out of dance halls, jazz clubs and hotel ballrooms. It seemed that the speakeasies would have a free night without the interference of being raided by the authorities, although they made a token raid on a couple of places that by all accounts, were pre-warned of a visit.

Sam had already met up with Eddie who had brought along a couple of his mates. Sam tagged along, always one step behind Eddie who seemed to know all the places that sound advice given, for not going in they went in anyway. Even Pat and Sandy seemed eager to venture into establishments that were deemed unsavoury. Sam started off on the cautious side but ended up having a damn good time. Dancing with near naked ladies and being propositioned by some. Sam had never been with a lady regarding the pleasures of the flesh and was up until that moment rarely in the company of girls who were worldly in that department. There was an instance while talking to Pat amid bedlam that a good looking lady caught his eye, dressed in a shimmering gold dress with an ostrich feather attached to a golden band that adorned her head, a head of long blonde hair that cascaded down her back. She looked at Sam and smiled.

"Don't even think about it Sam," Pat said, "you wouldn't be able to afford that one anyway."

"Expensive," said Sam.

"Very expensive," replied Pat. "If I was to be that good looking, had a body that words couldn't describe and had the morals of an alley cat then I would be expensive."

"Patricia!" Sam said sounding shocked, "does that mean you would charge me for your favours?"

Pat raised her eyebrows.

"Well, how much is expensive?" Sam asked with a straight face.

Pat didn't reply she grabbed his hand, "Let's get out of here the others are leaving anyway." Through the crowd Pat saw Sandy and pointed to the exit, Sandy nodded and turned to a lad she was with, he followed her out. Eddie and his two mates led them down an alleyway to a Honky Tonk where there was more music and dancing.

Some of the couples Sam noticed were dancing that close that the affection displayed was a little more than the shaking of hands. Sam, by then when taken onto the dance floor by Pat, was uncertain as to which couples to follow. Those dancing apart, or those whose friendship was already established, he chose the latter, the problem being, when he held Pat that close, the warmth of her breath, the feel of her body in his hands, was, where the need to make love to her came high on the list of things to do when the lights went out. Nonetheless if Pat was offended by the closeness of swaying hips she would have pulled away, she didn't, then again in all fairness the dance floor was packed.

After a few drinks in the Devil's Den, they left the establishment and made their way to Times Square. The crowds numbered in their thousands and everyone seemed in good cheer, except those whose timing was out, those who had peaked too soon were left behind, being somewhat ill, throwing up in shop doorways and the like, having been abandoned by their supposed friends. At ten to twelve Sam whose hand was entwined with Pat stood in the centre of the crowd in Times Square.

In the darkness search lights were scanning the sky, their beams like shards of light shining through the branches of trees on sunny days. The countdown begins and ends, with the searchlights turning on to the clock on the Paramount building. 1927 became 1928. There were lots of hugs and kisses, shaking of hands and shouts of "Happy New Year." Sam grabbed Pat and kissed her with as much attention to detail as he would feathering a goose, and Pat played the part of the goose to perfection.

With her party dress in disarray and her fragile mind all over the place, she looked at Sam and through tears of joy and sadness said.

"Don't you bloody leave me Sam Pryce, as I don't know how to get home." They looked around, people were starting to leave, "Can you see Sandy?"

"No, can you see Eddie?"

"He's over there!" Sam looked in the direction where Pat was pointing, he saw him and attached to his arm was the blonde lady that supposedly had the morals of an alley cat. Eddie waved and gestured with his hand that he would give Sam a ring. Pat was getting anxious over not being able to find Sandy.

"She was with a bloke the last time I saw her," Sam said.

"Yes, I know she's been with him a few times, he will look after her."

As they walk to Pat's apartment, Pat slipped her right hand into Sam's.

"It's been a long road," Sam says.

"Sam, it isn't that far."

"No, I mean it's been a long road for us to get where we are, tell me Pat are you happy, are you settled?"

"That's a double edged question Sam I love my job it's exciting and rewarding but as for being settled…," she paused.

"You miss your Mum," Pat stopped walking and looked at Sam.

"You really are a deep one aren't you Sam?" she smiled.

"Is that a failing on my part? You miss your mother, don't you?"

"Jesus Sam, I could hug you for that, how did you guess?"

"You told me on the ship and we hadn't even set foot on American soil then."

"Did I?" they started to walk again.

"Yes, you'd had a little too much to drink and you cried when you spoke of her."

Pat squeezed Sam's hand, "Don't you miss yours?"

"Yes, I do, but I try not to dwell on it too much. We turn left here."

They walked without talking.

"I hope Sandy is okay," Pat said wistfully.

"She'll be fine, she's a survivor she knows what she's about."

"You could say that, she's a flitter."

This time Sam stopped.

"A flitter?"

"Yes," Pat laughed, "she flits from one man to another."

"Is she really, you mean she has alley cat tendencies." They both laughed.

"That's a lovely turn of phrase Sam."

"I didn't mean she was an alley cat just that she may have the tendencies of being one."

"Sam Pryce!" exclaimed Pat, not letting go of his hand, "that's my friend you're talking about."

"Well, you used the term flitting and I would say that flitting and alley cat are in the same category, or pretty close to it." They laughed again as they walked. Pat felt warm and comfortable in Sam's company. It seemed that they had been friends for a long time. She had enjoyed the evening and already knew how it would end. What the hell she thought, he wasn't the first to share her bed and he wouldn't be the last, and as for the consequence, she didn't want to think about it.

"Here we are Patricia." Sam said as he let go of her hand. A gas streetlamp lit up the steps to Pat's apartment. Sam hadn't noticed but it was the glow of the streetlights, vehicle headlamps and lamps from horse drawn buggies that had lit the way to Pat's home. As they stood facing each other, Sam became aware of the amount of movement on the pavement. People, their voices wishing everyone a happy New Year, he then became oblivious to their laughter and merrymaking, now as far as he was concerned there was only Pat and himself on the street. He was about to kiss her goodnight when she slid her arms around him and asked him if he would like to stay the night as she did not want him to walk home alone.

"Is it that you want me to stay the night, or that you don't want me to go home alone?" Sam asked.

"I want you to stay the night." Pat said as she led him by the hand.

The evening didn't go as Sam had planned. He reckoned that he would have been home by two o'clock, at the latest, instead it was ten in the morning when he turned the key to his home. He was unaccustomed to holding young ladies, never mind ones, in his case, void of their garments, and as exciting as it was to drive Mrs. Doyle's Packard model thirty, it wasn't a patch on the excitement he felt when Pat switched the lights on after she had taken her clothes off. And even that came second to what happened next and what happened next lasted pretty much all night. As much as he tried to understand the procedure that led to what had happened, one thing was for sure it certainly was not love, as many a soothsayer would have you believe, it was pure and simple unadulterated lust, or to put it another way, it was the call of the alley cat.

"Jesus Christ Pat, you were at it all night."

"No, I wasn't, Sam was, I wasn't."

"I really didn't think you were that kind of girl."

"And what kind of girl is that Sandy? I like him, what's wrong with that."

"Do you think he will want to see you again?"

"Yes, we are good friends, of course we will see each other again, like I said we are friends. Look we are not in love with each other, it was a physical thing and I had a good night. What about you Sandy?"

"I'm not like you Pat, sometimes I wish I was but I'm not, and that fellow I've been seeing for the last few months I won't be seeing him anymore." Pat stopped folding her clothes.

"You've finished with him?"

"You sound surprised Pat."

"Well, I can't say I liked him that much, what happened?"

"Nothing really, I just didn't fancy him anymore."

When Pat had seen Sam out and closed the door, there was no regrets, no thoughts of why she had let him stay the night and certainly no regrets that he had shared her bed. She'd had lovers before and one who had lasted three years, he was a factory worker, he treated her well, but there was something missing in their relationship so it ended. In the past ten months she had, as she liked to put it, been the subject of two men's interest both of whom she didn't see any more, but Sam, Sam, was different, she didn't love him, nor he her, but she did believe he would always be there for her. Would they share the same bed again, probably, and she would have no reason not to, that is until she found her soul mate. If that were to happen all well and good, if it didn't that would be fine too. No, she had no regrets, she loved every minute of his company, inside and outside her bed.

15

"Sam, it's Curtis here, I know I'm a bit late in wishing you a happy New Year but I thought I would leave it until I had some information regarding our banker friend."

"Happy New Year Curtis, I thought you wouldn't have any news for me till next week."

"Well, this business has been bothering me and I've had a lot of digging to do, almost to the point of breaking the law myself in obtaining relevant papers. But the answer to our question - was a bank draught signed by Mr. Gordon Doyle on Friday 15th of November 1912? The answer to that question is yes. The question to that answer - is it genuine or a forgery? If it's genuine how it was obtained, as Mr. Doyle was in a coma at the time of signing it. If it was genuine, it could not have been signed on the date stated, therefore it would not be a legal bank draft. The money, the amount being forty four thousand dollars was transferred out of Mr. Doyle's account on the Friday afternoon, into a joint account held by Mr. Doyle and Mr. Warburton. An account that was opened at the Bank of the United States, three months before Mr. Doyle died. But there seems to be something amiss, as a similar sum was deposited at the time of it being opened and withdrawn three days later. This sum of money was then withdrawn by Mr. Warburton from the joint account and transferred back into Mr. Doyle's account. I hope you don't mind Sam but I am reading this as I have written it down, so I'll carry on until I have finished then you can throw a few questions at me."

"That's fine Curtis I'm listening."

"Now where was I, ah yes, the funny thing is, that this account was not closed, leaving me to believe that this was a ploy, pre-meditated that Mr. Warburton would have access to Mr. Doyle's money through this joint account. Now we come to Mrs. Doyle's accounts. This one is straight forward. Mrs. Doyle, in this particular account has a total sum of ten thousand dollars drawing an average of 5% interest per year which means that the two charities Mrs. Doyle subscribed to should have received two hundred and fifty dollars each per year instead of the one hundred and twenty five dollars that they actually got. The other two hundred and fifty dollars per year, is explained away by Mr. Warburton as administration costs, which is absolute nonsense. That two hundred and fifty dollars over fifteen years amounts to three thousand seven hundred and fifty dollars, plus compound interest. I don't know, maybe another one hundred and fifty so that brings it to around three thousand, nine hundred dollars in total. Not forgetting that most of that figure should have gone to Mrs. Doyle's charities. Then we have a figure of forty four thousand dollars that ended up in an account under the name of Mr. Warburton in a branch of the Bank of the United States." For a moment there was silence.

"How did he get away with it?"

"You may well ask Sam but get away with it he did, for fifteen years and he would have got away with it for a damn sight longer but for good reasons."

"Go on you're dying to tell me," Sam said with a little laugh.

"Well, he didn't count on a clever shit like you, who believed what Willena had told you, then you telling me and I believed you, then we both told Joe, and he believed us. You see Sam, he wasn't bothered about what Willena knew, she could smell as many rats as she liked, but as she said who would believe her, she was a black house maid and her word meant nothing, now your word Sam…"

"My word, come on Curtis, I make wooden boxes for a living, my word would mean about as much as Willena's."

"Now, you just hold on Sam, since you have been in America you have made the acquaintance of a few important people, and I don't include myself, although I can pull a few strings. You have friends like Joe who is in the position of being able to ask questions and get answers. Look at those people at Mrs. Doyle's party, it is through you that I have got to know them and they have been immensely helpful to me in my business. Amongst others, there's Mrs. Doyle, whom I adore, she is a lady of means and I don't just mean financially. Sam, you have no idea of the position you have found yourself in."

"Yes, I have been truly fortunate, Curtis and I know it. But I am who I am and like my Aunt Megan has told me, no man is an island, everyone needs someone at some time."

"Very true Sam, very true. There is one thing I did forget to mention, that is mister smart ass Warburton is not around at the moment. He's gone on holiday to Europe for a couple of months, so we will have plenty of time to gather as much information on him as is necessary. By the way he has enough money to settle his debt regarding Mrs. Doyle. I will ring Joe and let him know my findings and will speak to you soon."

"Thanks Curtis, bye."

16

January, the snow came and went. February, the snow came and again it disappeared, well not exactly disappeared, most of it went down the drains and eventually ended up in the Hudson River. Sam's work had become a priority, working long hours and weekends. His work partner having two weeks off didn't help after cutting off his little finger on the bench saw. Sam's saving grace was that the young lad they had taken on was quick and keen to learn. His relationship with Pat was much as it was before. He did ring her a few days after their dalliance on New Year's Eve, to thank her for a memorable evening. We must do it again some time she had said, give me a ring in a couple of weeks. Mrs. Doyle arrived back safe and sound and on her arrival, he presented her with a woollen shawl, "Your old one may have sentimental value but it's gone thin and this one will keep you a lot warmer, I know it's not a black one but I thought pale blue a less morbid colour."

She smiled, "Thank you, Sam, it's very thoughtful of you."

Willena had arrived back home the day after New Year's Day, a day before Mrs. Doyle.

"I'm glad to be home, all this rich food is not good for my hips." She laughed, as Sam took her carpetbag and carried it to her room.

"I'll make a cup of tea Willena, it's nice to have you back."

Every few weeks Sam would arrange to meet Pat in the city, they would do much the same things, go to different hotels and dance halls but it was the jazz bands that drew them. The sound of trombones, double basses and saxophones, the whole ensemble that it takes to make up a jazz band. Then there were the big band orchestras, Sam had also become quite a dancer in this new revolution after the Great War. The dance floors were full of young people dancing to ragtime music, then there were the dances, the turkey trot, jitterbug, the shimmy and variations of the waltz and foxtrot. Sometimes they would meet up with their friends, mostly at the end of the evening when they would have coffee. After they would walk to Pat's place. Sam and Pat had become a couple, of sorts, as they enjoyed each other's company but there was no romantic involvement, and they both wanted it to stay that way. Sam would stay the night and walk home in the morning, all very uncomplicated.

He had called to see Joe and Pageant a few times, even staying the night on the odd occasion. He had given Joe the addresses of the people that were in his notebook, as with his contacts he would be in a better position to find them than most. He didn't have much luck with two of them but the people from Carno still lived at the address given, and he would be contacting them in due course. Curtis would call from time to time as much to see Mrs. Doyle as he would Sam and would always bring along a bottle of something. On one occasion, he gave her a bottle of Jack Daniels bourbon whiskey. He didn't say where he got it from, but Mrs. Doyle told him he probably bought it from a bootlegger who would have bought it from the gangster who purchased the Jack Daniels Company using the medicinal loophole to get around the prohibition law.

"Ask Sam," she said, "he knows all about the sacramental wine I have in the cellar. By the way there would be no Jack Daniels only for a Welshman by the name of Joseph Daniel, he was Jack's grandfather."

"Mrs. Doyle you never cease to amaze me."

"Curtis I am an old lady who has seen a lot, done a lot, learned a lot and may I add forgotten a lot, but thankfully things still come to mind." Before Curtis left, she had Sam go to the cellar to get Curtis a bottle of the wine that Sam had gotten rather partial to. On seeing him to the door Curtis informed Sam of Mr. Warburton's return, suggesting that they should meet to discuss their next move regarding Mrs. Doyle's money.

It would be another two months before events gathered pace and it was decided they would confront Mr. Warburton on his next meeting with Mrs. Doyle which would be in two weeks' time. Joe had written an affidavit for Sergeant Mahoney to sign and through the prison authorities had arranged a visit. Joe had told them that on reading the affidavit Sergeant Mahoney was visible shaken but refused to sign it.

"He is guilty alright," said Joe "he just needs another push."

That push came from a quarter that could not have been envisaged. Joe had written a letter to Mr. Brian Humphreys of North Street, Chicago explaining that he was writing on behalf of a friend stating that a Mr. Sam Pryce had been given an address by his mother's friend saying that if he was ever in Chicago to look them up.

Within days Joe had a reply, Brian Humphreys had emigrated with his wife Ann many years before and if ever Sam were to go to Chicago, he would be most welcome to call in. Mr. Humphreys went on to say that his son would be going to New York in two weeks' time on a business trip, and he would try and get him to call and see Sam, his name is Llewellyn but everyone calls him Murray. As soon as Joe read the name Murray Humphreys he was stunned, he read it again, the sons name, Llewellyn Murray Humphreys, he couldn't believe it. But it had to be, how many Llewellyn Murray Humphreys were there in Chicago? In his job as a newspaper reporter Joe got to know the names of the good guys and the bad guys, and Llewellyn Murray Humphreys was in the company of the Chicago Mob. By all accounts Humphreys the Hump or the Hump as the mob called him was one of Al Capone's' top men.

"Sam," thought Joe, shaking his head, "you've one hell of a surprise awaiting you."

In all fairness it was known to those that were privy to the workings of the gangs of Chicago and those of New York that Murray Humphreys would rather use dialogue than a gun but would not hesitate to use one as a last resort. He had great trust in the corruptibility of people in authority. Joe had read documents about him, he was a likeable man, one who men of the law could deal with. He had once made a statement saying that the difference between guilt and innocence in any court is who gets to the judge first with the most. Joe had read the letter two or three times before it sank in that Sam had connections, all be it through Murray's father, that he could claim an allegiance with them, both being born within a few miles of each other. This has implications Joe thought as he poured himself a locally distilled whiskey and grimaced as he swallowed, reminding himself not to buy another bottle of the stuff. Joe reached for the phone and dialed.

"Hello operator could you put me through to the Correctional Facility, Sing-Sing Prison, I wish to speak to Louis Laws the warden if he's available. My name, yes, it's Joe Fleming a reporter for the New York Times. Yes, I will hold… hello, Mr. Laws it's Joe Fleming here, you may not remember me, I was present at the execution of Ruth Snyder and I spoke to you a couple of weeks ago regarding an interview with an inmate by the name of Charles Mahoney, yes that's right I did see him but something has come up and I need to see him again. Well anytime really at your convenience. Yes, that will be fine, two thirty next Wednesday."

Joe put the phone down and a big grin spread across his face, now we will see if you won't sign? Joe was in a quandary whether to inform Sam about the letter he had received from Brian Humphreys. He decided not to until he had seen Sergeant Mahoney, however he did ring him and Curtis telling them to hold off with their meeting with Mr. Warburton as things were progressing better than expected.

On the Wednesday Joe drove the thirty miles to the village of Ossining where Sing-Sing prison is located, he was taken into the same room where he had spoken to Charles Mahoney two weeks before. The room with its whitewashed walls and grey stone floor, was, Joe guessed to be around twelve feet square, there was no windows, just two doorways opposite each other with a light pendant hanging from the ceiling, beneath that, a large crudely made table, the only thing it had in common with other tables was that it had a top and four legs. On each side of this table were two wooden chairs, one being occupied by Charles Mahoney. Behind him, in front of a closed door stood a prison guard, tapping with precise timing a black baton against his right leg. Joe sat opposite Mahoney, he placed his briefcase on the table and looked up, he could see Mahoney was unsettled, his eyes were darting all over the place. Joe took out the affidavit and placed it onto the table.

"I told you I won't sign that piece of shit," he says, "I haven't changed my mind."

"Well maybe I can change it for you, tell me do you know anything about a man they call The Hump, Humphreys the Hump?"

Mahoney's face dropped, "Never heard of him."

Joe smiled, "Well, I'm just telling you now, that Mr. Murray Humphreys has taken an interest in your dealings with Mr. Warburton. You see, a friend of his father is on a visit from England and it so happens that he is visiting another friend, guess who it is?"

"I haven't got a fucking clue."

"Come, come, Charles, I told you the last time I was here what this is all about, it isn't you we want, we want Warburton, anyway the person who is going to benefit from all this is the wife of Mr. Doyle the man you and your cohorts defrauded, I told you all about this two weeks ago."

Joe reached into his briefcase for a pen and turning the affidavit the right way up for Mahony to sign, placed his pen alongside the document.

"Well, I have been instructed to tell you, that if I walk out of here without your signature on that paper things may happen. Mr. Humphreys tells me that he has," Joe paused, "associates he likes to call them, inside this prison and they owe him some favours, and looking after you would be for him a favour settled."

Mahoney started to fidget and Joe was waiting for a response that he knew was coming.

"It was fifteen bloody years ago," Mahoney said as he looked at the paper in front of him. "How can I trust you not to take this further?"

Got him! Joe thought.

"You can't," he said sarcastically, "But I can vouch for the man that has made that promise." Joe waited.

Mahoney hesitated then reached forward, picked up the pen and signed it. Mahoney placed the pen down on the table and looked up.

"And the Hump?"

"I'll ask him to call off his hounds. He'll be visiting New York on business next month - maybe you would like to meet him?"

"That motherfucker," Mahoney sneered, "why don't him and his boss stay in Chicago, they got no business coming here. I'm guessing his day will come sooner than later."

"I'll tell him you said hello Mr. Mahoney." Joe picked up the affidavit and slid it into his briefcase, he screwed the cap back onto his fountain pen and placed it into the breast pocket of his suit. He then stood. "Thank you for your co-operation in this matter Mr. Mahoney I'm sure all concerned will be grateful, especially Mrs. Doyle."

"How is that woman still alive?" Joe heard Mahoney mutter.

"Now Charles, this business as far as you are concerned is closed." Mahoney was still sitting in his chair as Joe with his back to him turned.

"It is customary when two opposing sides come to a conclusion on a related matter, they shake hands, but I think on this occasion it would serve no purpose, so I will bid you good day Mr. Mahoney." The guard opened

the door and Joe walked out leaving Mahoney to ponder
his future. Was that guy bluffing he wondered, was it all
bullshit? He knew the Hump had contacts in Sing-Sing
and not all of them were prisoners.

"Who the fuck was this guy anyway? Have I heard
of the Hump?" he grunted, "Jesus Christ, even Pinocchio
has heard of the Hump and he's a lying bastard."

"What is done is done," he said under his breath and
rose from his chair.

17

Sam was at work when the phone rang.

"Good afternoon, Archelli's coffins, Sam speaking."

"Sam it's Joe, Mahoney has signed, just got back into the office left Sing-Sing an hour ago, can we meet up Saturday morning at say ten- thirty at your place."

"Yes, yes, how the hell did you do it?"

"I have a lot of explaining to do, so it's best if we are all together."

"I will be here, I mean at home, well done Joe. Do you want me to ring Curtis?"

"No Sam I need to speak to him on another matter so I'll see you Saturday. Bye."

Sam couldn't believe it, he wanted to shout it from the rooftops but they had all had sworn not to tell anyone about Mrs. Doyle's financial affairs. And what would their next move be, in having Mr. Warburton pay the penalty of being the thief that he was?

Sam had mentioned it to Willena if she wanted to be present when Joe and Curtis called. He had told her that Charles Mahoney had signed the affidavit that Joe had drawn up, admitting his part in the fraud perpetrated on Mrs. Doyle. He explained that all was now in place to confront Mr. Warburton with the evidence of his guilt. Willena declined saying that she really wasn't needed and in any case she had made arrangements to take Mrs. Doyle for a trip out in her wheelchair, it's chilly but dry, she had said and the fresh air will do her good. We will be gone for an hour and a half so you will have time to discuss what you need to discuss.

For several months Willena had been taking Mrs. Doyle out for Saturday morning walks except when she wanted to have a ride in the car which during the winter months was not that often. Sam was pleasantly surprised as to how keen Mrs. Doyle was for her morning outings with Willena, also the difference in everything about her from the lady he had first met. Sam didn't mention that Joe and Curtis would be calling and as he saw Willena close the garden gate he felt a pang of guilt. Soon after, Joe and Curtis arrived Sam lead them into the kitchen and as they sat around the kitchen table Joe immediately from his briefcase placed the all-important document on the table.

"There it is gentlemen our *coup de grace*," Joe passed it around for Sam and Curtis to read. There was nothing in it that wasn't known to them. It was a document of two pages, it was factual, precise and condemning, the dates and figures had been checked and rechecked, nothing was overlooked and to see Charles Mahoney's signature on the bottom of it all was something Sam would not have believed.

"So how did you do it?" Joe smiled.

"With a little help from a past neighbour of yours."

"Past neighbour of mine?" Sam beamed. Joe then told them about the address that Sam had given him. His letter to Mr. Brian Humphreys and the letter he received back. Sam didn't know the family from Carno and he had never heard of Humphreys the Hump. Curtis smiled when the name was mentioned. But it didn't matter, as to have a connection with a man who didn't know that the threat of his name was enough to make Mahoney sign a paper that would bring to an end years of criminal activity.

"So, what happens now?" Sam asked.

"We make an appointment to see Mr. Warburton," Curtis said as he scanned the pages of the affidavit. "I have never met nor seen the man; I could tell him that I needed some advice on what to do with a considerable amount of money that needs a home. I will have everything prepared all the figures and dates so that like Mahoney he will have no choice but to do our bidding."

Sam sat listening to Curtis, he like Joe were men at the top of their profession and it dawned on him that his contribution to the impending downfall of Mr. Warburton was very little, he thought that only for these two men, who due to the circumstance of his meeting them on board ship would never have met each other and the conclusion to Willena's worries was entirely in their hands.

"Now Sam, it is imperative that you accompany Curtis and myself, reason being, is that he knows who you are, as I'm sure Curtis will agree. From the beginning he will be on the offensive. There will be no need for you to say anything as your presence will be enough. In the event of us not getting immediate satisfaction, if he starts stalling for time, he will be warned that this matter will be pursued through the courts." Joe glanced at Curtis.

"Absolutely agree."

"Now all that remains is for Curtis to arrange a meeting with Mr. Warburton… Curtis."

"Well, it's Saturday today, he will probably have a full diary for Monday and maybe Tuesday so it will be," Curtis paused "Probably Wednesday. How is your diary looking for Wednesday Joe?"

"I have a couple of appointments Wednesday morning, say in the afternoon."

"The bank is in Liberty Street, so I think it best if I pick you up Sam, I will give you a ring, and you Joe, I will let you know Monday afternoon."

Soon after they had gone Willena and Mrs. Doyle arrived back. Sam welcomed them with a hot cup of tea. Mrs. Doyle got out of her wheelchair unaided, Sam taking her by the arm sat her down in front of a roaring fire that he had lit first thing on getting up. On the first opportunity, he told Willena about Joe and Curtis' visit. They both hated the secrecy that was kept from Mrs. Doyle, and Sam could see Willena was on edge wishing sometimes, she said, that she had never mentioned the whole sorry business. But she knew in her heart of hearts that she could have never lived with the thought of that evil man getting away with treating Mrs. Doyle the way he had. She was fearful of Mrs. Doyle resenting the fact that they had both, herself and Sam, gone behind her back interfering with things that had nothing to do with them. Sam wasn't sure if his words of assurance allayed any fears she may have had, but he told her that he would stand by her in exposing Mr. Warburton.

For the rest of the weekend Sam pottered around the house doing jobs from a list Mrs. Doyle had given him on the Friday. He didn't see Pat on the Saturday night as she and Sandy had been invited to a wedding party by one of their work colleagues. Sam could have gone, but Pat had told him that he would be amongst a lot of her nursing friends, so he declined. Pat not being too disappointed, suggested that they met up on the following Saturday afternoon in the city.

It was three thirty when Curtis rang the workshop, as he suggested might happen, a meeting had been arranged on the Wednesday at three o'clock but rather than picking him up from home he would pick Sam up from his place of work. If Sam would take a change of clothes, he wouldn't lose too much time from work. On the Wednesday Sam drove to work, he informed Jimmy, the new lad that he would be taking a few hours off in the afternoon and they wouldn't see him till the following day. Sam may have been at work but his mind was on other things. There were a number of if's going through his mind, what if they had missed something, what if he decides to go all the way and take it to the courts, I don't have the money to pay lawyers he thought, and neither

Joe nor Curtis could be expected to finance a court case with no guarantee of winning. We were all strangers to the city and Mr. Warburton, he guessed, would probably know the type of lawyer that would have a damn good go at getting him off. Still Joe and Curtis would never compromise their position if they didn't think they had a watertight case against Mr. Warburton.

Curtis pulled up into the workshop yard at half past two. At three o' clock they were stood outside the Federal Reserve Bank of New York. On entering, they were directed, on the ground floor, to a door with the name, Mr. Lance Warburton engraved on a brass plaque. Curtis tapped and entered. Lance Warburton rose from behind a large leather topped Chesterfield desk, his smile disappeared when Sam entered the room behind Curtis and Joe. Curtis was the first to speak.

"Good afternoon Mr. Warburton, my name is Curtis Clark, investment banker for the Bank of America, this is Joe Fleming newspaper reporter for the New York Times, and of course you recognise Mr. Sam Pryce who resides at the home of one of your clients a Mrs. Margaret Doyle." Warburton shot a glance at all three, before offering them a seat. As they sat in the three seats that were in the room, Lance Warburton sought sanctuary behind a desk that offered him a buffer as to what was to come.

"And what can I do for you gentlemen?" he asked toying with a pencil, turning it over in his fingers like a magician.

"I will come straight to the point," said Curtis opening his briefcase, "we are here in connection with the fraudulent misappropriation of monies from the accounts of Mr. and Mrs. Doyle." Curtis now started to read from a sheet of paper that he held, "On the 15th of November 1912, a sum of money, being forty four thousand dollars, was deposited in a joint account being held…"

Warburton interrupted angrily, "What the hell is this all about, it was a legal transfer of money?"

"All in good time Mr. Warburton you will have your opportunity, but at the moment I would like to finish what I have to say." Curtis then went on to tell Mr. Warburton his findings, and the further Curtis went on about the fraud the more agitated Warburton got. At one stage he rose from his seat threatening Curtis that he would call security. At which point Curtis smiled and told Warburton that the New York Attorney General Mr. Albert Ottinger, a friend of a friend, had been unofficially notified of the fraud perpetrated on Mr. and Mrs. Gordon Doyle, who were, Curtis reminded him past members of the Four Hundred and that Mr. Ottinger would be kept informed of progress as it happened. Warburton looked stunned and sat down, not to say another word. Curtis also told him of his investigation regarding Mrs. Doyle's charity money. When he had finished, he asked Warburton if he would like to comment, Warburton stared at the three of them.

"I, I think you've got this all wrong," he spluttered. Now it was Joe's turn.

"Before you do make a statement Mr. Warburton I think you should read this." Joe had already opened his case and taken out the affidavit signed by Charles Mahoney. He stood up and taking one stride placed the paper on the desk in front of Mr. Warburton. He read it in silence then placed it back on the table.

"You can if you wish, contest this accusation, it is your prerogative, but I must warn you that if you insist on taking this to court it will cost you everything you have got," Joe shrugged, "But if you settle out of court… like now, you may leave yourself enough to live on and we will take no further action. Of course, you will resign your position in the bank with immediate effect and you will write a personal letter to Mrs. Margaret Doyle explaining your regret that you will no longer be looking after her financial affairs and hoping that the action that you have taken and the financial reimbursement agreed will suffice."

Curtis then placed a copy of the financial calculations in front of Warburton and read from his copy, going through the figures slowly and precisely. Warburton didn't look at the paper in front of him, he just stared at the table. After reading the financial summary Curtis stood.

"Now Mr. Warburton if you will accompany me to your branch of The Bank of the United States, we can make arrangements for money to be transferred, just remember that if you decide to take it to court you will probably spend some time in prison, plus you will be bankrupt." Lance Warburton stood up shaking. Sam opened the door and they all walked out, they walked through the foyer sidestepping customers as they made their way to the revolving door of the bank's entrance.

On the sidewalk Curtis walked with Warburton keeping up with the brisk pace that Sam had set. Within ten minutes they were standing outside the Bank of the United States. Sam and Joe stood outside the building as Curtis and Warburton entered. When they came out Curtis winked at Sam. With butterflies in his stomach Sam walked behind the three of them as they made their way back to the Federal Reserve Bank where Curtis deposited the bank draught into Mrs. Doyle's account. The last statement Curtis made to Warburton was to remind him of his commitment in the writing of a letter of resignation to the bank and a letter to Mrs. Doyle. Then the three of them watched a man who had paid the penalty for his wrongdoing walk to his office and close the door on a career that had, up until then, served him well. Unlike Joe and Curtis, Sam didn't feel the need to rejoice in the downfall of Lance Warburton, although he deserved it and maybe more, but he did feel a relief that it was all over, and the final figure including some interest, sixty three thousand, six hundred and fifty dollars.

On closing the door behind him, Lance looked at his desk, he all but stumbled to his chair. He opened the bottom drawer of his desk taking out a bottle of bourbon. He unscrewed the top and holding it to his lips he gulped the fiery liquid, he coughed and slumped heavily into his chair. Lance had always prided himself on his quick thinking, but this time no answers came. The dates, the figures and names, could he have got away with it? He shook his head. The two things that were undeniably in their favour was the affidavit signed by that policeman Charles Mahoney. They never mentioned what had become of the doctor John Danson, but no doubt they knew his whereabouts. Albert Ottinger, Albert bloody Ottinger, even his name sent a shiver through him, get him involved and that would mean a certain stay in the house of corrections. He thought of the figure, sixty three thousand dollars plus interest. He drank another mouthful of bourbon. If he sold everything and pooled what he had left he could just about manage. Lance had a lot to think about and not much time, there was his resignation, a letter to Mrs. Doyle, everything that must be done would be done, if not, he had no doubt they would be back and next time it would be for his head. He had to make sure it never made it into the newspapers as that reporter Joe Fleming would have no compulsion in having his name in the news. He was under no illusion that this would have a devastating effect on his lifestyle, so it was a question of damage limitation as it just wasn't going to go away by itself. Lance drank the last of what was left in the bottle then taking out a white sheet of paper from the top drawer of his desk, he would, with the pen that signed off the largest portion of his wealth, put pen to paper.

Dear Mrs. Doyle,

Sam, Joe, and Curtis called at a little cafe a short distance from the bank, they sat at a table to discuss the aftermath of the meeting with Mr. Warburton, both Joe and Curtis were as pleased as punch.

"I thought for a moment, just for a moment, that he was going to throw us out, then you placed the affidavit in front of him, from then on I knew we had him. And what's this regarding Albert Ottinger, the State Attorney General, your timing was perfect Curtis."

"Well one of my work colleagues knows someone who is an associate of his, so I dropped him a line telling him, without naming names, about this situation, asking his opinion whether I should pursue it or not."

"Did you get a reply?"

"Surprisingly, I did."

" What did he say?"

"Just six words."

"Six words, go on Sam you ask him what the six words were," a broad smile crossed Curtis's face.

"And what were the six words Curtis?" asked Sam with the beginnings of a grin.

"Most definitely and keep me informed. Regards Albert."

All three laughed and again congratulated themselves on a job well done. Sam raised his coffee cup.

"Joe, Curtis, can I say that your performance in Warburton's office was a pleasure to witness and I think that maybe the pair of you have taken up the wrong profession. But it is not over yet, the question being, is how are we going to tell Mrs. Doyle and when."

"I have been thinking about that Sam," replied Joe, "obviously it would be better if Mrs. Doyle received a letter from Warburton first, but how long do we wait? Firstly, I have no doubt Warburton's letter will be sooner rather than later, he won't want this getting out. I don't know how he will explain his actions but I can guarantee that it will be in such a way that it won't look as bad as it really is. Lance Warburton I'm afraid has a devious and calculating mind." Curtis placed his empty cup on the table.

"I think we will give him until tomorrow, in any case tomorrow night we should confront Mrs. Doyle with an explanation as to what we have been up to." Soon after, they got up and went their ways, Curtis dropping off Sam at his workplace. Sam checked the building, the lads having finished work for the day, then he got in Mrs. Doyle's car and drove home.

At six o'clock Willena walked into the drawing room, Mrs. Doyle casually looked over the top of the newspaper she was reading.

"A letter for you Mrs. Doyle, a young lad has just dropped it off." Mrs. Doyle folded the newspaper and placed it on the little table by her side. A letter at six o'clock she thought, most unusual. It was a white envelope with the words, The Bank of America embossed and Mrs. Doyle's name handwritten in black ink on the front. Willena handed Mrs. Doyle a white bone letter opener, one she had bought her from Macy's many years before, she then turned and walked out of the room. Margaret slit open the envelope and read the contents of the letter.

Dear Mrs. Doyle,

It is with regret that as from today, the thirteenth of June, I wish to inform you that I will no longer be available to oversee the administration of your various accounts held at this bank. Mr. Curtis Clark an investment manager for the Federal Reserve Bank of New York, an acquaintance of yours I believe, and an associate of his, a Mr. Joe Fleming, had been informed of an administration error that may have occurred in one of these accounts. The information given to them has unfortunately been proven to be correct. Also, your late husband Mr. Gordon Doyle, a man of whom I had the greatest respect, had it seemed, unknowingly to yourself, inadvertently left a considerable amount of money languishing in an account at the Federal Reserve, how this money had not come to light sooner I do not know, but I now find myself in the unenviable position of having no choice but to resign my position at this bank. I know this may come as a surprise to you as it did to me.

Of course Mr. Clarke's account of what has happened may vary from mine, but the conclusion is that a figure of sixty three thousand six hundred and fifty dollars, being the sum presented to me by Mr. Clark, and I have no reason to question this figure, has been paid into your account.

The portfolio of your accounts and relative papers may be picked up at this bank by yourself, or

Mr. Curtis if acting on your behalf, at your earliest convenience.

May I apologise again for my error and I wish you well for the future.

Yours sincerely
Lance Warburton.

Mrs Doyle was confused, she read it again, nothing made sense. Lance Warburton was in her house just two weeks ago and nothing was said, he seemed his usual self and really there was no need for him to call by, but he had been calling every so often ever since Gordon had passed away. He had been Gordon's banker for several years before his death, and at the time of his death Lance had been overseeing his banking affairs. She vaguely remembered some controversy over a sum of money but as far as she knew it had been sorted out. In any case she was at the time, not in a fit state, nor had the inclination to be bothered with anything. Gordon was dying and financial matters were the last thing on her mind.

How on earth, she wondered, had Curtis and Joe got involved. She knew Curtis worked at the Federal Reserve, maybe there was a connection, and what was the information they had received and from where had it come from? It seemed from his letter that Lance had overlooked something, whatever it was it must have been serious as to warrant him losing his job. Then a thought crossed Margaret's mind, had Lance taken advantage of her trust in him. Maybe Sam knows someone or something? Willena: Margaret knew she didn't like Lance and she could understand the reason as Lance could be a little obnoxious at times. If Willena had a fault it was that she thought everyone should speak to people like they would have people speak to them, a lovely thought but in the real world it was not always so.

She placed the letter on top of the newspaper she had been reading and waited. Sam was working late that night, she anticipated the back door opening and Sam's voice calling Willena as he always did, then he would open her door and ask how she was as he always did. It had become a habit of his, one that she looked forward to ever since he had started work. She didn't have to wait long before she heard the back door being opened, and Sam calling Willena, then her door opened and Sam with a smiling face saying, "Hello."

"Hello Sam," Margaret said, "and how did your day go?" Before he could answer she asked him if he could call Willena as she needed to speak to them both. Instinctively Sam knew that she had received word from Mr Warburton.

When Willena arrived, Margaret handed Sam the letter, "Sam, I would like you to read this letter and after you have read it, I would like to know if you know anything about its contents. Willena I would like for you to read it also." Sam was conscious of a slight shake in his hand as he read the letter, after having read it, he passed it to Willena. Willena stood stone faced as she read the letter, after reading it she looked up. Margaret found herself smiling and she saw in Willena's face that they both knew something of Lance's letter.

"Well Sam," she said calmly, he didn't speak for a moment but could sense that Willena was on the verge of tears so he held her hand.

"Mrs Doyle I will tell you everything I know. Some months ago, Willena came to me in some distress and at first, she wasn't going to tell me, but I insisted I wanted to know what was bothering her, so she told me that she feared Mr Warburton was being dishonest with you regarding your finances."

Sam went on to tell Margaret everything, about asking Curtis and Joe for their advice, about the whereabouts of the witnesses that Lance Warburton had brought into the house. He also told of the charity money, the affidavit condemning Sergeant Mahoney and how Joe got him to sign it. He told her of Curtis' investigation of Mr Warburton himself. During Sam's explanation of the letter Mrs Doyle sat with a solemn face and tears ran down Willena's face. Sam insisted that all this was done to put a stop to Lance Warburton taking further advantage of her. He explained that they didn't tell her of their suspicions until it was proven, so as not to cause her any anxiety and distress. And it was Curtis that told Lance Warburton at their meeting earlier that afternoon that he must resign his position at the bank and forward a letter to you explaining the situation.

For a moment Mrs Doyle did not speak and when she did it was to ask Willena to go into the cellar for a bottle of champagne.

"Sam, you go into the glass cabinet and get out three champagne glasses. We're going to have a toast, I don't know what we're going to drink to, but we will think of something when our glasses are full."

While Willena was in the cellar Margaret asked Sam if he could give Curtis and Joe a call on the telephone. "I know it's late, but could you ask if they could call around and tell Joe that I would also like Pageant and Billie to come along." Sam went into the hallway and made his calls.

"Curtis it's Sam, Mrs Doyle has received a letter from Warburton."

"God that didn't take him long."

"Mrs Doyle handed it to me when I got home, his version of events differ slightly from the truth, Willena has read it as well and to be honest, we didn't know how she would react."

"And how did she react Sam?"

"Well after I had told her everything, she has just sent Willena to the cellar for a bottle of champagne."

"Well already I am feeling happy, Sam, there is still one or two things that I have to sort out with her but that will be easy, now that everything is out in the open."

"Curtis, she has just asked me if it was possible for you to call tonight as I'm pretty sure she has a lot to say."

"Sam I'm on my way, see you in fifteen minutes. Bye."

Sam put the phone down then picked it back up, he gave the operator Joe's number, it rang a couple of times, then he heard a young girls voice.

"Hello Billie, it's Sam here."

"Hello Sam and how are you?"

"I am well Billie and how are you?"

"Good," she said, "would you like to speak to my Daddy?"

"Yes Billie, I would, thank you," Sam heard her shout her father.

"Dad it's Sam," a moment later Joe's voice was on the line.

"Hello Sam, Mrs Doyle has received a letter hasn't she?"

"How did you guess?"

"I had a funny feeling, I told Pageant when we were having tea that it wouldn't surprise me if Mrs Doyle hadn't heard from him, and how does she feel about it? I presume you have told her."

"I have told her, but more importantly she has instructed me to ask if you, Pageant and Billie could come over tonight. I have rung Curtis and he is on his way, I know it's short notice and it's getting late but if you can come over, I would be very grateful. Willena has just come up from the cellar with a bottle of champagne so that will give you some indication as to her feelings." Sam could hear Joe relaying to Pageant some of what he had said, and he overheard her reply, saying that they should go as it was important to Sam, as it was to everyone else.

"Sam, we will be there as soon as possible."

"Thank you, Joe, I appreciate it. Bye."

On Sam's return three lead crystal flute glasses were filled to the brim with sparkling champagne, Willena handed Sam one.

"Well, what shall we drink to Mrs Doyle?" Sam asked.

"Are Curtis and Joe coming?" Margaret asked.

"Yes," answered Sam.

"Then I think we should wait, in the meantime, we will dispense with the toast until they arrive and just drink the bubbly."

Willena raised her glass, "Thank you, Sam," she said.

"For what?"

"For believing in me."

"Isn't that what it's all about, to believe in your friends? Cheers," he said as he tasted the sparkling wine and when the bubbles hit his nose, he realised he had never drunk champagne before.

It was nine o' clock when Curtis bid Mrs Doyle Goodnight. Joe, Pageant and Billie had left a half hour before. All Mrs Doyle's questions had been answered. The rationale of her understanding of what had happened was remarkable considering her age, Joe made the statement to Sam while Curtis was in a discussion with Mrs Doyle about her future banking arrangements. Mrs Doyle perfectly understood the reason Willena was reluctant to say anything for all those years and it was the trust she had in Sam that finally made her say something. Even then they wanted to know for sure that Lance Warburton was not the man Mrs Doyle thought he was. It was when Sam eased the cork off the second bottle of champagne, that Mrs Doyle made a surprising announcement.

"Gentlemen, Willena, Pageant, where's Billie?" Mrs Doyle asked,

"In the kitchen, hunting down Willena's cookie jar," said Joe with a little laugh. Margaret smiled.

"It seems I have some money in the bank," Mrs Doyle again smiled, "money that I didn't have yesterday. Now," she paused, "what am I going to do with it. Each of you in your way have contributed to the downfall of that good for nothing man and the increase in my fortunes, partly," she looked at Sam, "It seems, that Sam's connections with the Chicago mob had something to do with it. Still, we are where we are, but I promise you this, each one of you will benefit from my good fortune."

Mrs Doyle smiled "I know you didn't do it for gain or reward, but at the same time there was no need for you to have done what you have done. I won't join you in another glass of champagne but I will celebrate the fact that I am fortunate in having friends, that in the time that I have known them, which is but a blink of an eye when considering the years I have lived and the people I have met during that time. Joe has suggested that I tell my friends, the ones that you have met in this house, to keep them fully informed of the decisions I will make, not that I must tell them, but I can see Joe's reasoning for this. And now I will say goodnight and I sincerely thank you Curtis, Joe, Pageant and Billie for coming over at such short notice. Curtis, we will discuss further your suggestions regarding this windfall of mine if you could make arrangements with Willena."

Sam lay awake that night thinking of the day's events. He couldn't believe that things went as planned by Curtis and Joe, and as for the letter from Lance Warburton, it was as if he had written it to Curtis' dictation, apart from the half-truths. As for Willena, her manner was that of someone who had lost a penny and found a sixpence. He had been conscious of her squeezing his hand when they had faced Mrs Doyle over what he thought might be an inquisition as to their conduct, as it turned out the inquisition that he had feared never happened, in its place was a grateful and thankful lady who celebrated the outcome the only way she knew how, with a bottle of something from the cellar.

18

Three months had passed since the Lance Warburton affair and true to her word Mrs Doyle had made a gift of one thousand dollars to both Joe and Curtis for the work they did in exposing Mr Warburton. She knew they didn't want any reward for what they had done, but she made a point of telling them that she would be offended if they were to refuse her offer. She also give Pageant three hundred dollars to go shopping with and one hundred for Billie to put in her bank account. As for Sam she smiled and just said that she had plans for him. Her banking was now in the hands of Curtis who pointed out that it wouldn't be prudent of him to be personally involved in her financial affairs so with Mrs Doyle's permission he would hand over her accounts to a trusted colleague of his. He would still be her advisor in all her financial matters, and that her accounts would be open at any time to be inspected by persons of her choosing. Willena had become very close to Sam and had admitted that the worry over Mrs Doyle's banking affairs had gone. She fussed over him like a mother hen, not that she didn't before, but now it seemed there was more purpose in her life. Mrs Doyle had told her friends about Mr Warburton, and to say the least they were shocked at his behaviour, and applauded Sam and his friends for their concern over Mrs Doyle's welfare, suffice to say that they started to invite them to some of their own social gatherings.

Sam was busy at work as more and more orders were coming through. Was it that more people were dying, he wondered, or was it that word was getting around? There seemed to be a buzz in all manufacturing industries and it had been that way for the past twelve months, the American economy was booming, people were spending their money on consumer goods, which in turn was good for factories, assembly line workers were in full flow and the stock market was awash with speculators money, but how long would it last. Some people were even borrowing money to put on the stock market. So, it was little wonder why Sam couldn't understand the increase in the turnover of coffins, as one thing was for sure, people weren't dying to beat each other to the pearly gates in his coffins. Sam's income was in the region of two thousand a year and rising, but he still wasn't letting go of his dream. To have his own business was everything to him now, and to see that figure triple, when he was to eventually open the doors to his own workshop.

He noticed the leaves on the lime trees had started to turn colour in the last few weeks, and it was cooler than it had been. He thought of the winter months ahead, at least he would be in the dry and any inclement weather would not interfere with his work. His mail that week had consisted of letters from home, and there was one from Grace that had arrived that morning. As he entered the house, he called Willena, she caught him in the hallway as he turned the door handle to the drawing room where he would see Mrs Doyle.

"She's in bed," Willena said, "she was feeling a little under the weather so she went to bed."

"How long has she been there?"

"About an hour."

"I'll knock on the door just to see how she is; I don't like it when she is unwell."

"I don't think you have to worry yourself Sam as she was all right fifteen minutes ago, just let her answer before you go in." Sam gave the door a quiet knock, immediately he could hear Mrs Doyle's voice.

"Come on in Sam." It was said in a bright and cheerful way that Sam dismissed doubts that he had over her being ill. When Sam peered round the corner of the door, Mrs Doyle was sitting up in bed, reading a book.

"Hello Mrs Doyle, Willena told me you'd gone to bed."

"I felt a little tired so I thought I would go to bed and read for a while."

"Is there anything I can do for you?"

"No thank you Sam I have everything I need, and how was your day?"

"Very good we seem to be getting more orders from other undertakers now, and we're having a job to keep up with the work."

"You will have to put your prices up."

"That side of it has nothing to do with me Mrs Doyle."

"It will one day Sam, it will one day."

"Hopefully, Mrs Doyle, there are a few things I would do differently, but why should I give other people my ideas."

"I agree Sam, you would be putting more money in your boss' pocket. You're twenty in December, do you think you could handle a business by then?"

"I could handle a business now Mrs Doyle, except of course the laws of taxation and any legal requirements, but there are people I could find to look after that side of it."

"Sam, you sound very confident."

"I am good at what I do Mrs Doyle."

"I'm sure you are Sam, by the way did you ever hear anything of, what was his name, Humphreys the Bump?"

"Humphreys the Hump," Sam said with a chuckle, "No I haven't but I have dropped his parents a line, saying who I was and where I lived, also the names of my mum and dad. I don't suppose they know them; I don't know how they could." Mrs Doyle invited Sam to sit on her bed and as they talked Willena came in with a cup of coffee for them both, telling Sam that she was doing some steak and eggs for tea. Sam stayed for a little while then on hearing Willena call he went for his tea. After his meal Sam went to his room and opened a letter from Grace, he sat on his bed as he read it.

Dear Sam,

Thank you for your birthday card, I received it last week three days before my birthday. Mum, Dad, myself and John, he is a lad I have been seeing for the last couple of months, nothing serious, anyway, we went out for a meal to an Italian restaurant that has just opened on Lord St, it was a little more refined than mum's roast rabbit at the Admiral Rodney. We had a break in last Sunday night, someone forced the back door open at about 3 o'clock in the morning. Dad being a light sleeper woke up and went downstairs with a stick in his hand, one he keeps in the bedroom for such occasions. The intruder fled before dad got to him and he only saw his back. Nothing was stolen, just the back door lock was broken. Thank goodness that sort of thing rarely happens.

Sam didn't read anymore, but he did read again the line about her going to an Italian restaurant with a lad called John and for some reason he didn't like this John. He knew it was coming but it didn't make it any easier, but there it was in her own handwriting. Of course, he seeing a young lady call Pat didn't count, so naturally he didn't tell Grace he was seeing someone, that would be a little bit like cheating wouldn't it. His thoughts now were that he would tell her he was seeing someone, but at the same time he knew he wouldn't. He also thought that he was being ridiculous, Grace was a little older than him, why on earth shouldn't she look for someone who would pay her attention, someone who would treat her well and more than anything, be there for her. He put the letter down, but he still did not like the thought of her seeing someone.

On November the 6th Herbert Clark Hoover became the 31st President of the United States. Sam wasn't at all into politics and didn't even know what party Herbert Hoover supported until he became president. It had been a busy time for Joe, reporting from conventions in New York State and further afield. Joe would tell Sam and Curtis stories about these conventions and the politicians that attended them, some full of optimism, some talked of doom and gloom and some never getting off the fence.

Both Joe and Curtis were supporters of Mr Hoover, Joe even remembering some of his quotes. He gave some examples, as they sat having a drink, in a coffee house one block away from Joe's home. One being, "Blessed are the young for they will inherit the national debt." There were others, but the one that Sam liked best was, "All men are equal before fish." He didn't quite know what Mr Hoover was implying with that one, but he liked it. Curtis was at the time seeing a lady by the name of Isabelle. Sam had never met her, but it seemed Curtis had been seeing her for a few months before mentioning that he had a lady friend. Both men, Curtis and Joe would discuss the American economy and it was this discussion that got Sam interested in the subject. Politics and its implications on the future wasn't something that he had taken much notice of, but if it was going to have a bearing on his future then he needed to know a little about the subject. Curtis mentioned that the stock market was going crazy and he felt that the good times could not go on as it was, he felt sure it would end, but when?

Throughout October and November Sam kept a close watch on the stock market. People were still investing money but he did notice from the newspapers that the purchase of consumer goods had levelled off and that farmers were producing too much food. Workers' wages had stopped rising and, in some cases, had started to go down and by Christmas there was some apprehension about what would happen in the year to come.

Sam again had his birthday party at Mrs Doyle's house, the same people were invited and the same people attended plus three others. Those being Isabelle, Curtis' lady friend, Susan the blonde girl that Eddie had been seeing for nearly twelve months, and a male friend of Sandy's whom he had met a few times while visiting Pat. Mrs Doyle's business friends didn't seem to have the same sense of wellbeing as they did the year before, as much of the time they were in discussion with Curtis, quizzing him about the safety of their assets and the impending gloom that could be upon them. One of them, Clive Peters, who made his living from the stock market dismissed any suggestion that things were going to turn "arse about face" as he put it. He explained that even the President of the United States poured scorn on the doom mongers. House prices had been steadily falling for the last two years and there had been an increase in the number of businesses going bankrupt, this was pointed out by Frank Trevor who knew what he was talking about seeing that he was in the business of property development. There will always be businesses going to the wall insisted Clive, nothing new about that.

"Well, I'm glad I'm out of it all," he said through a mouthful of Dean's cake, "these are damn good," he added. Mr Lance Warburton's name was never brought up. Mrs Doyle had instructed that his name was never to be mentioned in her house again. Dean had started work as the pastry chef at the Astoria Hotel, but like Sam he wanted his own business, he wanted a delicatessen in the city and nothing he said would stop him from achieving his goal. Eddie's girlfriend, the blonde girl, was nothing like the expensive girl that Pat had put her down to be, in fact Pat got on very well with her. She was still an outrageous dresser, always trying to be one step ahead in the fashion stakes, which made her a subject to be condemned by some. By all accounts Eddie had fought for her honour on more than one occasion. Pat had asked her why she would set herself up for comments that would upset her? Her answer, "Because I like getting dressed up. I work in dungarees on a production line all bloody week and I like to do my thing on a weekend, and anyway Eddie likes the way I dress." Well, there's no answer to that thought Pat and, in a way, she admired her for her stand against conformity, and there were many like her, who would always put the glitz into Saturday night's downtown. Noticing Isabelle standing on her own Sam went over. Curtis had introduced her to him when entering the house, she seemed quite shy and reserved, impeccably dressed, and looking very elegant. Sam wasn't sure if she drank alcohol or not, but if she was going out with Curtis it would be a foregone conclusion that she did. On his approach she reached for what looked like a martini from one of the tables that held little snacks that Willena had put out. She smiled.

"Curtis tells me that you met on the ship coming over. In fact he has told me a lot about you."

"All good I hope," said Sam with a smile.

"Indeed," she answered, returning his smile, "he also mentioned that you make coffins."

"I do."

"A bit of a dead end job," she giggled.

"You could say that," Sam laughed.

Then without being asked, she went on to tell Sam her life story. Born on a ranch in Texas, went to boarding school in Austin, then she attended the University of Texas in Austin, passing out as a schoolteacher. She added with some pride that she was one of the main cheerleaders to the universities football team, the Texas Longhorns.

"I'm from a long line of ranchers, longhorn cattle ranchers, my great grandfather was given land, as he was a Texas Ranger. He died in the Battle of the Alamo mission, San Antonio in 1836,"

"The Alamo!" Sam said with surprise.

"Yes, the Texas Rangers went to help Bill Travis defend the mission against General Santa Anna's Mexican Army, but he died along with James Bowie, and…."

"And Davy Crockett," Sam said excitedly.

" Yes, and two hundred others," added Isabelle. "You've heard the story Sam."

"Yes, hasn't everyone, the story of the Alamo is legendary Isabelle."

"I suppose it is."

"Anyway, you're a long way from home, how did you end up in New York?"

"I was seeing a lad who wanted to see the bright lights of New York, as the bright lights of Austin couldn't hold a candle to the ones in New York."

"Very good Isabelle a nice line, I mean, couldn't hold a candle to the ones in New York." Sam smiled, "So, you came over with him?"

"I did, and we spent two years together before he started cheating on me, and then, when he would have too much drink he would come home and hit me."

"Sounds like a nice sort of guy, why didn't you go home?"

"Because I had a big fight with my parents before I left home, dad said he was no good, but I didn't listen, and I didn't want to give him the satisfaction of saying I told you so."

"How did you meet Curtis?"

"At the Cotton Club three months ago, you were all out celebrating something, and he asked me for a dance."

"He's a awful dancer," said Sam with a grin.

"Don't I know it, he kept telling me not to keep putting my foot under his, I asked him why he wanted to dance being as he wasn't very good at it, and he said he just wanted to hold me."

"And his dancing, has it improved any?" Isabelle looked at Sam and raised her eyelids.

"It's his timing, he just hasn't got it."

"So," said Sam, "what do you like about him?"

Isabel thought for a moment. "He's attentive, treats me like a lady and I would like to think he would never raise his hand to me."

"Isabelle, Curtis would never do that."

"No, I don't think he would Sam," Isabelle replied thoughtfully.

"Well, I hope you two get on, as Curtis needs a companion."

"And the girl you are seeing?"

"Pat."

"Yes, she seems a nice girl."

"She is a nice girl," Sam said glancing over to see her talking to Pageant.

Isabelle then excused herself as Antonio Archelli came over.

"Sam, could I have a word, your employer tells me that he is thinking of selling your workshop and the coffin business."

Sam was stunned. "It's the first I've heard of this!"

"Well, it's not public knowledge yet and may not be for a number of weeks. He needs some capital for another investment and he thinks that if he is going to sell, now would be the time to do it. I hope you don't mind me telling you but I think you should know, properties he said had been over valued and if he were to leave it, he wouldn't even get what he paid for it." As Sam listened, his first thoughts were that he would be out of a job and he would be joining those who had lost theirs. Unemployment was going up and for the first time he felt vulnerable to what was happening.

"Have you told anyone else?" he asked, "how many people know?"

"I have no idea how many people know about it and I've only told you, but knowing Yosef, I'm pretty sure it will happen. Listen Sam, I think we will be going into uncertain times and it's just a thought, this could be an opportunity for you, see Curtis, he's the financial wizard, maybe he could advise you."

Sam's head was spinning. This was an opportunity but there was no way he could buy Mr Acker's property. The rest of the evening was a blur, as solutions of him being able to acquire his own business would enter his head only to be dashed by the realisation that he didn't have the collateral for a loan. Antonio placed his hand on Sam's shoulder. "You will find a way Sam, there is always a way, in the meantime I will find out as much as I can and let you know." That night Sam lay in Pat's bed, they had made love and Pat fell asleep soon after, but Sam just stared into the blackness, he could not see anything but his name on a billboard above the double doors of his workshop. He could see a queue of people lining up to take away his coffins. He wondered how much it would cost to buy freehold the workshop and everything in it. If prices were going down, how far would they drop, and for how long would the drop continue? One thing was for sure, God wouldn't be turning off the tap of people dying.

19

Christmas carols had been sung and church sermons preached. Fires made cold homes warm, and extra blankets had been taken out of cupboards and placed on beds. Sam had worked late into January before Yosef let it be known that the workshop and its contents would be up for sale. Sam had spoken to Curtis of its being for sale some weeks earlier and Mrs Doyle had got to know through Antonio at about the same time.

"And how much money do you have Sam?"

"Just under two thousand dollars, Mrs Doyle."

"And how much does Curtis think you could buy it for?"

"Well with prices falling he thinks it could be bought for between nine and nine and a half thousand."

"Will you be able to get a mortgage on it?"

"Maybe, I have been saving for the last two years, and I have to thank you for how much I have saved, but I don't think it will be enough."

"Well, if you need some money to add to it, you know I can give you some."

"If I did that Mrs Doyle, you know you would get it back."

"I know Sam, I know. When will you be making an offer?"

"I will be going to see Curtis on Tuesday, and he will make an offer on my behalf on Wednesday."

"I could do with speaking to him myself, I'll talk to him in the morning, I don't think I have his number. I'll get Willena to ring him, if you could give her his number in the morning."

"I will do that Mrs Doyle and thank you for your offer of a loan."

At midday on the second Saturday in February Curtis and Isabelle had called and picked up Sam. Mrs Doyle and Willena had left the house a half hour before, they had caught a taxi and were going to Antonio Archelli's home as he had invited them to celebrate his wedding anniversary. As Sam turned the key to Mrs Doyle's home, he thought about asking Curtis again if he had heard anything about his final offer, but thought not to ask. For the last two weeks, since he had been laid off he had rang him often, asking for news. The workshop was empty. The last coffin had gone, picked up on the Wednesday and they hadn't done a stroke of work since. Although they had been paid up until the Friday. So why Curtis wanted to go to the workshop Sam didn't know, except to say that he wanted to tie up a few loose ends. As they pulled up into the work's yard, Sam was feeling deflated. He looked at the building and wondered if he would ever have his own business.

Reaching for the lock, still having a key, he noticed the door was slightly ajar and as he swung it open, he had the biggest surprise of his life. There inside, cheering and shouting were all his friends, even Mrs Doyle and Willena. He couldn't believe it.

"What on earth is this all about?" he asked, turning to Curtis wondering what was going on.

"Welcome to your workshop Sam." Everyone was still cheering.

"I don't understand, my workshop?" Curtis was one step behind him.

"Yes, it's yours." Sam was in a daze. "The workshop, the business, it's all yours." All were gathered around him, those that didn't have a drink in their hand were clapping, and those that did, put them down and clapped.

"The business is mine?" said Sam not quite taking it in, a drink was placed in his hand.

"Yes," answered Curtis, "Mrs. Doyle has bought you the freehold, the building, and everything in it, and it's all in your name." Sam was dumbfounded, shocked that something like this could happen to him. He looked at the lady who was his friend and who was now his benefactor. She was seated on a chair and stood when he walked over.

"Can I give you a hug Mrs. Doyle?" he asked.

"Of course, you can."

As he hugged her, he whispered, "Why did you do this Mrs Doyle?"

"Because I can," she whispered back, "because I can." Then as she sat, Antonio Archelli and his wife came over.

"Congratulations Sam," he said as he extended his hand.

Sam took it, "And congratulations to the two of you on your wedding anniversary, it is your wedding anniversary," he paused, "isn't it?"

"It is," Antonio said laughing, "thank you Sam."

Joe and Pageant expressed their wishes that Sam should be successful in his new venture. Pat planted a big kiss on his cheek and squeezed his backside. Eddie came over and wished him well for the future. Sam still not believing his good fortune was at a loss as to know what to say or do so he showed everyone around the workshop explaining the process of how they make coffins. The scent of pine and cow hoof glue hung in the air, noticed, and mentioned by Isabelle as she congratulated Sam on his successful bid.

"You are well aware that it was Curtis, who was responsible for my acquiring this place?" he smiled, using his hands to indicate the building. "My friends, the food and drink, you knew all about it didn't you?" he said holding her arm.

"Yes, along with everyone else."

"When was the deal done?" Sam asked.

"Lunchtime on Thursday."

"And the food, Willena's idea I suppose?"

"Who else, she suggested it to Mrs Doyle, and it went from there." At that moment Ian, Tom and Charly walked in, and on seeing Sam they immediately walked over, Isabelle stood to one side as they approached.

"And how the hell did he pull this off?" Ian said looking at Isabelle.

"You had better ask him," she answered smiling, never having met Ian before.

"Ladies and gentlemen," Sam called out, "I don't think many of you have met my workmates before, this is Ian and Charly, and the young lad is Tom. Like me they too have been laid off work, and again like me, they can start back on Monday morning if they have a mind to." A big cheer went up as Sam made the announcement.

"I knew you wanted this place Sam, but I didn't think for one minute that you would get it."

"Well, Ian, Tom, Charly, do you want a job?"

"Same time Monday morning?" asked Tom.

"You had better believe it, I need you guys," said Sam excitedly, "It will be a new beginning for the three of us."

"Thank you, Sam," Tom was smiling, "I didn't think I would be able to get another job like this."

"You boys go and get yourself a drink and a sandwich and I'll speak to you later."

Willena was sorting out sandwiches on Sam's workbench when he went over to her.

"Sam I'm so happy for you."

" Willena, I'm lost for words, I've been told you knew all about this?"

"I did, and everything is turning out just fine, isn't it Sam?"

"It sure is Willena, it sure is."

As Sam did the rounds, he stopped and was talking to Eddie when Curtis approached carrying a folder.

"When you have a moment Sam, I have some papers for you to sign."

"It looks like you have some business matters to sort out Sam." Eddie grinned.

"The wheels of industry," Sam said laughing, "Come into the office Curtis," he said still laughing.

"You have an office!" Joe had overheard the conversation.

"It's over there," Sam pointed to a tiny room with a window, at the back of the workshop.

"That's your office!" exclaimed Pageant.

"Now don't you start," said Sam.

"This is where the money is earned, not in there." On closing the office door, Curtis laid the folder on a little table and brought out a folded document.

"This is the deeds to the property Sam, and I have a couple of papers that I need your signature on. This," he took out another paper, "is the bill of sale," he handed it to Sam, who immediately looked at the bottom line.

"You got this place for eight thousand two hundred?"

"It took a bit of doing, but yes I got it for that figure, and I have opened a business account for you, and that is the figure you have in it." He handed Sam a bank book, Sam opened it and was taken aback.

"There's six thousand eight hundred dollars in here," he said looking at Curtis.

"Yes, Mrs Doyle has been very good to you Sam, she instructed me to transfer that sum into this account."

"Jesus, I don't know what to say."

"This money is for outgoing expenses before any return starts coming in. Money in your personal account has not been touched. Mrs Doyle rang me last week and told me what she wanted, and I have just done her bidding." Sam was stunned. "She has asked me, for you to say nothing about this money, as it is something, she would prefer you to keep secret, if you understand."

"I do understand Curtis, bless her."

"Look Sam, Mrs Doyle is an old lady, and I think she has no need of money, well not the amount that she has got, and she wants to leave it, or some of it to someone who will make good use of it. And it seems Sam that you are the one."

"How can I repay her Curtis; I have nothing to give." Sam was on the verge of tears when Curtis rested his hand on Sam's shoulder.

"You have already given her what she has needed for a long time, you have given her your time, your patience and your friendship, what more could anyone give."

"I like the old lady."

"Don't we all Sam, don't we all. Now when we go out of here, don't thank her, not here, you thank her when you get home. Now I need a drink." Sam then signed what papers Curtis placed in front of him and replaced everything back into the folder.

"And you Curtis, could you send me your bill for all the work you have done." Curtis looked at Sam and smiled.

"It's all been taken care of Sam."

"You mean."

"It's all been taken care of, that's what I mean."

20

Sam went to bed that night exhausted, and to say the least a little inebriated. Pat's head was drawn to her pillow as if it were part of her. Sam closed his eyes for minutes, or so it seemed, before opening them. Pat had already left for work.

"I can earn more money if I work Sundays," she had always said.

Sam drew back the curtains and looked at his watch, a quarter to nine, he said to himself, and I must walk home. Pat had left a note on the bed.

Good morning Sam, thank you for a wonderful afternoon and evening, no doubt you will have a busy week next week, give me a ring and let me know how you are getting on. Love Pat. PS - Lock the door on your way out.

As soon as he stepped onto the road outside Pat's apartment he thought of the previous afternoon and knew that those few hours were life changing. He said a little prayer as he walked home, "God grant me that the decisions I make are good ones, and if they are not, the strength to overcome them." Sam had not spoken to God for years, he tried to remember the last time he had prayed, when he left Sunday school he thought? It was all so sudden, his priority was to stock up on his coffins. He would contact all those regular customers that were already on the books and let them know that they were back in business. He may have lost some to his competitors, but he needed to come up with new ideas and not rely on the way it had always been done. He opened the door and called Willena.

"I'm in the kitchen," a voice called back. Willena would spend most of her time in the kitchen and Sam often wondered what an earth she did in there. He found her with her hands in a mixing bowl,

"Making some cakes to give to the church," she said smiling. Sam went over and give her a peck on the cheek. "Well," she asked, "Did you enjoy yourself last night?" Joe gave Mrs Doyle and myself a lift home." Sam sat on a stool opposite Willena.

"It was all a dream, and I remember asking Curtis how I was ever going to repay Mrs Doyle for what she has done for me".

Willena with her hands still in the mixing bowl looked up, "I remember as a child, I once wanted a pretty dress, one I had seen in a shop window, I knew I would never possess it as it was so expensive, but I wanted it just the same. My mother never said a word to anyone, as little black girls didn't wear dresses like that. I remember I even prayed at the foot of my bed. The next day a parcel was delivered addressed to me, my mother helped me unwrap it." Willena again looked up.

"And inside was your little dress."

"That's right Sam inside was my little dress, my world was my little dress. Do you know how I came to have it?"

"I have no idea."

"Mrs Doyle was bringing me a glass of water when she overheard me praying for the dress, and she bought it for me, don't ask how she knew where I had seen it, maybe I told her, I can't remember as my mum didn't tell her and it has remained a mystery to me, but I did thank her. She had given me my dream Sam, much like she has given you yours, and before you say anything, that act of giving has stayed with me. Cost doesn't come into it, for her Sam, I think it was like buying a little dress all over again." Sam left his seat and walked around the table, he wrapped his arms around Willena's expanding waist and gently gave her a hug, he didn't speak, there was no need.

Sam knocked on the lounge door and entered, Mrs Doyle was, as always sitting in her chair, she looked up and on seeing Sam she smiled.

"Good morning Sam, and how are you?"

"Very well Mrs Doyle and yourself?"

"Good," she said, "Good." Sam went over and kissed the top of her head.

"Mrs Doyle," Sam stammered, "I know I thanked you yesterday but I feel the need to thank you again for what you have done for me."

"Sam, you thanked me many times yesterday so you don't need to keep thanking me, all I want you to do now is to make a success of what you have, I am as excited as you are about it all, just let me know from time to time how things are going."

"You can be assured of that, Mrs Doyle, now I'll have myself a late breakfast then I will go to the workshop and get things ready for tomorrow morning so I'll see you later."

"You do that Sam, see you later."

21

"How many have we in stock Tom?" Sam asked.

"Eight pine, six elm and six oak."

"Charly could you give Tom a hand. I need four pine taking out front, somebody is coming to pick them up, they're going to Staten Island, then if one of you could start bringing me in enough boards to replace them. We seem to be making more and more pine coffins than we used to."

"It's because they are the cheapest," said Ian, "people don't have the money like they used to."

"I guessed it was that. Half the coffins we turn out now are pine and it could be even more." It had been two months since Sam had started back to work. His business had, for the first few weeks been slow but after the seventh week it was getting nearly as busy as it used to be. Sam didn't mind as it gave them a little time to change the workshop around making it more like a production line. Sam had discussed with the boys the need to smarten up the outside of the building, to take down the old sign, replacing it with a new one, one of his own, one with his name on it.

"What are you going to put on it?" asked Ian.

"I have been thinking about that, Tom go to the office and get me a pencil and paper." They were standing around Ian's workbench as Tom passed over a pencil and paper.

"This is what I want on the sign," said Sam as he laid the paper on the workbench, he started to draw the vision that was in his head. When he had finished, he handed it to Ian, immediately Ian started to laugh, then he gave it to Tom who, passed it on to Charly, both like Ian started to laugh.

"Are you serious about this?" asked Ian.

"Don't you like it?" said Sam sounding disappointed at Ian's comment.

"I think it's great, and you Tom?"

"I love it."

"Well, I like it too. You need a sign writer now Sam."

"I have contacted one, and he is calling tomorrow morning. Now we have to decide what colour to paint it."

"Black," said Ian.

"No," answered Tom, "we need a brighter colour, how about blue Ian?"

"Well, I suppose black is a bit of a morbid colour, so yes blue, why not."

"Why not," said Sam, "blue it is then."

The following morning the sign writer had called and had made some suggestions as to the sign's layout. Two days later he was back, the boys had erected a scaffold and a ladder had been placed against it ready for the sign to be taken up and screwed to the weatherboarding. As the scaffolding was up Sam suggested they paint the weatherboarding at the same time, brown seeming to be the obvious choice. All that was needed now was the sign. Friday lunchtime the sign writer arrived, the sign was taken off his truck and manhandled up the ladder, it was levelled and screwed onto the front of the building above the double doors. Everyone stood back and commented. It read,

SAM'S COFFINS
COFFINS TO BE SEEN DEAD IN

Throughout the fourth week a number of people walked in, passing comments of the new sign. The vast majority approving, some saying that in times of despair a statement like the one above the door was refreshing. One or two said that it was in bad taste, but overall, it was an accepted statement.

In June there was a definite despondency in the economics of New York State. President Hoover's popularity was decreasing by the month. Banks were getting jittery, bankruptcies were going up, and the number of jobs available to the unemployed were going down. Food kitchens were becoming a source of sustenance for those that needed to subsidise what food they could afford. More and more farmers were walking off their properties as they weren't making enough to pay off their loans. America, the largest economy in the world was now looking rather sick. Sam was starting to get worried; his business was doing well although they didn't make anywhere near as many oak coffins as they used to, and he had to reinvent the making of his pine coffins, insofar as to use inferior timber on the cheaper ones and do away with brass name plaques and handles. Calico was now used to line the inside of these coffins instead of the finer and softer material that he still used on the dearer ones. Sam kept his profit margin. They were cheaper, but they still took much the same time to make. The only way to make them even cheaper was to do away with the linings altogether.

It was in mid-June just after two o'clock on a Tuesday when Tom opened the office door and told Sam that someone had called to see him and was out in the yard. When Sam stepped out, a man, a tall man in a camel coat was standing by a green Lincoln Continental, either side of him were two well-dressed burly men, both wearing black fedora hats. The gentleman stepped forward on seeing Sam.

"Mr Sam Pryce", he said holding out his hand, "Sam Pryce from Montgomeryshire, Wales, UK?"

"It is," said Sam as he shook his hand.

"My name is Murray Humphreys. I've come down from Chicago on business so I thought I would call and say hello, you wrote a letter to my parents some months ago and my father asked if I could stop by and see you."

"Pleased to meet you Sir," Sam said.

"And you too Sam," he said smiling, "I see you are in the business of people that are done with paying taxes and drinking hard liquor."

"Yes Mr Humphreys, although I never thought of it like that," Sam smiled. They talked for a while about Sam's home, and stories that Murray's father had told him about his life in Wales before he immigrated to America.

"I must go there someday," he said warmly. "Now, I have a business proposition to make to you. Could you supply me with your top of the range coffins? I will need four of them ready to be picked up on the first of every month."

Sam was surprised that Humphreys the Hump was standing in his yard, let alone placing an order!

"You need four coffins be ready to be picked up on the first of every month?" he asked looking bemused.

"Yes."

"And the size?"

"Just your average size Sam."

"With all the trimmings?"

"With all the trimmings."

"Starting on the first of next month."

Sam smiled.

"On the first of next month," Murray repeated.

"Shall I open you an account?"

"That won't be necessary, you will be paid in cash when they are picked up."

"And who do I make the bill out to Mr Humphreys?" a broad grin spread over the Humps face.

"Think of a name Sam, think of a name. Remember the first day of every month."

"Very good Mr Humphreys, it will be done." Sam then shook his hand. Murray then walked to the Lincoln. The back door of the car being opened by one of the men sporting a fedora hat. He got in, closed the door, and wound the window down, smiling he pointed over Sam's head to the sign above the double doors of Sam's workshop.

"I like it, I know some people that would look very good in your coffins." With that, the car gently pulled out of the forecourt and was gone. Sam turned and glanced up, for a moment it reminded him of the sign outside the Admiral Rodney, of course his picture wasn't on it, but nonetheless it was his sign. Inside the workshop the boys had seen Sam talking to the stranger in the camel coat and were inquisitive as to who he was.

"That gentleman is Chicago's Mr Al Capone's right hand man, Mr Murray Humphreys, or to call him what his friends and enemies call him, Humphreys the Hump."

"Jesus, Sam are you associating with gangsters?" asked Tom excitedly.

"Now hold on Tom, how I got to know him is a long story, but to be associated with him may be too strong a word, anyway, he has placed an order for four coffins to be picked up on the first of every month, wheels within wheels Tom, wheels within wheels," Tom looked at Sam not understanding, "It doesn't matter Tom it doesn't matter."

One week before Murray's coffins were to be picked up Joe and Curtis called in to see Sam. It was unusual for them to call without giving him a ring, and by the look on their faces Sam could see they were concerned about something. Sam took them into his office.

"You obviously haven't come to order a coffin," said Sam jokingly.

"No, it's a bit more serious than that," said Joe, "I'll let Curtis explain."

"I don't know if you have been following the news Sam, but I believe the country is heading for a major depression, and I'm fearful there will be a run on the banks."

"Run on the banks?"

"Yes, people will be drawing all their money out and sticking it under their beds."

Sam looked confused, "And this concerns me?"

"It could do, because it could be that if you're the last to go to the bank they may not have any money to give you."

"So, you think it might be wise to take all my money out before everyone gets the same idea."

"Well at the moment it may be safer under your bed than in the bank, these are unprecedented times and no one really knows what will happen."

"Is that your opinion Joe?"

"Everything is pointing that way Sam and I would hate to see you lose the money you have."

"Does that apply to Mrs Doyle as well?" Joe looked at Curtis.

"I think it would be wise if she were to do the same."

"Have you spoken to her about it?"

"No not yet but when it happens it will happen quickly."

"And the stock market?" asked Sam.

"Well, that will be the crux of the whole thing, if that goes and everything is pointing to it, I think the consequences will be enormous. Joe and I sold what shares we had a couple of months ago."

"And you put your money under the bed?"

"Something like that Sam. And you, how are things in the coffin business?"

"Good, as I have told you we have experienced a downturn in the quality stuff we are turning out, an increase in the cheaper ones which has not affected our output and business generally is good. I was thinking at one stage of putting another man on as it would free me to follow up on the enquiries we are getting, but I will leave it for a while, at least until things have settled down."

Curtis and Joe stayed for another fifteen minutes or so chatting then left. Curtis saying that he would call and see Mrs Doyle stating that he would like Willena present while he explained things to her. The next morning Sam stood outside his bank, he entered as the doors were opened for business. He didn't close his two accounts but left one hundred dollars in each one, so as to save time re-opening them when the panic was over. He placed the cash, his entire fortune, in the footwell of the car and drove home. He did not look inside the bag as he didn't want to think too much about it.

Curtis had been to see Mrs Doyle and explained the situation to her, Willena being present throughout. Curtis, because she had a substantial amount of cash reserves said she could do one of two things, or even both, she could draw it all out in cash, or she could buy property. Curtis told her bricks and mortar don't disappear. Mrs Doyle took it all very calmly asking would things really be that bad and Curtis saying that she shouldn't really take that chance. Within the following two weeks Mrs Doyle had bought two condos in Manhattan, and withdrew all her cash, there was a lot of cash.

This moving about of money seemed unreal, more and more people were losing their jobs. Queues could be seen at soup kitchens as they had been for some time. Women with children to feed were undercutting the local street girls to put bread on the table. But the revellers still went out on Friday and Saturday nights. Street entertainers with their caps on the pavement still entertained people with money and there was still plenty of them.

On the first of July as Murray Humphreys had said a vehicle pulled up and drove away with the four coffins that had been ordered. An invoice had been made out to a Mr S Samson. They were as Murray had ordered, good quality, with all the trimmings including a red velvet inlay. A man then handed over cash and said would return on the first of the following month.

At this time unemployment had become a major problem and the number of homeless people grew sharply. Shantytowns sprang up close to free soup kitchens.

Hundreds of people lived in these ghettos, they became
known as Hooverville towns named after Herbert Hoover
the president who was widely blamed for the catastrophic
events that had befallen them. Deaths by disease and
malnutrition had increased, suicides had become more
common, and the bodies of the John Doe's, unidentified
people, were left in the city morgue for weeks before being
placed in a shroud and buried in places set up for that
specific purpose.

For the next few months things got worse, then on the
24th and again on the 29th of October the stock market
crashed. Wall Street, the financial district of New York
was in turmoil, there was, as Curtis had predicted, a run
on the banks, everyone with money in them were drawing
it out, until there was nothing left. Many businessmen
were in financial trouble and overnight some people lost
everything. Many small banks were looking increasingly
vulnerable.

Sam's business was booming and some weeks later
another man was hired. He extended his workshop installing
two more work benches and built new racks to take an
increase in pine boards. Thirty percent of his coffins were
purchased by people with little money but they still wanted
their loved ones to be buried, in even a half decent coffin.
To make them cheaper he dispensed with brass plaques
and handles. There was no internal cloth linings and the
handles were of timber nailed to the sides of the coffin.
Sam had the boys working long hours and weekends. He
paid them well and they admitted that they were lucky in

having a job that wouldn't disappear overnight. And in this light, they were all instrumental in working as a team even making suggestions that would speed up their output without compromising the quality of their work.

"Cash is king," said Joe as he poured over the depressing news that he himself had written for the New York Times. "I don't understand it," he said, "You would think the people who have been investing money for years would have seen it coming. It beggar's belief. And you Curtis, how are things going at the bank?"

"It's bloody catastrophic! I don't know if I'll have a job in six months' time."

"You don't think the Federal Reserve will go under do you?"

"Your guess is as good as mine Joe; it's been a few weeks now since the fall of the stock market. Some banks will fail when their debts become greater than their assets."

"So, who is making the money Curtis?"

"Sam Pryce," said Curtis with a laugh.

"Talking of people making money I heard a story the other day about a man who played the stock market. He was walking in the city and stopped to have his shoes cleaned, anyway, as the shoeshine kid was shining his shoes he was telling this gentlemen all about the stock market, this happened only a few months ago, he told him what stocks to buy, the gentleman listened and thought that if a shoeshine kid is telling him what stock to buy it's time to get out, so he sold every stock he had and made a million."

"Who was he?" asked Joe.

"Does the name Joseph Kennedy ring any bells Curtis?"

"Yes, I have heard of him, his timing was perfect wasn't it?"

22

Sam was working on a coffin lid, when Tom answered the phone, he put the phone down and rushed from the office.

"I think you had better go home Sam, that was Willena she sounded in a state, it's Mrs Doyle, Willena has found her on the floor." Sam dropped the spokeshave he was using and rushed out. As he drove home, he feared the worst. He drove through the rain going as fast as he dared, thinking thoughts of Mrs Doyle lying on the carpet. His car skidded on the gravel nearly hitting the garage door as it stopped. Willena was kneeling beside Mrs Doyle weeping, as he placed his hand on her shoulder she cried out.

"She's gone Sam, she's gone." Mrs Doyle's prone figure lay in front of her chair, her little table had been tipped over along with a cup and saucer, the tea it contained soaking the carpet, with some being spilled over a newspaper. A red apple with a piece cut out of it had rolled across the floor, Mrs Doyle still clutching the knife she had been using. Sam bent forward, he could see she was dead, and there was nothing anyone could do. Willena kept telling her to get up as she would make her another cup of tea. Sam felt empty and numb and his thoughts were of Willena. She had lost her companion, someone who was her reason for being where she was. He took a deep breath.

"I'll phone the doctor," he said softly and unhurriedly.

"Don't leave me with her Sam," she whimpered.

"I won't leave you, I'll be back in a moment." Within twenty minutes the doctor called and within another twenty minutes he was gone, saying matter-of-factly that at the age of ninety six she had had a good and long life. It was as Sam suspected, a heart attack. Willena had taken Mrs Doyle a cup of tea and the newspaper. Fifteen minutes later she found her lying on the floor whereupon she immediately rang Sam. Sam carried her to her bed and laid her out, crossing her arms and closing her eyes and jaw, rigour mortis set in. While the doctor was making his assessment of Mrs Doyle, Sam rang everyone he could think of that would have wanted to know about her passing, some he got hold of, some he didn't. Her three lady friends and the couples that had attended his parties phone numbers he found in her little book that lay beside the phone. Willena was beside herself, and Sam was at a loss as to what to do, so he just hugged her and told her that everything would be alright.

Sam had taken care of the funeral arrangements, calling the local undertaker, one he knew. Mrs Doyle's funeral was a low key affair. Mrs Doyle's lady friends helped Willena put on food and drink at Mrs Doyle's home for those who had attended the funeral. A lot of Mrs

Doyle's past and present friends were there including a few Sam had never met. It seemed strange that Mrs Doyle herself was not there, watching over her own funeral, maybe she was? As she seemed to be the catalyst that held everyone together. She was buried next to Gordon in the Marble Cemetery in Manhattan. She was lowered into her grave in one of Sam's coffins. He looked up and was pleasantly surprised to see, standing some distance away, his workmen with their hats in their hands and heads bowed knowing that indirectly it was the lady in the coffin that had given them their jobs. It was Willena that had invited them back to Mrs Doyle's for refreshments, they in turn accepted her invitation on condition that she visit them from time to time for a cup of tea at the workshop.

"That would be lovely," she said smiling, it being the first time Sam had seen Willena smile since the death of Mrs Doyle. In the first week after Mrs Doyle's death, he had written home to his mother, Aunt Megan and Grace, telling them of her demise and it seemed that they had written back by return, as a couple of weeks later three letters arrived on the same day.

Two weeks after Mrs Doyle's funeral Sam had a phone call from Mr Antonio Arcelli, asking Sam if they could meet.

"It's regarding Mrs Doyle's will. I had a call from her solicitors this morning, I don't know if you knew but I am the executor of Mrs Doyle's will."

"No Antonio I didn't know, but I guessed it would be one of her older friends."

"Well, I had a call, and the gentleman asked me to contact you and Willena. An appointment has been made in the city for the day after tomorrow at two thirty, will that be convenient for you?"

"Yes, yes, that will be fine, I will tell Willena and bring her with me."

"It's a sad business Sam. Mrs Doyle changed her will some six months ago, she made a few changes and I think the two of you, like the solicitor suggested, should be there when her will is being read." Antonio gave Sam the address saying he would see them both at two thirty on Thursday. Sam told Willena of the phone call, and their presence being needed at the reading of Mrs Doyle's will. At first, she didn't answer.

"I knew she had changed her will," she said looking at Sam. "I know she had left me the house and some money to keep it, but as for anything else I know little apart from a few personal items for her friends."

Sam, Willena and Antonio were shown into a plush office on the twentieth floor in one of those buildings that people gaze at in the city streets.

Three chairs were placed around a big table where the gentleman in a grey suit sat looking through papers that were on his table. He stood and introduced himself, being very business-like in his approach to the subject of Mrs Doyle's will.

"Getting straight to the point, regarding Mrs Margaret Joyce Doyle's Last Will and Testament. I will read it then at the end I will hand a copy to Mr Arcelli to oversee the execution of said will."

Mr Summers as that was how he introduced himself spoke for half an hour. A lot of it was legal jargon but to put it in a nutshell, Mrs Doyle's will, was such that she had left the house and contents to Willena with a condition that Sam could stay as long as he wished and upon the demise of Willena the house would pass to Sam. There would be a sum of fifteen thousand dollars to pay for all expenses needed to run the house in the years to come, this included a weekly sum for Willena herself. The two properties that Mrs Doyle had bought with the money withdrawn on Curtis' advice were left to Sam, along with another five thousand dollars. Curtis and Joe were left five thousand dollars each. Her other properties were to be sold off and the money given to charities. Some personal keepsakes were left to her lady friends which Willena was well aware of. Sam was surprised when Mr Summers mentioned Dean, leaving him five thousand dollars to help him acquire his own business. She bequeathed one thousand dollars each to four people Sam didn't know, one thousand to Billie, the same to Eddie and even leaving five hundred to Pat. What remained of the cash would be given to Willena's church, on the proviso that she would have the final say in how it was spent.

The legalities of Mrs Doyle's will would rest with Mr Antonio Arcelli. There were other things discussed between Mr Summers and Antonio that were beyond the comprehension of Sam and Willena so they just sat and listened. It was mentioned that nothing would be sold from within the house so as to leave it as Willena had always known it, this again was something Mrs Doyle had assured Willena of many years before. Sam glanced at the lady sitting by his side, he had held her hand throughout the reading of Mrs Doyle's will, her eyes were full of tears as she turned her head, as she looked at Sam, she smiled and squeezed his hand.

Outside the three of them stood on a wet New York sidewalk, all thinking different thoughts, then Antonio turned to Sam and Willena.

"Well," he said with a sigh, "I think Margaret couldn't have left a better balanced will, she discussed it with me some time ago and asked me for my opinion. I told her I was content, not as you understand that I had any influence in this matter. I have, as you well know, known her for many years, and will oversee her last wishes as best I can. You may think Sam that she seems to have taken care of you and your friends in a manner that may have surprised you. But you see, all her long standing friends, and there isn't many of them left, want for nothing, and all this," he looked at the brief case in his hand, "is a reflection of her regard for you and those friends you have.

As for you Willena," he said smiling, "we have known each other for much the same time and I will always be here for you. Sam you are young and I think you came along at a time when Margaret needed something in her life and for three years you gave her what she needed, a renewed zest for living." Antonio shook their hands saying he would be in touch. As he walked away Willena took Sam's hand.

"He's a good man, now can we go home Sam?"

"I couldn't think of a better place to go."

On the way home Sam thought about the three weeks since Mrs Doyle's death. The hours he had spent listening to the stories Willena had told him about the life she had spent with Mrs Doyle. Sometimes he felt that he had intruded into a life that he had no business to be part of, other times it seemed, as she told her stories that he had grown to be part of that life. It was when Willena had asked Sam if he would be moving on now that Mrs Doyle was not there anymore that he realised that that was a question she was justified in asking. Would he stay because he wanted to stay or would he stay because of the financial benefits he would reap? No, he would not be moving on, he would stay, and for two good reasons, firstly, he liked his home and the security it gave him, secondly, because of Willena, she was his friend, she could be counted on and they got on well together and he would not desert her. Of course, he would like to go back home for a visit and that would happen in the next couple of years or so. Then he thought that maybe she would like him to move out even though Mrs Doyle requested that he could stay as long as he wished. But he wouldn't stay if Willena didn't want him there, after all it was her home now.

"Would you like me to stay?" he asked.

"What kind of question is that?"

"Well, I'm only asking, like you asked me if I would be moving on."

"Sam you must know that I want you to stay," she hesitated, "I have lived my life being needed by someone and if you left, I don't know what I would do."

"Well," said Sam, "that puts us in the same position doesn't it."

"Meaning?"

"I want to stay as much as you don't want me to go, am I right." Willena chuckled.

"Yes, you are right, it would drive me crazy living in this big house on my own with no one to look after."

"Now let's get one thing straight, you are not my servant, you will not fetch and carry for me, in fact I am young enough to be doing a little of that for you."

"Alright Sam we will look after each other."

Every Friday Willena went into work with Sam. She had been doing his books at home but had asked him if she could do them in his office as it made more sense, and anyway it would get her out of the house. She got on well with the lads and they enjoyed seeing her on a Friday on account that she would always bring in a cake to share amongst the boys. Tom even asking for the recipe for her cherry cake.

In the eighteen months since Mrs Doyle's death Sam's life had become one of responsibility and hard work. The recession had bitten hard into the lives of the American people. Unemployment was at record levels; businesses were still going bankrupt and there seemed to be a despondency that seeped through the population like a plague. But Sam was always encouraged by the resourcefulness of people who would never give up. The ingenuity of some to make a dollar where they could, and Sam was up there with them always thinking of ways to maintain his share of the coffin market.

Six months previously while visiting Curtis and Isabelle, she was telling him about her childhood on her father's ranch. She spoke dreamily of the ranges she would ride mustering the cattle that would be taken to the railhead to be transported to the towns and cities for slaughter. The rodeos where cowboys on horseback would ride like they were glued to the seat, of the roping and branding. She spoke excitedly of the gymkhanas, that as a teenager, she would enter.

"I would like to see all that someday," he had said.

"Well, there's a little bit of cowboy in all of us," she answered.

"Are you a city girl?" Sam asked seeing that he had touched on something that was close to her heart.

"Do you know Sam, I don't think I am."

"Will you go back to Texas?" Sam saw her fiddle with an engagement ring that had been on her finger for only a few weeks.

"I would love to go back, but only if Curtis came with me."

"How do you think he would feel about that?"

"We have discussed it, but at the moment it's his work that keeps him here."

"Could he not get a job in Austin?"

"We haven't thought that far ahead yet, but as things stand with banks going to the wall, and as long as the depression lasts, I don't think we will be moving far."

For a few days Sam had thought about the conversation with Isabelle. He imagined her as a young girl riding the open plains, and her saying that there was a little bit of cowboy in all of us. If that were true as it surely was, then there must be a few cowboys in New York State. That being the case maybe he could take it one step further and have some of the old cowboys in the State taken to their resting place in a coffin for cowboys. His mind was racing as he thought over how to do this. Coming up with an idea of branding with hot irons the names of the deceased on the pine boards of their coffin lids. The coffins would be plain, nothing fancy as he didn't think cowboys did fancy. Maybe a finishing touch would be to brand a cross below their name. The initial cost of the branding irons would be expensive as he would have to have every letter in the alphabet along with numbers from one to ten so that he could brand the year born and the year they died. Within a month Sam was advertising his coffins for cowboys and the response was such that he had to employ a girl full time in the office to handle the amount of enquiries that were coming through. Another carpenter and a yard man were taken on too. The condos that had been left to him by Mrs Doyle were rented out to two of his workmen both of whom were married, thus giving Sam some guarantee of a rent structure that was beneficial to both parties.

It was the last day of June when Sam answered the phone, it was Pat she was clearly distressed as she told Sam of news from home.

"It's my Dad Sam, my Dad has died," she was sobbing, "Mum didn't tell me he had been ill for some months. He forbade her to tell me, saying it was something he would get over. But he didn't and now he is dead, I have to leave America Sam, she will need me."

"When will you be going?" for a moment Pat didn't answer.

"As soon as I can get a ticket."

"Will you be coming back?" Sam already knew the answer. There was a slight pause.

"I don't know Sam, I really don't know. Where are you?"

"I'm at work, do you want me to come over?"

"No but if you could call tonight, maybe I will be in a better state of mind."

"I will come straight after work," Pat heard the click as Sam placed the receiver down.

"No Sam I don't think I will be back," she sobbed.

In the last six months they had been seeing less of each other and Pat was getting restless and although they were the best of friends, she wanted more from this relationship. It wasn't Sam's fault and it wasn't hers. She had been here four and a half years, and now it was time to go back home. If anything was to happen to her mother while she was in America, she would never forgive herself, so she would get herself a one way ticket on the earliest ship sailing to Liverpool. She was sad about her relationship with Sam, they both knew it wasn't going anywhere, but their friendship was genuine and she would like to think it would always be so.

One week later Pat reluctantly accepted a first class steamship ticket from Sam and sadly sailed out of his life. As he watched her wave goodbye, his thoughts turned to a similar scene when he waved goodbye to Grace at Liverpool docks. Pat was a good friend, and indeed was still a good friend and always would be, but still it was a shame that their friendship wasn't enough. As Pat waved farewell, she cast her mind back over the last four and a half years, to say the least it was an adventure like no other, but deep down she had always known that she would go back home one day. She was not surprised when Sam handed her a first class ticket, it was typical of him to do such a thing, and to refuse it would be pointless as it was given in good faith. Pat watched the American shoreline disappear. She turned and looked at a setting sun that slowly sank below a still sea, and for the second time she stood on the deck of a ship, pondering what future life had in store for her.

23

Grace laid Sam's letter on her bedside table.

"Why do you torture me so" she sighed.

She hadn't received a letter from him in months, and after all this time she wondered why he still wrote to her, more to the point why did she write back. He told her about all the money he had been left and of the continuing success of his business but not once did he mention or hint that he was seeing someone. She thought it unnatural if he hadn't been intimate with someone, or at least had a lady friend. She felt as though he had cheated her out of four years of loving. Most of her female friends were married, some with children, and those that weren't were in long term relationships. "And you Grace" she said to herself, "are you not in a relationship yourself?" Grace had been seeing Richard Smith for the last twelve months, she had even for the want of more descriptive words, lost her innocence to him. "So what," she thought, but ever since their night of passion and their continuing physical relationship, he had been pestering her to marry him, but she had been reluctant to commit herself. "Damn it," she thought, "he is good to me and he has a good job and he loves me." Should she throw caution to the wind, hope for the best and marry him? He had asked her many times to marry him and she had always put him off, but now she had decided was the time to live her life. She got up off her bed and reached for Sam's letter, she crumpled it up in both hands then dropped it in a little basket by her bed.

That night Grace went to the cinema and watched Dracula. It was not really her kind of film but as she watched Bela Lugosi pursue Helen Chandler and sink his teeth into the white flesh of his victim, she wondered what it would be like to have a dominant lover like Dracula. The man sitting next to her was far from being a dominant lover. She understood the need to be attentive but now and again she wished he would ravish her. He had kissed her goodnight under the watchful eye of Admiral Rodney. She went upstairs, took off her clothes and went to bed but not before reaching into her waste basket to retrieve a crumpled piece of paper that she then ironed out with her hand on her bedside table. She then placed Sam's letter in a drawer that held all his others.

"Well," said Grace frowning, "do I have your approval?"

Mary smiled, she had seen this coming for some time and was pleased that Grace had finally put to bed the torch that she had carried for Sam. It wasn't that Grace had not had a good time being single, on the contrary, she had had a bloody good time. A lot of young men had called at the Admiral Rodney seeking her affection. Some Mary approved of some she didn't, and of those that Grace had chosen to court, their time together was short lived. Mary had suspected that her daughter had always compared her suitors to Sam as it was always the case that when things started getting serious, she would finish their relationship. That was until Richard came on the scene. He was, as George put it, a nice enough fellow but lacked fire.

Richard worked in the office of the Cunard Shipping Line. They met one Sunday afternoon when she had gone to the docks with a friend whose family were seeing off some relations that were immigrating to Canada. It was the first time Grace had visited the docks since the day she had seen Sam wave goodbye to her over four years before. At first, she was reluctant to go with her friend as she knew it would bring back a memory that had taken her years to get over. As coloured streamers drifted from the upper decks of the passenger ship the memories of Sam's departure filled Grace's mind. She listened again to the shouts and cries of departing individuals who were leaving family and friends. Grace lifted her hand and waved. She didn't know the people she had come to see off but she waved just the same. She had often thought of what it would be like to sail away and start a new life. To be one of those who had thrown their hand to the wind letting that very wind take her on a journey, one that she had longed for. She knew it would never happen but to wish for something beyond her world didn't alter the fact that she wanted it. Grace looked around, to her left stood her friend waving and shouting. To her right a young man whose face was expressionless but whose eyes told their own story. For a moment she took in the sight of someone who she had suspected was there not of his choosing. He looked at Grace and smiled.

"Friends?" he said nodding towards the ship. Grace wasn't sure if he meant his friends or hers.

"Not really," she answered deciding that he meant was she saying goodbye to friends of hers. "Just people I know," she hesitated "and that isn't altogether true, I don't know them at all, they are friends of my girlfriend's family, I'm here as a favour to her just to see them off. And you?"

"My eldest sister is on that ship. We were never that close. I wish her and her family well of course but I am not that upset about seeing her go, we are indifferent to each other. As I said we were never that close, it's a pity really but that's how it is."

He looked back at the ship as its siren sounded, "You live around here?" he asked.

"Not far and you?"

"A ten minute walk, I work over there," he said pointing to a large building that stood at the entrance to the docks, "the Cunard office is on the ground floor."

"I know where it is, I pass it every morning on my way to work."

The ship's siren sounded again as it started to drift from its moorings.

"And where do you work?"

"I work this side of the city at Pearson and Simpson Accountants office," Grace answered.

"And you live?"

"Just up the road at the Admiral Rodney."

The young man smiled and raised his eyebrows, "Not exactly my kind of pub and please don't take offence."

"None taken," said Grace "it's not exactly my kind of place either but there is something about keeping all the rats in one nest."

"And that is?" enquired the young man.

"Well, most of them have been banned from everywhere else so the Admiral Rodney is the only place where they can spend their money." Grace's friend give her a nudge.

"We're going."

"I'm coming," Grace said as she turned to the young man, "nice to have made your acquaintance Mr?"

"My name is Richard and yours?" he asked as he removed his hat.

"Grace."

"Grace, well Grace until we meet again," Richard replaced his hat and re-joined the party of people that had come to the docks to see his sister leave a rather depressed Britain.

Exports had halved in the industrial areas and the war was responsible for depleted coal stocks. In 1925 Britain was importing more coal than it was mining, unemployment was on the rise as living standards were falling and the gap between the rich and poor was getting wider. The facts and figures of the British economy mattered not a jot to Grace and the deprivation of the poor and unemployed was not her concern. She was a fully qualified accountant, there was a good return on beer sales at the Rodney and all in all life was good. As for living standards falling, the exact opposite was happening in Grace's household. One could say that she lived a relatively privileged life as her personal financial outgoings were all but zero. Her parents would forgo any living costs incurred as Grace would do bar work most nights of the week apart from most Friday and Saturday nights.

Her friends were of mixed social standing and were a generation of young people who were rebellious against the society that preceded them. They were flamboyant, decadent, and outrageous and some promiscuous to the point of being obscene. Birth control was within their reach and this many would argue was the reason of the unacceptable behaviour of the young of the late 1920's, which in their defence would argue back that past generations had done the people no favours and it was their turn now and they were making the most of it. Smoking and a large gin was now the order of the night along with marijuana and the pleasures of the flesh. And where on the ladder of indulgence did Grace place herself? About halfway up she reckoned. Some of her friends had reached the gutter that the ladder was placed against, but not Grace, sure she had fumbled a bit down the back alleys of some dance halls but she had always got off that train before it reached its destination. But she had partaken in a little bit of everything else. On most Friday and Saturday nights Grace could be found with her friends in some of the smarter entertainment establishments in the city. Grace was a woman of the new world, a woman that could vote for a government that would reshape the country. A woman of financial independence. A woman that was classed as an 'it girl', one of the bright young things, by men that would give anything to be intimate with this darling of the dance floor.

The Grafton, Adelphi and Reece's ballrooms were venues that Grace would frequent. Her red dress would shimmer under the revolving lights of the Grafton, her bold red lipstick would match the red feather boa that would flow sensually over her naked arms and snake through the air as she twirled around and around on one square foot of the timber ballroom dance floor. Her red Mary Jane dance shoes would show off her nude coloured stockings, stockings that would be one shade darker than her natural skin. It was moments like this that Grace would feel free, she would throw back her head, close her eyes and abandon her everyday existence. She relished the idea of being a woman, a woman in the throes of being a female in every sense of the word. It was she who would be the predator of men and not the men who would assume their own importance in being a good catch for the likes of herself. Grace had learned a long time ago what men were about, after all she was a landlord's daughter and her preconceived notion of men hadn't altered until at the age of eighteen when a certain young Welshman walked through the door of the Admiral Rodney. Soon after his departure Grace started to look for a life outside the walls of the bar swilling establishment that was her home. Of course, she had fond memories of some of the men that she had known, some had seen her in her mother's arms as a child. Some had seen her first birthday and lived long enough to see her twenty first. Most, she had seen laugh and some she had seen cry. She had concluded some time ago that drink was like a double edged sword, too much of it would bring out the worst in some people, in others she had seen the best of humanity.

Sometimes on quieter moments in the pub she would listen to men telling their stories. Some would pour out their heart, telling tales of life, death, regrets and sometimes things that they would only tell God himself. She often wondered to whose benefit did they tell their tales because it certainly was not hers. She didn't want to know the man sitting opposite her had stuck a bayonet into the chest of a German soldier or how his friend in the trenches was blown apart in front of him. Yes, these men had a story to tell if they chose to tell it. She could see it in their drunken eyes, but why tell her? She didn't want to know; she didn't want to go to bed at night with the thought of their nightmares, but on many occasions she did do. But the thing that really pissed her off was that some men would come into the pub the following night as merry as can be and not even remember talking to Grace, never mind telling her about all the shit that they carried around with them in their heads, and another thing if they did remember telling her they would just say, that stuff I was telling you about last night, forget about it, and they would say it with a smile. Forget about it, Jesus Christ, some of those stories she would tell her friends would give her fucking nightmares and they wanted me to forget it. I swear to God while talking to me you would think they were talking to their Docker mates.

Grace did not have long to wait to see the man in the brown suit, that very night, he, with two of his friends, came through the door of the Rodney. It was a wet Friday night, a night when she would have normally been in the city, but that night, the Rodney was host to the sixty fifth birthday party of a regular patron, Roger Brown, a now retired Docker who had been a regular at the pub for many years. He was at a loss for words when he entered at his usual time of six thirty. All his family and friends were there to greet him. The party was in full swing as Jimmy Taylor, another pensioner, started doing his foot tapping dance. The ragtime music that he danced to was made up of other locals playing instruments that were often played in public houses. The squeezebox accompanied by someone playing the spoons and someone else on the Jews harp. Then there was the resident singer belting out songs that everyone knew. As it happened, he was singing an Al Johnson song as Grace handed three pints of beer over the counter.

"Didn't expect to see you so soon Richard," she said as she took his money, "You made a special trip to see me?" she added with a smile then turning her back she pressed some keys on the till.

"You could say that," he answered as she handed him his change.

"I thought this wasn't your kind of place."

"Well," he said before lifting his pint, "you were right about me coming to see you, I didn't think you would be here as it's Friday night but I thought I would take the chance."

"And your friends?" Grace asked looking at his companions who had moved away from the bar.

"I told them that I had met a pretty girl down at the docks and that if I saw you again, I was going to ask you out."

"And what makes you think I would accept your invitation? Two bottles of stout John?" she said taking her eyes momentarily away from Richard.

"Well," he shrugged, "if I didn't ask, I wouldn't know."

24

Sam received Grace's letter stating her intention to marry. He read it over and over, he wasn't surprised at the news, he had been expecting it for some time but to actually read the words of her intention was numbing. He poured the last of the red from the bottle he had brought up from the cellar. For nearly five years he had guessed that she secretly waited his return and as he sat in Mrs Doyle's chair pondering his own future, he was aware of a feeling of being abandoned and was resigned to the fact that if she did wait his return, she would wait no longer. Why did he assume that Grace was waiting for him? Their letters had been sporadic and always were, but there was something undeniable, that Grace would answer his letters by return of post something he had never done.

It had been nearly twelve months since Pat had returned to England, she had written a couple of times and that was it. Since her departure Sam had played the field so to speak, there was always a young lady on his arm, but none that had stolen or broken his heart. In most cases the only hearts to be broken were those of the girls that had fallen in love with him. He was now seeing a young lady that he had met at a debutante ball at the Astor. Sam was there at the invitation of Joe who was mixing business with pleasure reporting on the goings on of this prestigious event and on this occasion, Joe was accompanied by Pageant. Just how he got a ticket for Sam he didn't know and at first was hesitant about accepting it but curiosity and discretion being the better part of valour he became the ninth member of a party that was to sit at a table to celebrate the coming of age of the daughters of the rich and famous. Sam sat next to Pageant and during the course of the evening became increasingly impressed with her knowledge on most subjects while talking to people of various professions, be it in the arts, literature or business. As for politics to which everyone in the room had some opinion or other, Pageant, to the annoyance of some, would stay clear of admitting her own political preference.

"Just how do you do it Pageant?" Sam whispered after finishing his main course of Beef Wellington.

"Do what?" asked Pageant placing her napkin on the table.

"Being able to converse in any subject that people bring up and to do so in such a way as to not make yourself look as though you don't know what you are talking about."

"Sam," she said, looking around making sure everyone on the table was preoccupied in their conversations, "I'll tell you a little secret of mine," Sam bent forward, "I was about fourteen when I read a book about the Geisha of Japan. Maybe you haven't heard of the word."

"No, I haven't."

"Well, they are a class of female entertainers who from a very young age are trained in the traditional styles of the performing arts. This lasts for many years and the number of subjects taught are too many for me to explain here." Pageant leaned back as a waiter placed a Baked Alaska dessert in front of her and Sam.

"This looks yummy," Pageant said prodding the meringue topping with her dessert spoon. "Anyway, one of the subjects was the ability to indulge in conversational skills that is to say that whatever the subject their guests were discussing they would have a basic knowledge of that subject. The host of the parties and gatherings that the Geisha were invited to were mostly men, rather rich men, businessmen of high standing and their like. As it was, the Geisha would have been informed beforehand of who their hosts would be and would have brushed up on subjects that were of interest to them. Thereby, in the likelihood of such subjects being discussed the Geisha were able to voice a comment if asked. But first and foremost, they were entertainers, skilled in dance, singing, reading poetry and all being able to play an instrument manly a banjo like instrument called a shamisen." As Sam listened the dessert plates were being cleared away to be replaced with tea or coffee. Pageant stopped briefly to take a sip of tea before popping into her mouth a Fargo chocolate mint.

"And what other activities did these young women get up to?" Sam asked with a grin. "Was sleeping with the guest part of the deal?"

"As it turns out Sam they probably did, but as a fourteen year old, the book that I read didn't mention it, but maybe I misunderstood the word favours, which I recall was mentioned a few times. But they were not street walkers, fallen women or hookers," Pageant insisted, "they were courtesans, a far more respectable word."

"Much the same thing." Sam said smiling.

"Much the same thing," Pageant answered back.

It was at this point that the band started to play, and an announcement made. Everyone stood and applauded. The debutantes left their tables and gathered on the ballroom floor, with their long flowing white dresses and a corsage fastened to their left wrist. They were indeed a splendid picture. After another announcement, the lady's escorts accompanied them, and as the band played a slow waltz the lights dimmed and white dresses seemed to float above the ballroom floor moving in time to the music. There were a good many Cinderella's on the dance floor, some already having found their Prince and many more looking for them.

"Sam do you still send out coffins for Mr Murray Humphreys?" Joe said sitting in Pageant's vacant seat. She, having accepted an invitation to dance from a gentleman unknown to Sam.

"Yes, I do," Sam answered looking rather surprised at the question, "four every month, why do you ask?"

"Have you had any problems, I mean have there been any questions?"

"Asked by who?" Sam now sat upright in his chair.

"By people from the Prohibition Department. I know it's nothing to do with me but one of my colleagues in Chicago sent a message last week, apparently there was a fire at a crematorium in Chicago a few days ago".

"Go on," Sam wondering what was coming next.

"Well, it seems there were two coffins at the crem, one held the corpse and the other…" Joe stopped talking for a moment to have a sip of his orange juice laced with gin.

"And the other?" Sam prompted Joe.

"The other held a few bottles of bootleg whiskey."

"Don't tell me they put the wrong one through the flames!" Sam said with a laugh.

"It seemed so. I didn't tell you before now, as I wanted to find out what happened."

"You don't think it was one of mine," Sam said raising his eyebrows.

"I'm afraid it could well have been, you see Sam your coffins were being used to smuggle whiskey from New York to Chicago."

"Shit," Sam said as a little colour drained from his face, "do I have anything to worry about?"

"No, you don't, although they paid you in cash. It was a legitimate contract between yourself and the people who paid you, was it not?"

"It was."

"And you had no idea what was going on?"

"No, I didn't ask questions, I didn't want to know, but what you tell me holds no surprises."

"My informers tell me that from the beginning or pretty well early on, it was suspected that those coffins were carrying contraband liquor. They were stopped early on, and on that occasion the coffins were empty, then apparently some bribe money was paid but not before the vehicle was stopped again. This time Mr Humphreys' men were ready. They had word that an overzealous agent would stop the vehicle again, and well, they did stop it only to find that Mr Humphrey's men had called at a hospital to pick up some body parts before they were sent to be incinerated, two amputated legs I believe. They were placed into one of the coffins with a sheet over them with only their feet showing. For good measure, a decomposing rat was thrown in."

"What happened?" Sam was on the edge of his seat listening.

"The agent had Humphreys' men raise a coffin lid, all he saw was two feet, and the smell was enough to convince him the coffin contained a corpse."

"And the other coffins?"

"The agent didn't even bother to look. After that little episode they weren't stopped again except on the odd occasion when corrupt police were seen to be doing their job."

"And the two coffins at the crematorium?"

"As I have said, one held a body, but the wrong one went through the furnace. It seems that this coffin was the last drop, as it went from one place to another delivering the bootleg whiskey along the way."

"How many bottles were in the coffin?"

"My friend, Charles Schwartz, he's a reporter for the Chicago Daily News, reckons, or so he was told that a half dozen bottles went up along with your coffin. The raids on illegal bootleggers and their properties in Chicago have increased dramatically in the last twelve months, ever since Hoover appointed a man named Elliot Ness to head a team of Prohibition agents. This man and his team, Charles tells me, are beyond bribery and have coined a phrase, calling them The Untouchables."

"So, the bootleggers are having a hard time of it?" Sam interrupted.

"Well, they don't have it as easy as they used to, and having said that, I don't think prohibition will last that much longer. I think the law will be repealed sooner rather than later, I'll give it another twelve months or so."

Sam looked around, the younger generation had taken over the dance floor, gyrating hips, flared skirts and quick music. The piano player was doing a medley of dance music that had feet tapping in time to each ivory key that was struck by the lightning hand of the piano man's fingers. Sam had held back on gracing the floor with his version of the swing dance as he needed to have a partner, someone that could follow his moves. Then he saw her, the stunning blonde he had seen when she was first presented at the beginning before they were all seated. She was dancing with a lad who didn't know where to put his feet and she in contrast knew exactly where to put hers. Sam didn't take his eyes off her. He was standing some twenty feet from her when the music stopped and the lad she was dancing with moved away giving another man an opportunity to move in. Sam was tempted but resisted, he wanted to catch her eye first, but how with all those strutting males seeking her favours?

"Excuse me," said Sam to an elderly gentleman standing next to him on the edge of the dance floor, "that young lady," he pointed, "who is her father?" The gentleman looked.

"Aah Savannah's father is Herbert Celeste, the gentleman sitting over there," a casual finger was pointing at table twenty seven.

"And what line of business is he in?"

"Was in," the gentleman said with a grin.

"Was in," said Sam raising his eyebrows.

"Yes, he lost a lot of what he had."

"The stock market?" Sam suggested.

"That and other things."

"Other things?"

The gentleman looked at Sam and smiled.

"Fast cars and slow horses were his downfall, still he's got plenty left. Are you Irish?" the man added tilting his head.

"No, I'm Welsh."

"Been here long?"

"A few years."

"And how did you get a ticket for this little get together?"

"I have contacts," Sam said smiling.

"And to what is your interest here?"

Sam leaned a little towards him and whispered, "I'm looking for a virgin."

The man placed his hand over his mouth and gave a discreet cough, "My God," he uttered "I like your style but I think you're in the wrong place, as I don't think you'll find many in here." Sam looked at him still smiling, "mind you most debutantes' fathers would like to think that their daughters are still…" he hesitated.

"Intact," said Sam raising his eyebrows.

"Precisely."

Then a long white gloved hand tapped his shoulder and he was whisked away onto the dance floor, presumably by his wife Sam thought. His concentration was now on Savannah. Her dance partner this time was rather good looking and his footwork was on a par with hers. They danced as if they had been doing it for years and the rapport they had suggested they had been friends for a long time. He glanced back at table twenty seven, the man Sam had seen presenting Savannah, her father, was seated, behind him stood another young man who was bent over talking to the gentleman sitting. When he stood up, Sam smiled as the lad was the image of Savannah's partner, "so" Sam said under his breath, "Miss Celeste has twin brothers." In the next half hour Sam had, as time would permit, put into practice the ways of the Geisha as explained by Pageant. All he had to do was to ask Joe to tell him everything he knew about the Celeste family before making his next move.

The note was slipped under his door. Willena gave Sam the envelope as he walked in after work. It was sealed with just his name handwritten on the front of it. He slit it open with a letter knife and read its contents.

Sam, it has come to my attention that you have been seeing Savannah Celeste for the last couple of months and unknown to Savannah her father does not approve. It has come to the point where I, as a friend of Mr Celeste, must ask you to refrain from seeing her again. Usually, Savannah has the good sense to liaise with her own kind but it seems that she has become infatuated with you and will not listen to good advice. You must understand that to pursue this relationship is unwise and may I add unhealthy. Counting on you to do the right thing and hoping common sense will prevail.

Sam smiled to himself, he had in the last few weeks detected a disapproving mood in the family and he knew from pretty much the beginning that seeing a young man of his standing was not something her parents had in mind for their daughter. From the moment she had accepted his hand for their first dance Sam with his good looks and Rudolph Valentino charm, along with his ability to put his feet where Fred Astaire would put his, had set fire to Savannah's curiosity in him. Savannah was the kind of girl who loved being the centre of attention and getting what she wanted would propel her to that end. Their relationship was more physical than it was anything else and Sam knew they lived in different worlds and that one day soon she would move on. Sam was annoyed at the contents of the letter that was pushed under his door but having thought about it, he was going to milk the situation for what it was worth. The following Friday night when Sam went to pick up Savannah, he was greeted at the door by her father, unusual he thought.

"Hello Sam," he smiled, "Savannah is upstairs getting ready, come on in," As Sam brushed past him, he closed the door, "Sam," he said leading the way, "I was wondering if I could have a word with you." This is it, thought Sam smiling, "Come into my office."

Passing two doors from the hallway, Herbert stopped and opened the door to his office.

"Take a seat Sam." Immediately Sam detected a change in Herbert's manner, "I will come straight to the point Sam," the smile having left his face. "This relationship with my daughter, how serious do you think it will get?" Herbert stood behind a large desk and behind him, a comfortable looking desk chair. Sam looked up, the smile on his face gone,

"I beg your pardon," Sam said looking surprised.

"I think you heard me Sam," Herbert leaned forward, his hands placed flat down on the desk in front of him, his posture intimidating. "Well," he said raising his voice for a moment. Sam was silent as he looked at the ink well and papers on the desk. Then raising his gaze, and with a slight smile, he answered,

"I think I'm in love with her," he lied.

"Love her, you hardly know her!" he snarled.

"Well enough to fall in love," Sam said, "and she loves me."

"Correction Sam, she is infatuated with you and that has got nothing to do with love."

"That may be so Herbert, but I believe, you yourself weren't courting long before getting married."

There was a slight tremor in Herbert's voice as he struck the top of his desk with his fist, "That's got fuck all to do with you."

"And your wife," said Sam standing to his full height, "she is the daughter of a wealthy industrialist who I believe had words with you about marrying his daughter, as you at the time were not a good prospect for anyone's daughter, let alone his, need I go on?" Herbert stood open mouthed as Sam spoke of a period in his life that he would rather forget. Herbert sat down, his thoughts were of Sam, what else does this heap of shit know of his past.

"Look Sam," his demeanour having changed yet again, "Savannah's mother and I had her late in life and we just want the best for her." Sam now leaned forward, reversing the roll, and knowing exactly what to say, placing his hands on the table, he stared into Herbert's eyes.

"I understand your dilemma Herbert, but if I wanted to be rid of someone I didn't want around, I would throw some dollar bills on the table and tell them to fuck off." Herbert didn't say a word. He just opened a drawer and reaching in brought out a bundle of notes and placed them on the table.

"Come, come, Herbert, you know as a businessman I cannot accept your first offer," Herbert, his face now contorted with anger, reached into his drawer and pulled out another bundle.

"I didn't think you would," he said with resignation. Sam slowly picked up both bundles and placed them in his jacket pocket.

"I think that concludes our business, of course I cannot deprive Savannah of her evening's entertainment but I can assure you I will keep my end of the bargain." With that Sam turned and walked to the door, on opening it, he turned, "If we should ever meet again, I suggest we are civil to each other. Goodbye Mr Celeste, nice doing business with you." Sam closed the door.

Herbert sat for a moment, thinking if nothing else Sam Pryce had stood his ground. He raised himself from his seat and cursing shook his head, "Son of a bitch."

Outside, Sam sat in his car waiting for Savanna, as he didn't think it prudent to wait inside. He smiled to himself, thinking of what had just happened. He was surprized at how smart ass Herbert Celest had caved in when the tables were turned. He was also surprized at his own behaviour, but Herbert had crossed a line and Sam wasn't having any of it. As for the money he didn't need it and he didn't want it. A grin of satisfaction spread across his face. "That's the quickest bundle of notes I will ever earn." He said under his breath, "and I can get rid of it just as quickly.

"And where are we going tonight." Sam said, as Savannah slid seductively into the passenger seat of his car. With wide eyes she looked at Sam then wrinkled her nose.

"Your place where else!"

On the way home he called in at a church where people with very little would come and collect food parcels. He never said a word to Savanna as he pulled up outside a makeshift tent alongside the church. Without getting out he caught the attention of a clergyman. Sam beckoned him, and as he walked over, he went into his jacket pocket. With the car window down Sam handed him the money that had been in Herbert Celest's desk drawer. "For the cause," he said placing his car into first gear.

"Bless you," the Clergyman said with a smile.

"You're blessing the wrong man" grinned Sam as he pulled away.

"What was that about?" Savanna asked.

"Just a little spare money I had".

"That was a kind gesture",

"Wasn't it just?" answered Sam smiling. Savanna, a little confused smiled back.

That was the last night Sam was to sleep with Savannah, maybe sleep was the wrong word! In the morning she dressed and as she looked at herself in the mirror she sighed.

"I'm going to miss our lovemaking."

"Me too," said Sam.

They didn't speak as he drove her home. Then just before she got out, she smiled.

"Sam, it was great fun, but it was just one of those things."

Nice line Savannah, Sam thought. She then again wrinkled her nose and got out.

25

At one thirty on Saturday 23rd of January 1932 the church bells of Liverpool Parish Church began their peal to celebrate a wedding. Grace stood on Chapel Street with her husband of thirty minutes and turned. Through the falling snow she looked at the gothic church spire that had witnessed their exit. The building looked as it always looked, the bells sounded as they had always sounded, with both making no exception to the happy couple that had just made a commitment to love each other till death were to part them. Grace had not thought of Sam for months, he had known of her wedding plans and she dismissed his letter offering his congratulations that had arrived some time earlier. This she thought, as she stood shivering in the cold would finally put an end to any wishful thinking that she had harboured for she couldn't think of for how many years.

"Come on Grace darling," he said as he opened the door of the fancy car that her father had hired. That night as they lay in each other's arms they talked of the day's events and of the future. It was their first night in their rented home on Union Street not far from the church they were married in, and a ten minute walk from the Admiral Rodney. It was a strange but satisfying feeling being together, away from the restraints that living with her parents entailed, of course it was their home too, but this was different.

George and Mary stayed up late. The pub had been closed all day in recognition that the landlord's daughter was getting married. Mary sat silently holding a full glass of sherry. The warmth from the coal fire comforted her as she dwelt on the years that had passed.

"You look sad," George said as he sat down in his chair. Mary looked at him.

"I am," she answered, "Things won't be the same again, do you think we should sell the pub?"

"And do what?"

"I don't know, maybe live a normal life."

"Well," he said with a sigh, "I must admit it has crossed my mind, we have talked about this before but when is there a good time to do it and where would we go?" George looked at his wife, a tear ran down her face.

"Maybe now is a good time to go, I am tired George, God knows we have worked hard for what we have and it isn't as though we are destitute. We have been putting money away for the last twenty years, saving for the moment when we can put our feet up and let the rest of the world go by, well at least put one foot up."

It's true thought George, they had worked hard and had put up with a lot of things running the pub. "Give it two more years Mary and I promise we will do as you wish."

"You promise George?"

"I promise."

Six months later Grace walked through the door of her terraced home. Work was finished for the week and she was looking forward to the weekend. It was Robert's birthday and she had booked a table at a restaurant on the way home from work. It would be the first time that they would be eating out since getting married. She put the kettle on the stove and looked out of the window, people were hurriedly walking home from their own place of work, probably like her, glad the working week was over, that is, she thought, if they had a job to walk home from. The homes across the road were like hers, a row of stone terraced houses that stretched down the road and around the corner. She took off the cardigan that her mother had bought her for Christmas, it was warm, the temperature had risen over the last few days and everyone was making the most of it. A half hour later Robert walked in.

"Hi honey," he said as he kissed her on the cheek, "love you," he whispered as he took off his coat. He had told her that, every day since their wedding and if he did miss one, he would tell her twice the following day. They walked out of their door at seven thirty turning left into Chapel Street. Ten minutes later entering the restaurant. They were shown to a table on which lay a printed card saying reserved, by its side a fancy silver scrolled candlestick, the red candle it held was already lit giving off a soft orange glow, next to it a tall narrow glass vase with one single stemmed rose. They sat opposite each other and as browsing the menu Richard looked up.

"You're not on the menu Grace."

"You can eat me later," she said with a grin.

"I'll hold you to that," he said giving her a wink. After a lovely meal of Chicken Chasseur and a bottle of wine, they closed the door to Sally's restaurant and decided to go for a drink. The public house, a short walk from the restaurant was full but they managed to find seats in the saloon bar. The atmosphere was welcoming. The patrons Grace noticed were a generation younger than those of the Rodney, with more couples enjoying each other's company. After drinking two gin and orange, Grace suggested they leave. Daylight was fading when they stepped out of the Rose and Crown, last orders having been called sometime before. The late evening shadows were long as Grace and Richard made their way home, they talked and laughed and talked some more. There were few people on the street, chinks of light could be seen through the windows of homes whose curtains were not fully drawn. Now and again raised voices could be heard from within the houses that ran parallel to the pavement, a lone figure approached and past, his stumbling walk suggested that he had had too much to drink along with the slurred, "Good evening" he said as passing. Two more men came into view they stopped and looked around, for no reason Richard turned, there was no one on the street, he felt uneasy and squeezed

Grace's hand, she was chatting away saying how much she had enjoyed her meal.

"Got a light guv?" the taller of the two asked as Richard and Grace came alongside them,

"No, I'm sorry I don't," Richard let go of Grace's hand. Without warning, the shorter of the two lunged at Richard pushing him against the wall of one of the terraced houses, the other man grabbed Grace and cupped his hand over her mouth as he held her from behind. The wall stopped Richard from falling over, he grabbed the strangers coat collar, then felt a searing pain in his stomach. The short man lashed out and struck Richard on the face causing his head to hit the brick wall, his legs then crumbled. Falling to the ground his head, with a sickening thud, hit the cobbled pavement, the man then rifled his pockets taking Richard's wallet from his inside jacket pocket. Grace looked on in disbelief, mortified as to what was going on. With all her might she tried to break free, then like a ragdoll she was thrown to the ground, the man grabbing her handbag as she fell. Her screams echoed up the street and must have been heard from within the houses that fronted the pavement. Doors were opened as people rushed out. There were shouts for help, as people ran to do what they could. A man knelt by Richard's side and lifted his head.

"Jesus Christ," he uttered as he gently laid his head back from where he had lifted it. Blood flowed slowly between the cobbles of the pavement. He rose, "This man is in a bad way", he said, as another man came and stood by his side. Two women were comforting Grace who was still on the ground unable to get up due to her ankle.

"It's broken or badly sprained", said one, Grace was calling for Richard but he didn't answer. She could see him lying there, he was not moving. More people had gathered around, nearby curtains were drawn wide letting light onto the pavement. Grace was helped over to where Richard was lying, she knelt by his side pleading for him to get up, she lifted his head then noticing her bloodied hand, she gave a mournful wail and began beating his chest. A voice could be heard.

"It's Grace from the Rodney, it's Grace from the Rodney, Stan, run and get her father, run as fast as you can, did anyone see what happened?"

"I saw two men run up the street, these two were in the Rose and Crown earlier on, they had been for a meal at Sally's."

"I think he's dead."

Grace heard that last word and fear filled her very being. Time stood still and in what seemed ages another voice stood out.

"Stand aside, stand aside," a policeman said loudly, "the ambulance has arrived." He stood over Grace and placed his hand on her shoulder. "Come on miss," he said softly, "let these men take him to hospital." Grace was lifted by the two women that had not left her side.

"Grace," she recognised her father's voice, "Grace are you alright?" George held his daughter.

"They've hurt Robert," she cried, "They've hurt Robert."

Robert was taken to the Royal Infirmary, Pembroke Place and was pronounced dead on arrival. Grace's ankle was in plaster for six weeks and she never again set foot inside the house that she had shared with Robert. It was cleared by George, Mary, and some of George's regulars. It was heart breaking for Mary to collect Grace's things, her clothes, pots and pans and wedding presents, some not even opened. They were placed in cardboard boxes and taken to the Rodney, being put into the spare bedroom to be opened by Grace as and when she felt the need to.

After two months, Mary wrote to Sam explaining what had happened, also mentioning that she was worried about Grace, saying that she didn't think she would ever be the same again, ending her letter asking if he could write, as it may help in some way. For the first few months Grace would have flashbacks of the night her life was torn apart, the recollection of events were etched in her mind. Sometimes she would wake up hardly able to breathe, remembering a stranger squeezing the life out of her and fondling her breasts as he did so. She remembered the blood, Richard's blood, congealing between the pavement's cobbled stones, the cries and shouts of people as they scurried and stood about as her husband lay dying, killed by a man who had stolen his wallet. Going back to her home was not an option and going back to the Admiral

Rodney was nearly as bad. For weeks after the funeral the atmosphere in the pub had changed, it was nothing like it used to be. It surprised Grace as to the behaviour of the locals, they couldn't do enough for her mum and dad, bunches of flowers were brought in every other day for Grace, some by men who Grace thought didn't have a decent thing about them. Robert's parents called a few times, but it was too distressing for them to maintain the bond that had grown between the two families, so their meetings diminished rapidly over the coming months. A fund was set up for Grace and unsurprisingly money was handed over the bar. Grace may have had a roof over her head but it was a roof she didn't want, she wasn't ungrateful, but it was all driving her crazy.

After four months George and Mary decided that they would sell up and move away. It was a decision jointly made, but where would they go? The countryside appealed to them all and financially they would be able to buy a little place somewhere and make a new start. There were some reservations that George had, not least the question of work. Although the depression was still with them there was signals that the country had turned the corner and in any case work in towns and cities was much harder to find than in the countryside. One of George's customers, a gentleman, who from time to time would call in and having heard of George and Mary's decision to sell the Admiral Rodney and move to the country, happened to ask where they would be moving to.

"We haven't decided," George answered, "Have you any suggestions?"

"I have," he said lifting his pint, "Shropshire."

George smiled, "Yes a lovely part of the country, spent my childhood there. To be more precise a little town on the Welsh border called Bishops Castle."

"Never heard of it."

"Take a trip there George, you won't regret it."

It was mid-October when the big move came. The removal lorry was full and was now in transit, travelling the one hundred miles to their new home in the very town that was suggested to George. They had bought a little three bedroom stone cottage in the middle of Bishops Castle, an interesting place eight miles from the Welsh border and ten miles from Montgomery, the county town of Montgomeryshire. Grace felt relieved to have left behind the accursed place that had caused her so much heartache. Within a week, George, because of his knowledge and experience in the pub trade, found a part time job in the local brewery, The Three Tuns, established in 1642, the oldest licenced brewery in Britain.

Before leaving Liverpool, Grace received a letter from Sam, in it he wrote of his sadness of the news of Richard's death and his hope for Grace's future happiness. Amongst other things, he mentioned his forthcoming trip home, he was hoping it would be in April. His intention was to stay for six weeks and would call to see her if it would be all right. He asked Grace to pass on his good wishes to her parents. Sam was not sure how to end his letter, so he wrote:

> I've never forgotten you Grace, keep your chin up and I'll see you in April My love and thoughts.
> Sam.

When Sam had read Mary's letter telling him of Richard's death, his thoughts of Grace were uppermost in his mind. How sad, she must be devastated. She had found someone to share her life only to lose him in such a tragic circumstance. But in the back of his mind was a thought that surprised him, she was free, free to love again. Sam did what Mary had asked and wrote a letter to Grace. It was the right thing to do and he would have written anyway, but it was nice of Mary to think that he could be of some help, even if it was only a letter.

He had already planned his trip to the UK, sailing the third week of April for a stay of six weeks. The business was running smoothly and he felt that he could disappear for eight weeks, including time spent on the ship, without any problems. As for the financial side of Sam's business Willena would as she had done for the last two years oversee its weekly incomings and outgoings, and the boys were quite capable of seeing to what was needed to be done.

Willena had often mentioned in the past six months, about Sam taking a trip home. "I think it would do you good, you need a break from all this and I'm sure your mom would be over the moon." As the weeks went by Sam was becoming more anxious about leaving the business for so long. He had on various occasions gone away visiting other parts of the state but a few days away was the most he would allow himself. Sam had visited many parts of New York State but this was a little different. Still, he had made up his mind, even to the point of writing home letting everyone know that he would be paying them a visit. During the last two months before his leaving, Sam had arranged for someone in his absence to do some of the work that he would have been doing. Having seen his standard of work Sam was content to let this happen. Three weeks before his departure Sam had paid for a first class return ticket and now all he had to do was bide his time. Biding his time wasn't an easy thing to do, he was finding it hard to sleep, all kinds of thoughts would flash through his mind, things that he hadn't thought much about over the last few years. His brother and sister, whose image would last in his mind for the length of time it took to read the few words that they had written. The rolling hills and green fields, he thought about his old school friends, where were they now and what were they doing? And then there was Grace, she was the centre of many of his thoughts, would any of them be realised.

Two weeks before his boat was to sail, Sam called to see Curtis and Isabelle. He hadn't seen them since their return from Isabelle's father's ranch in Texas. Curtis was full of stories.

"And how did the natives treat you, Curtis? No doubt they sat you on a horse and let you get on with it," he said with a laugh.

"They started me off sitting on an old nag that could hardly walk. It was all very embarrassing, it wasn't even moving and I fell off. Much to the amusement of the cowhands that had gathered to watch a greenhorn make an exhibition of himself. But I persevered and by the end of our stay I was riding the prairie like one of those chaps who rode the Pony Express."

"How did your father receive you?" Sam asked Isabelle, she looked at Curtis and smiled.

"Well at first, he wondered what the hell I had brought home, especially after his trick on the old nag, but although they come from two different worlds, he was impressed with Curtis' determination to succeed. And just before leaving he told me that I would be a fool to let this one go, of which Sam," she looked up, "I have no intention of doing so."

When Sam left their home, he thought about all the new friends that he had made and what part they played in his not missing home as much as he maybe should have. "I've had a busy few years," he muttered dismissing any thoughts of guilt. Sam had several phone calls wishing him well on his journey and his last Saturday night was spent at home. Willena had suggested that he gathered his friends for a farewell meal, this he did and was surprised to find that most had the same idea of bringing along a book for him to read on the journey.

"The docks." Sam said as he placed two large suitcases in the boot of the taxi."

"You're going to England."

"That's my intention," answered Sam as he closed the car door.

"Going for long?"

"Two months."

The taxi driver, not a talkative person, only spoke again when he told Sam how much the fare was, this he paid, then taking his suitcases he walked through the departure gate.

26

Sam's voyage took him back to when, as a naive eighteen year old, he trod the decks of another ship. How much he had changed in that time he didn't know, but now he felt more mature and confident in everything he did. He remembered his Uncle Bill telling him the last time they were together that the next time they were to meet he would be in the company of a different man, one who had lived in an adult world, a world where he didn't have his mother or anyone else to wipe his arse when things went wrong. Of course, he did not see it then, but he saw it now.

On a beautiful May day Sam set foot on British soil. The first thing he noticed was the total lack of the American accent and found that he had to concentrate on what people were saying. It was early afternoon and Sam hadn't made plans as what to do, should he catch a train? To where? It crossed his mind to stay the night at the Admiral Rodney but decided against it. He knew that Grace did not live there anymore but maybe if he were to call he could get more information about what happened the night Richard and Grace were robbed. He looked at his watch. If he could leave his cases, he would have time to go to the Rodney then come back and catch the trains that would take him to Shrewsbury. He would hire a car and go to Bishops Castle to see Grace, then onto Llandyssil. Sam picked up his suitcases and walked the short distance to the station where he left his luggage in a locker and bought a ticket to Shrewsbury. The train would be leaving in an hour and a half from platform two.

The three thirty train left on time and Sam settled back and reflected on the story he had been told by a gentleman at the Rodney. The men responsible for the death of Robert had never been caught. There were suspicions, but it was hearsay and you can't hang a man on hearsay. Grace's handbag had been found in the churchyard of the church they were married in six months before, there was nothing in it and was returned to Grace. She had burnt it in a fire that she lit in the pub's backyard before they moved away.

At Shrewsbury the train stopped and Sam got off, he left the station noticing on the way out a sign, Godfrey Davies Car Hire. In the station yard was a little shed with more signs advertising the company's cars. Sam did the deal giving the gentleman a forwarding address, that of his parents and paying cash, peeling off one pound notes from a role he had in his hand. The gentleman took note of Sam's passport, then taking his money, including a bond that he would get back on return of the car. He handed him the keys. Sam noticed a road map on the passenger seat as he slipped the car into first gear.

He drove out of the station yard turning right then left under the railway bridge. Within ten minutes he was in open countryside heading south west to Bishop's Castle. There were few cars on the road as he drove the remaining twenty miles to Grace's home. Bishop's Castle two miles, the signpost said, as Sam slowed down to overtake a horse and cart. He was now getting anxious about everything, his appearance, what would he say, would she be at home, would anyone be at home? There were a few cars on the street as Sam drove into Bishop's Castle, parking opposite a greengrocer's shop. He got out and stretched his legs. He was hungry but didn't have time to eat. People were going into and coming out of shops. A dog chased a cat, both running under a horse who stood motionless awaiting his master's call to move on. He having delivered a bag of potatoes at a shop opposite. The afternoon was warm as the sun shone through wispy clouds. In the gutter two jackdaws fought over a piece of bread. Sam looked up the road, two women were talking, they stopped on his approach.

"Excuse me, could you tell me where this is?" Sam read Grace's address, written on a piece of paper he held.

They looked at each other.

"Yes," said one, "It's just up the street to the left of the market hall, go around the corner then left again and it's just down the road on your left."

"Isn't that where the new people live?" said the other.

"Yes, he works with our Clive at the Three Tuns, sad business about their daughter, Grace I think her name is."

"Thank you," said Sam as he leaves them, overhearing the words about Grace as he walked away. He followed the direction the lady had given him and found himself standing outside a little cottage. Tudor House, that's what it said painted on a piece of board screwed to a little white gate. Butterflies were in his stomach as he lifted the latch opening the gate and strode the six steps to a green front door. He raised his hand and knocked. The door was opened, Sam recognising Mary immediately.

"Hello Mrs Holloway," he said with a grin, and with a broad smile spreading across her face she answered.

"Sam," she cried, "it's been a long time, come on in, what a lovely surprise." Mary held out her hand, Sam took it and with a warm feeling seeping through his body she led him into the lounge.

"I'll put the kettle on, you fancy a cuppa."

"I do," said Sam as he stood looking at a photograph of Grace standing on the mantelpiece above the fireplace.

"George is at work," she said excitedly, her voice coming from the kitchen, "and Grace has gone for a walk, one sugar in your tea Sam?" then added, "are you hungry?"

"One sugar will be fine Mrs Holloway and please don't bother with…."

"I'll make you a ham sandwich," she said before Sam had finished answering whether he was hungry or not.

"Do you want mustard on your ham?"

"Thank you that would be lovely." Sam went into the kitchen as Mary was spreading some mustard on a sandwich. She cut it in half then placed it onto a small plate.

"Sit down Sam," she said as she placed a tea strainer over a cup before pouring the tea. She asked when Sam had arrived in Liverpool.

"Eleven o'clock this morning, I caught a train to Shrewsbury, hired a car and drove here."

"You haven't been home then?" she asked with surprise.

"No, I thought I would call first as it's sort of on my way home. I called at the Rodney before catching the train. A gentleman told me all about what happened, it was quite upsetting. How is Grace?"

Mary handed him his cup of tea.

"She hasn't got over it yet which is understandable, but she is better than she was." Sam then changed the subject and asked how they were finding it living such a long way from home and in new surroundings.

"Well, it's different," she answered, "And we have settled in really well. Of course, it is a lot quieter here, a slower pace of life which is to be expected."

"Are you glad you moved?" Sam asked as he finished his sandwich.

"Oh yes, it all got too much for us in the end and Grace couldn't get out of there fast enough."

As they talked Sam was anxious to see Grace. George would not be back for another couple of hours and he wanted to meet Grace on her own, as Mary had told him she had gone for a walk. "If you go now you may catch her coming through the kids' playing field, you can't miss it. Go to the bottom of the main street and turn left, she must walk through the field to get home. As I know she is looking forward to seeing you again."

Sam drank the last of his tea and stood thanking Mary before leaving. "Come back with Grace", she said as he closed the little garden gate behind him. Ten minutes later he was seated on a wrought iron bench watching some children doing what children do on a playing field. To his right and in a far corner of the field he noticed a stile and a footpath that lead into the woods. He looked at his watch, half past four, he was hoping to be back home by five but that wasn't going to happen. A figure approached the stile and got over it, it was a woman, she wore a dark skirt and a white blouse. It's Grace he thought, but it wasn't. Soon after another lady did the same.

"Hello Sam," startled he stood, behind him was Grace.

"You were looking at the wrong stile Sam, I got over that one there." Turning she pointed to another stile at the opposite end of the field, "I have been watching you for some time." Sam stood open mouthed, not believing it was Grace who was speaking to him. He looked into her eyes.

"Grace," her name stumbled from his mouth, he didn't know what to say.

"Well," she said, "aren't you going to give me a hug?"

Grace had moved from the side of the bench, standing now within arm's reach of the young man that had held her over six years earlier. Grace had seen him sitting on the bench after she had gotten over the stile and for some minutes had studied the stranger, her curiosity was raised when she noticed he was staring toward the far stile and never took his gaze from it. She couldn't see his face but there was something about him. She skirted the field stopping every so often not taking her eyes off him. It was when he turned his head that her suspicions, that it could be him were realised. She knew he was due to arrive but didn't have a definite date. Her thoughts of Sam were that of a lost love and for the last few years had become no more than that.

An hour and a half later, with mixed emotions, Sam drove home. The rolling hills of Montgomeryshire were in front of him as his thoughts drifted from Grace to seeing his family, then back to Grace again. They had sat on the bench and talked for an hour. Grace wanting to know what Sam had been up to in the intervening years. The subject of Grace's traumatic experience was discussed briefly, Grace seemingly not wanting to go into much detail and Sam not wanting to hear any more than what he had already been told. He was at ease in her company and within minutes the apprehension he had felt before meeting her had gone. She told of the new life she wanted and when he gave her a hug, he had a feeling of wanting more. As they walked to Grace's home, they passed his car parked on the street.

"Fancy going for a ride sometime?" he asked.

"Is that yours?"

"No, it's not mine, I have hired it for six weeks."

"I would love to, where would we go?"

"I don't know, maybe I'll take you home to meet my Mum and Dad and Aunt Megan of course." Grace stopped.

"Are you serious?" she smiled.

"Why not, you are a friend of mine aren't you?"

"That would be nice," she said.

George had still not arrived home when Sam said his goodbyes, promising he would call in the evening on Wednesday. He gave Mary and Grace a peck on the cheek then walked to his car. Sam was now in familiar surroundings as he drove through Montgomery town, he noticed four cars on the main street and in the late afternoon the clouds had the beginnings of a ruddy tinge that would last until sunset. Two men stood outside the Upper House pub as Sam slowly drove past. They looked with curiosity, no doubt wondering who the stranger was as very few cars were seen passing through Llandyssil. He parked the car in a layby opposite his parent's house, one that would be used for parking up the steamrollers when roadmen would come to repair the road. Sam's homecoming was heralded as something like the second coming and word spread just as fast. His mother was beside herself with joy and pride. His sister wept, and his father praised God for bringing his son home safely. His brother was not so verbal in his excitement but nonetheless he was eager to hear the stories that he would tell. Sam's joy at being home lasted for the few days that it took to meet everyone. After his family, Aunt Megan was the first he was to meet, her hug was an extension of the hug she had given him when he went away, tears were in her eyes as she held him at arm's length.

"My goodness you've grown Sam."

"I'm still the same height Aunt Megan."

"Maybe, but you have a bit more meat on you now. You were a boy when you went away and now… and now."

"He's a man" said Bill taking hold of Sam's hand and shaking it.

"And how are you, Sam?"

"I am well Uncle Bill, and yourself?"

"Good, now come and sit down and tell us all about yourself." For an hour Sam spoke of his life since leaving, he elaborated on the things that he had already told them in his letters.

"I have been truly fortunate Aunt Megan, the money and the property that Mrs Doyle left me in her will has enabled me to live a life beyond my expectations. I have met some wonderful people, some of whom, with their help have given me an opportunity to succeed in my dream." As Megan listened to Sam's stories she wondered how much of an influence, if any, she had had, in the way he had conducted himself in his adventure.

"Aunt Megan," Sam had broken her thought, "Would you mind if I were to bring a friend, a young lady to visit?"

Megan looked at Bill, she smiled.

"A young lady friend, you haven't been back two minutes and you want to introduce us to your girlfriend."

Sam laughed.

"It's not quite like that, she's a friend and she's a young lady, do you remember me mentioning the girl I met at the Admiral Rodney? The pub I stayed at the night before I sailed to America, well she lives with her parents in Bishop's Castle now, I called to see her before coming home and I asked if she would like to go for a ride in the car, she said where to and I said here." Sam went on to tell of the tragic events that had befallen Grace, mentioning that he had kept in touch with her over the time he had been away, then asking if they wouldn't mind putting her up for the night, that is if she would like to stay.

"Does your mother know?" asked Megan raising her eyes.

"She's alright about it, I will stay at home and I thought if you're agreeable she could stay here."

"I can't see why not," said Bill, "how old is she?"

"She's twenty five, a few months older than myself."

"In that case I can't see a problem," again Megan smiled.

"I am going to see her tomorrow evening, I will ask her then. Now don't read too much into this Aunt Megan as I have too much going on in my life to think of any romantic involvement."

A half hour after Sam had left Grace George arrived home, he placed his lunch bag on the kitchen table.

"And what's the matter with you two?" he asked.

"We've had a visitor," said Mary smiling, "go on Grace tell your father who's just called."

"It's Sam, he left about fifteen minutes ago."

"Sam, American Sam!" he looked surprised.

"He's hired a car."

"He's hired a car for six weeks. Not short of a bob or two then."

"George don't talk like that."

"Just joking."

"He went to meet Grace on the playing field."

"And how did you find him Grace."

"Much the same," she answered, "not that I really knew him, probably a lot more worldly than I remember him."

"He probably saw that in you too, he's done a lot of living in the last six years. That makes him twenty four now," George said deep in thought, "and if he doesn't know his own mind now, he never will."

Grace went to bed that night with her mind full of Sam, but with the thought that she would not let her heart rule what was going on in her head. The big question was, did he feel obliged to call and see her and for no other reason than that they had kept in contact with each other and to pay a debt he thought he had regarding his night's board and lodging. Or did he have any ulterior motive? After all he would be going back to America in six weeks and would probably not come home again for many years. She took a deep sigh, "so enjoy the moment Grace," she said to herself.

The news of Sam's return was spoken of throughout the village, and the talk in the pub was of him being a rather wealthy young man. Some saying he was showing off by driving his car around like some Lord of the Manor. Sam was disappointed to hear of such talk and was disappointed that some people would think like this.

"Sam," Megan said handing him a cold lamb chop, "I want you to think about a question I'm going to ask." Sam, chewing on his lamb chop, give her a curious look, then nodded his head. "What does the meaning of success mean to you?" Sam smiled, this was typical of his Aunt Megan. As he was growing up, she would ask him questions, questions that no other person would ask and he had learnt a lot from the questions she would ask. He thought for a moment.

"To achieve your goals," ending the word goals on a higher pitch.

Megan smiled, "Could you elaborate?"

"Well, if you set out to do something that is within your capability and you succeed isn't that success?"

"And where do you think money comes into it?"

"I don't know if money does come into it," he shrugged, "if to make money is your objective and you make money then you have achieved your aim, but having said that, if you are good at something, money usually follows anyway." Sam looked up after placing the bone from his lamb chop on a plate, "But I don't think that being successful automatically means financial gain. I have a successful business and I make a lot of money, but I couldn't have done it without the financial support given to me by Mrs Doyle and I am fully aware of that fact." For a moment Megan did not speak.

"You know Sam, I still think of you as the young lad you were when you went away and not the person you are now," Megan paused, "A lot of people would use the word success and money in the same sentence, not that they would be wrong, but you didn't and to me it shows how mature you have become. Those people that have accused you of showing off, are people that probably know you and let's face it everyone knows everyone around here, but their ability to applaud your success without turning it into jealousy is a problem that they live with, and of those people, how many would refuse your offer of a drink down at the pub, probably not a one. So pay no heed to those people Sam. Few know you better than I and when you leave again, I know I may never see you again. As sad as that is, you have a life to live and you must live it."

For the first week Sam did the rounds calling on people he knew and some his mother insisted he visit. Their joy in seeing him was evident in the way they greeted him with long handshakes and questions by the dozen. Cups of tea and cake were always on offer, along with homemade wine ranging in taste from rhubarb to elderflower. As arranged, he had called for tea at Grace's home. George now with greying hair, asked if he would like to stay the night.

"If not maybe you can stay one night before you return to America."

"I would like that," said Sam looking at Grace. During tea, the subject of his stay at the Admiral Rodney came up, George telling him that the two men he had measured up for coffins had died, along with one or two others that were there that night. It was when George was laughing at the scene of Sam with a tape measure that Grace got up from the table and excused herself. Mary looked at George and then at Sam.

"I'm sorry Sam," she said, "but sometimes when talking of someone dying Grace gets a little teary. She will be alright in a minute."

"I'll go to her," said Sam as he rose from his seat.

"She will be fine," said George, "sometimes we forget."

Grace was in the sitting room drying her eyes when Sam walked in.

"I am sorry Sam," she said, "I get like this sometimes, I can't help it."

"You don't have to apologise Grace I understand perfectly," he placed his hand on her shoulder, "no one is insensitive to your feelings Grace, and it's moments like this that a hug can make it better, would you mind?" he smiled.

"Feel free," she said returning his smile. On returning to the table Sam spoke of a little matter regarding his debt.

"Don't forget the interest!" George remarked with a grin. Sam went into his pocket and brought out a roll of notes.

"And you can put that away," Mary said with a raised voice, "it was a pleasure to have had your company then, as it is to have it now, you wouldn't want to offend us would you."

Sam sheepishly put his money back into his pocket.

"In that case," he said, "I would like to repay you by having your permission to take your daughter out of your hair for a couple of days."

Sam looked at Grace sitting opposite, "You may be aware, if Grace has told you, I have asked her if she would like to go for a ride in the car to meet my parents. But what I didn't mention was, I would now, like her to stay the night. She would stay with my Aunt Megan, of whom she has heard me speak, which is a ten minute walk from my home." Sam stopped talking for a moment, "That is if you're agreeable and of course if Grace would like to stay the night."

"I would love to," Grace answered almost before Sam had finished speaking.

"I have no objection," said Mary "and Grace is over twenty one."

George looked at Grace then at Sam, "You couldn't take her away for a bit longer could you Sam?"

27

Sam's father, unlike his Uncle Bill, seemed distant. It wasn't that he didn't try to engage in conversation or want to know of his son's adventures, it was just that the conversations he had with him didn't flow as they might have. He now lived an insular life. Even Sam's mother had told him that he was not the same after coming home from the war and there was little laughter in their home. He treated his mother well and she had got used to the quiet life he now liked to lead. He hardly ever went to the pub and did not see Bill as often as he used to. Never going shooting anymore his shotgun, Sam had noticed, had gone from above the fireplace, its resting place now being in a cupboard under the stairs. His main love was his garden. Jim would enter its produce into local shows winning more than his share of red ribbons.

Grace sat in the passenger seat of Sam's car. The distinct smell of leather from the upholstered seats entered her nostrils along with other scents that the wind blew in from her open window. She closed her eyes, the purr of the engine and the gentle vibration of the car itself put Grace in a mood of calmness, she glanced at Sam and snuggled deeper in her seat. The overriding feeling of being in safe company delighted her, she felt as though she had known Sam for a long time which she had, but most of that time she had dismissed him as someone that had fleetingly entered her life - held her for a moment and moved on.

"What are you thinking?" he asked without turning his head.

"Nothing," she smiled.

"You're fibbing," he glanced at her.

"Of course I am."

"Well, aren't you going to tell me?"

"Certainly not."

"Will you ever tell me?"

"Probably not, but that depends."

"Depends on what."

"I knew you were going to say that. Tell me about New York Sam," she said changing the subject, "I have read a little about it, maybe you could enlighten me a bit more."

For the rest of the journey, Sam told of the New York that he knew, tall buildings, the diversity of the people that live there and the way they live.

"It's a lot different from the life you had lived Sam," she said as she opened the car door and stepped out. Sam's introduction of Grace to his mother went as Sam had expected, being very polite and cordial and was pleasantly surprised at the way his father welcomed Grace, asking questions about the Three Tuns brewery where she and her father worked. Jim was taken with Grace's agreeable nature especially when she asked to see his garden explaining that since they moved to Bishop's Castle her father had become a keen gardener, as he had never really had a garden that he could grow anything in before. After lunch and Grace telling Sam's parents her life story, touching briefly on the reason for their moving from Liverpool, they walked to Megan and Bill's house passing the Upper House on the way. After climbing the hill with the cemetery on their left they stopped.

"Is that where Michael is buried?" Grace suddenly asked.

"It is", answered Sam, a little surprised that Grace had remembered the story of Michael. "We will see his grave later." He pointed to Megan's home two hundred yards further on.

There was a warmth in Megan's smile as she opened the door, a smile that lifted Grace, not that she needed lifting but her welcome was, she felt, touching and genuine.

"I've heard a lot about you Grace," she said, "Come on in, have you had anything to eat?"

"Yes, Sam's Mum made us some sandwiches."

Two hours later as they stood by Michael's gravestone Grace gazed at the village below. The church, a dominant feature of the village, stood with its spire ascending to the heavens, it was topped off with a cockerel, from where it oversaw the passage of time, and people who lived their quiet and, more often than not, uneventful lives. They would first enter as babes in arms to be given their names and in the end leave it in a coffin. The cockerel had witnessed it all. Grace laid her hand on the warm slab inscribed headstone; she knelt and slowly ran her finger along the chiselled letters that read his name.

"Michael Barry Gill, so this was the man who inspired you to follow in his footsteps."

"Well, you could say that," Sam said wistfully.

"And where do you go from here Sam Pryce?" she said rising from her knee, "I mean you have people here that love you and when you go back to America, I am fearful you may never come back."

"Grace," he answered with a sigh, "That very thought scares me too." He reached for her hand. "I know these people love me and I love them too and what I have here will stay with me, but I don't have a choice and if I did, I would still go." They stood in silence both content to stand for a moment taking in the sunshine that warmed their backs.

"The church," Grace said, "did any of your coffins go through its doors?"

Sam smiled, "That one there," he pointed to the gravestone next to Michael's.

"Mavis," said Grace letting go of Sam's hand.

"Yes, she was buried a few days before I left home."

"You must feel rather proud and don't tell me it was just another coffin."

"No, that one wasn't just another coffin, it was for someone rather special and yes it meant a lot to me."

As they walked through the village Sam pointed out the blacksmith's shop where Aunt Megan had lived before marrying Uncle Bill. There they popped in and said "hello" to David who was pumping the bellows of his blacksmith's forge. He stopped and stared at Sam, immediately calling out for Rose. He reached out a rough and calloused hand shaking Sam's as if there was no tomorrow. Rose came through a door at the back of the shop and on seeing Sam raised her arms.

"I declare," she said loudly, "it's Sam," David stepped aside as Rose gave him a hug. After a joyful greeting, Sam turned and introduced Grace.

They passed the undertaker's yard, where Sam had learnt his trade, the village school and the church. Grace looked up; she was fascinated by the cockerel on the top thinking that if it could only talk what stories it could tell. Set back and through the trees was the vicarage. Sam mentioned it was where, as a fourteen year old, Megan had worked. They walked on. Sam told Grace of his childhood and to Grace it sounded an idyllic life surrounded by loving people and a way of living that was a dream away from hers. Then he spoilt it all by telling her of the hardships that were encountered along the way. But she did not want to hear about them, she didn't want this fairy-tale to end but deep down she knew she couldn't have what she wanted and the fairy-tale would end and it was this that was breaking her heart. Mrs Griffiths the local gossip from Barlow's Cottage was out with her white enamelled bucket drawing water from the village pump.

"And this is your lady Sam?" she said smiling, "heard you had someone in tow. Welcome home and you Grace," she paused looking at them both, "have a good life."

"Take no notice of her," Sam said as they carried on walking, "Nothing happens in this village without Mrs Griffiths knowing about it, she means no harm, it's the way she is."

The smell of roast duck greeted them as they walked through the door of Sam's home, the table was already laid as Violet busied herself in the kitchen.

"Sit yourself down Grace," she said, "tea won't be long."

During their meal Jim asked if they would be going down to the pub later, adding that there would be several people there wishing to see him, suggesting that if they were going down, he and his mother would go with them.

"That would be nice," Sam said looking at his mother.

It was seven thirty when Sam opened the bar door. Immediately there was a lot of enthusiastic shouts and backslapping, as he made his way through the crowd. Behind him, Grace, a little surprised at the amount of people there grabbed hold of Violet's hand. Violet in turn led her to two chairs being vacated by men who had offered their seats next to Megan and Bill. Grace looked around the room she had seen this scene many times before at the Rodney, but this was different in the respect that there wasn't a face that she recognised. In the Rodney, she knew who could be trusted and who couldn't, who was a fighter and who wasn't, but here…? Bill was the only man she knew and as she looked at him, she felt his happiness. Was this the dream that she had had, a long time ago? But that was a dream that had fallen away a long time since, and now…?

"What are you drinking Grace?" she looked at an old man with some pheasant feathers sticking out of the band of the brown trilby hat he wore, he smiled.

"A port and lemon, thank you Sir," she managed to say returning his smile.

Hours later Grace a little unsteady on her feet slid her arm through Sam's as they walked the steep incline to Megan's home.

"Thanks for a lovely evening Sam", she stopped for a moment. "It must have taken a lot of courage to leave the life you had here?"

"And if I hadn't left, you wouldn't have been here to ask the question."

"No, I wouldn't but it doesn't answer my question."

"Maybe I was looking for something, it's a big world out there Grace, and maybe Michael and Megan brought out the need in me to see it."

"But the courage side of it, Sam where did that come from?"

"I don't know," he said with a shrug. "My mind was focused on the adventure of it all and not on any courage or bravado I may have had, although there was a moment when I wondered what the hell I was doing."

"And when did you wonder that."

"The night I stayed at your place." Grace stopped walking.

"The night you stayed at my place! God Sam you are human after all and I thought you didn't have a care in the world."

"I let my guard down a little that's all," he laughed. They had walked the steep hill and were now on flat ground when Sam suddenly stopped.

"Grace."

"Yes."

"What would you say if I were to ask," he hesitated, "if you would come back to America with me? Perhaps this isn't the right time to ask but I'm asking it anyway."

"Jesus, Sam, I need to sit down, you want me to go back with you to America, are you serious?"

"I have never been more serious in my life."

"Hang on Sam, you've had a few drinks and now on the spur of the moment you are asking me to go back with you, are you mad, is this some kind of joke." She was shaking as she let go of Sam's hand. "Don't you play with my feelings Sam, and don't you dare say things that cannot happen."

Sam reached for Grace's arm, "This is not a joke and neither is it a spur of the moment thing, as for your feelings they are the last thing I would hurt."

Sam looked into Grace's tearful eyes.

"I have already bought your ticket, in the hope that I wouldn't be travelling back alone. Listen, we don't have much time, I am not without Grace and I have spent very little of what I have on myself, not that money is an issue here, but if it can help me in persuading you to spend the rest of your life with me then so be it." Grace was stunned, and at first did not know what to say.

"You said that you have already bought me a ticket, is that a single ticket Sam?" There was a tremor in her voice "and how long ago did you decide that this is what you wanted."

"A while ago."

"It was after the death of Robert wasn't it Sam," she cried, "wasn't it, it must have been as before that, I was a married woman and out of your reach."

"Yes, yes, it was, it may sound callous of me Grace but you were free to love again and please don't think too little of me to take advantage of that fact."

"So, it's a one way ticket," Grace looked down at her feet, "just what is it Sam, what is it that you want from me?"

"Damn it, Grace, I want you to come with me, I want you to marry me, I want us to have a life together." She looked up, her eyes now wide open.

"You want us to be married?"

"Well…, yes."

"And how many words are there in, will you marry me,"

"Four", said Sam smiling.

"Well," answered Grace smiling back. Sam wrapped his arms around her and whispered,

"Will you marry me?"

"And when do you want an answer Sam Pryce," she whispered back. Sam held her at arm's length.

"As soon as possible. I don't want to rush you but there will be a lot to do if your answer is yes."

"This is all very sudden Sam and I suppose we won't have time to go through the ritual of courtship, so may I suggest we skip that part."

"I'll go along with that," Sam said gripping Grace's hand.

"Then yes Sam, I will marry you, have you mentioned this to anyone."

"No, you are the first to know," Sam laughed having realised what he had just said, "I mean no, I have told no one of my intentions."

That night they announced their decision to marry, firstly to Megan and Bill and then walked to Sam's home, catching his parents about to go to bed.

Grace pulled the bed sheets over her head, curled herself into a ball and wondered what she had agreed to. It wasn't the fact that she was going to marry Sam, it was the timing of it all. She had been a wife, a widow and would be a wife again all within the space of ten months and on the top of all that, she would be going to America. Her mind was now racing, where would they get married? Passport, she hadn't got one. Her parents, had Sam thought about them? How could she leave, her mother would be devastated. Grace unfurled herself and threw the bed sheets back staring with fearful eyes into the darkness, "my God what have I done."

"Grace are you awake," she heard Megan's comforting voice, half whispering from the doorway.

"Yes, Mrs Jones I'm awake."

Megan opened the door and walked in, the light from the hall casting a shadow of Megan as she approached Grace's bed. As she sat on the bed, she noticed Grace's tear filled eyes.

"Would you like to talk?" she asked softly. Grace sat up and covered her eyes.

"I feel like a…a peg in a game of solitaire," she sobbed, "and don't know which way to move. Three hours ago, I knew where I was and I didn't mind so much if I lost, but now losing isn't an option."

"Do you love Sam?" Megan asked.

"With all my heart and always have, but he was out of my reach, and I had a life to live."

"And now?" Megan asked.

"I would follow him to the ends of the earth, Aunt Megan," Grace looked up, "can I call you Aunt Megan?"

Megan, placing a comforting arm around her and sighed, "That sounds like a good idea Grace."

"But I'm fearful for my parents."

"Look at me Grace, I have known Sam all his life and when he leaves, I may never see him again, but I know that he wouldn't have asked you to marry him if he hadn't had thought things through and that includes the concerns of your parents. So, do not despair. I'm sure your parent's priority is your happiness. Give him the opportunity to answer what fears you have and if it turns out that it is not meant to be, then take comfort in the fact that he loved you enough to ask you to be his wife.

Now give me a hug and go to sleep and dream pleasant dreams."

Two weeks later at half past two in the afternoon on Saturday the 5th of August Sam signed his name in the registrar's book of marriages. On the line below would be Grace's name. He placed the pen down. The registrar covered his signature with a sheet of bloating paper and ran his palm over it. Stepping back Sam glanced around the room, there to witness the event of his marriage to Grace were his mother and father, Grace's parents and his Aunt Megan and Uncle Bill. This is what Grace wanted. She had done the white wedding bit before and now wanted nothing more than to be around the people who wanted nothing more themselves. Outside the sun shone and a warm breeze gently blew, scattering the coloured confetti that fell upon her head. She lifted the small net veil covering her face as Sam bent and kissed her on the cheek.

"Now Mrs Pryce," he said, "welcome to the rest of your life."

"Looking forward to it," she answered squeezing his hand. The registry office building on the corner of Broad Street and Severn Street in Newtown passed behind them as Sam's car with Grace beside him and Mary and George in the back seat drove out of town. Behind, in a car belonging to the landlord of the Upper House were Sam's parents, Megan and Bill.

The wedding reception was to be held at the Upper House. Twenty guests had been invited and were already in the bar as Sam's car pulled up outside. A cheer went up as they entered, handshakes and wishes for a happy future were said as Sam and Grace were shown to their seats. Sam had asked his Uncle Bill to be his best man, this being unusual in the respect that most young men of Sam's age would have had their best friend of a similar age to do the honours. As it was, after being away for such a long time there wasn't anyone Sam felt he could ask, other than his brother and he really didn't want the job. For Sam there was only one man who could fill the role, and that was his Uncle Bill. Grace's dilemma in choosing a bridesmaid was quickly settled as at first, she thought of asking a friend, one who had been a bridesmaid for her at the time of her marriage to Richard, but she had second thoughts thinking it wouldn't seem right and that it was such a long way from Liverpool. Grace's choice was to say the least limited, so she asked Sam's Aunt Megan, who when asked was thrilled.

The previous afternoon a young man riding a BSA Bantam motorcycle called at the village pub and handed the landlord four telegrams. These telegrams were placed on the table in front of Bill alongside other cards that he would read out during his speech. The telegrams, two from people who couldn't attend and two from America, one being from Joe and Pageant and the other from Curtis and Isabelle who in their telegram mentioned that Willena also sent her love and best wishes. Sam and Grace spent their honeymoon on the Welsh coast. Two nights in a hotel on the beach front in Aberystwyth. Their fun filled days and intimate nights were everything that Grace had imagined it to be, the thought of Sam's previous lovers never entered her mind, although in the past she had visualised him having it away with every girl in Manhattan. She had thought of Richard a few times and although he was her first lover and the one she had married, to that end he would remain, but that was then. Now as she gazed at Sam's naked body lying beside her, her thoughts were of someone she had met before Richard and she would not allow her past with Richard interfere with her future.

28

Paris in June was the same as Paris in July the only difference being that in July Sam and Grace would be on the high sea but for now as they took in the view of the Champ-Elysees from their hotel window Grace had come to realise that she had stepped into a different world. A world, but for Sam, was only accessible to her through words and pictures in a book. As she looked, she was in awe of her own destiny. Grace's passport had arrived two days earlier and was surprised to see that there was some French translation printed on it, giving rise to Sam's spur of the moment suggestion that they visit Paris.

"We have two weeks before we sail. A week in Paris would be nice don't you think?" Paris, thought Grace, was one of those places where the intellectual and wealthy would go to visit, a place where visionary people would unleash their dreams. Be it in the arts, fashion, or in the writing of poetry and books.

Famous painters she found would stand their easels on the pavements besides cafes and restaurants and could be seen squeezing lead filled tubes of coloured oils onto a pallet, before transferring them onto a canvas. Painting the image of the very people sitting at the cafe's small round tables. This is where the observer would while away his or her time drinking Americano coffee and smoking fashionable cigarettes, ones that were pictured on billboards leaning against the cafe's walls.

Outside their hotel looking west stood the Arc de Triomphe.

"The monument," Grace read from her visitors guide to Paris, "is a monument to honour those that died in the French Revolution and Napoleonic Wars, and beneath its volts lies the tomb of the unknown soldier of the Great War."

As she read, they walked, Sam not knowing a word of French was distracted from Grace's reading and was now listening to the passing conversations of people in the street. It amused him to hear little children who, holding hands with their mothers, chattered away in a language that made no sense to him. He had become familiar with foreign languages in America but here was a little different. When they reached the Arc de Triomphe they had a quick look around and headed back. In front of them, the Champs Elysees seemed to stretch for miles, the rich green leaves of the horse chestnut trees that lined the street on both sides were an added dimension, giving the scene in front of them a country look that only the colour green could give.

Grace, to Sam's surprise, had for two days her head stuck in a French phrase book, one given to her by Megan who had received it from Miss Mavis some years before her death. To Grace's credit she had become competent in being understood, practising her French on the street vendors who were selling everything from postcards, small souvenirs, cigarettes, newspapers, and magazines, one of which Grace bought, a Vogue fashion magazine printed in English. Halfway down the Champs Elysees they stopped and sat outside a café. Having spent a few francs on two expresso coffees and a cheese baguette they sat and for a while melted into their surroundings like the Parisians they were mistaken for. Sam looked at Grace, she sat with her eyes closed bathing in the warmth of the sun's rays like the geckos that clung to the cafe's wall behind her. He tilted his head and studied her face, she sat upright in a wicker chair, one of a dozen or more that were placed around the tables outside the cafe, her pose reminded him of Mrs Doyle in the portrait of herself, the one hanging on the wall of his home in Manhattan. Regal was the word he was looking for, with her long slim neck showing off the pale skin that adorned the rest of her body. Her bright red lipstick, acting like a beacon, attracting predatory males that strutted the sidewalk seeking unaccompanied females that would succumb to their smiles and flirtatious behaviour. This seemingly, their only reason for living. She opened her eyes.

"This is heaven," she said reaching for Sam's hand, "I will always remember this moment." Grace wore a wide brimmed, floppy peach coloured hat, it matched the flimsy sleeveless dress that followed the contours of her body stopping some inches above her ankle. Her hair was parted in the middle with finger wave curls that clung to the sides of her face. From the centre of her forehead wispy strands of curly hair fell to the bridge of her nose reminding him of the actress Joan Crawford. He kissed her hand as they rose from their seats. Grace picked up her visitor's guide to Paris and placed it in her shoulder bag.

Paris was more than Grace had imagined it to be, the numerous shops and stores along the Champs-Elysees were busy with tourists and holiday makers, fashion houses and perfume shops were many. Grace was like a little girl again, dragging Sam into couture dress shops just to have a look. Every now and again she would stop outside a perfume store, poke her head through the door and take a sniff, once emerging to give Sam a hug repeating again that she was in heaven. It gladdened Sam's heart to see her so happy and, in the end, told her that if they happened to come across another perfume store, she was to go in and buy a bottle. They did not have to go far.

"Look", said Grace excitedly pointing to a store sign, "Coco Chanel." Sam stood on the pavement as he had been ordered to, as Grace went in trying to look as calm and demure as the ladies who walked out.

The first full day in Paris ended in a small restaurant just down the road from their hotel. They had walked what seemed like miles from one end of the Champs-Elysees to the other and back again, as they walked, they listened to street singers and musicians, watching ladies in summer dresses and palazzo pants, some with parasols over their shoulders, who, every so often would twirl them like a carousel at a fairground.

Sam read the menu, an English translation of French dishes on offer. He placed the menu on the table and suggested they try frog's legs and snails. Grace, to Sam's surprise looked up and smiled,

"I was going to suggest the same, but maybe not tonight."

A bottle of champagne was brought to the table. The wine waiter, typically dressed in black trousers white shirt with a white cloth over his arm, poured out two glasses, these were drunk before their garlic mushrooms and toast were served. Another bottle of bubbly was drank before rising from their seats. Both feeling full on French cuisine that was both exciting and an experience they had never had before.

Hunger had another meaning as they climbed the staircase to their room and were now eager to indulge in a night of passion and lust, the latter word having been mentioned several times during the day. Grace went to the bathroom as Sam took off his clothes and lay on the bed. Grace appeared and with a seductive walk approached the bed lying next to him with nothing on but her Coco Chanel No5. There was no boundaries to their love making. In the five nights spent in Paris their love for each other grew, both physically and romantically, even the French language had a sexual charge about it. It could be heard well into the night drifting through open bedroom windows of hotels the full length of the street below.

"Yes," Grace thought, "Paris was a byword for romance and intrigue."

Their days were spent doing things that tourists do. Sam bought a Kodak Brownie camera and started taking pictures of everything they saw. The Eiffel Tower being a good subject to start with, then there was the Notre Dame cathedral, the Luxor Obelisk at the Plaza de la Concorde. Every day was filled with wonder. They strolled through the neighbourhood of Le Marais on the right bank of the River Seine to where artists would paint. Their canvases would be splashed with colour, then they would paint fine lines, with fine brushes to depict intricate forms, thus when finished, their paintings would become masterpieces in their own right. Avant-garde painters who saw things a little different bewildered Sam, Grace tried to explain the meaning.

"But a ball is round," said Sam, "So why is he painting a square one?" Sam was pointing to an artist whose canvas had a group of boys all with legs three times the length that they should have been kicking a square ball in a field of tulips. Sam stopped then smiled, "Because that's how he sees it?" He raised his eyes.

"Sam Pryce, I love you," said Grace wrinkling her nose. Sam went into his pocket and brought out his roll of notes.

"I think I'll buy it."

"You like it?"

"Not a lot."

"Then why are you buying it?"

"Because I may grow to like it and when I look at it in the future it will remind me of Paris."

"How much is it?" Sam made a quick calculation.

"Two hundred and fifty francs, about ten dollars."

"Well, neither currency makes much sense to me." Sam laughed.

"Yes, it's a bit confusing isn't it?" He peeled off a five hundred franc note.

The artist rose from his seat. He was an elderly gentleman with a mottled grey beard. On his head placed at an angle was a black beret, he wore an artist smock covered with flecks of colour, looking like the skyline above Times Square on New Year's Eve. He hadn't finished the painting and told Sam to call for it the following day. Sam added to his roll of notes the change given to him by the artist. On leaving and much to the delight of Grace he said, "au revoir." One of the few French phrases Grace had him repeating morning noon and night.

They visited the Louvre to see paintings and sculptures both of which they had only seen in books. Grace looked in wonderment at the Mona Lisa and the statue of Venus de Milo, not believing that she was seeing the real thing. Sam was overwhelmed, there was more stuff here than he could poke a stick at, yet he was enjoying every minute. Sam knew little of the Arts but the more he saw the more he wanted to see. The Moulin Rouge situated on the Boulevard de Clichy was a place to go. It said so in Grace's visitor's guide to Paris so on their next to last night at seven o'clock they, along with another couple, caught a taxi to the Moulin Rouge. It would be a fifteen minute ride into the Pigalle district of Paris. Their companions for the evening were American tourists. They had the previous evening introduced themselves as Louis and Charlotte Fontaine. Having dined at a table next to Sam and Grace, in the restaurant that they had frequented each evening since they had arrived in Paris. Sam had detected his accent as soon as they were shown to their table. He used the word, thank you, then corrected himself, speaking fluent French to the waiter. For a while they spoke English to each other. The man, Sam guessed to be in his fifties, glanced across the table and smiled.

"And what part of New York are you from?" Sam asked unexpectedly. The gent looked surprised.

"Tribeca, Lower Manhattan," the gentleman said smiling, "you know it?"

"New York is a big place," said Sam, "but yes, I know it."

"Tribeca, Baxter Street."

"Would you like to join us?" Sam interrupted knowing that he should have asked Grace first. The gentleman looked at his wife.

"That would be nice," she replied.

"You don't mind?" Sam whispered to Grace.

"Not at all," she whispered back. Sam rose from his seat as the couple joined them. The man, before sitting caught the waiter's attention and spoke a few words, the waiter then set up two places to accommodate Sam's invited guests. On sitting they introduced themselves,

Sam in return did the same, explaining their Paris trip was an extension to their honeymoon and they would be returning to New York in two weeks' time. Louis spoke of a long awaited holiday himself, spending money, money that had been left him after his father's death some three months earlier. Their conversation was casual, generating a friendly atmosphere, discussing their holiday as they had so far experienced it. Louis again mentioned his father saying that his grandfather had immigrated to America, leaving Paris many years ago and since that time had tried, with success, to maintain the French language within his family. Sam could not believe that Louis lived in the same district as himself and after telling him the nature of his business, Louis shook his head in disbelief.

"You don't make coffins for cowboys, do you?" Sam nearly choked on the quiche lorraine he was eating.

"Don't tell me," he spluttered, "that your father was buried in one of my coffins."

"He was," replied Louis hardly containing his laughter.

"A Frenchman in a coffin for cowboys, if nothing else your father had a sense of humour."

"He did," said Louis, raising a glass of red.

The taxi dropped them off outside the Moulin Rouge. The street, already busy with people looked like the promenade on any seaside town. It was still daylight, motor cars and horse drawn carriages were either picking up people or dropping them off. Grace noticed other review bars along the street. But the Moulin stood out with its windmill being almost as famous as the Eiffel Tower. Posters of dancing girls doing the Can-Can were fixed to the walls of the building, these, Louis informed Sam and Grace, were prints of paintings by Toulouse-Lautrec a famous French painter who had died over thirty years earlier. Outside the Moulin Rouge and other review bars, were ladies flamboyantly dressed, encouraging customers into their establishments.

After paying to enter, they found a table in the open courtyard, four tables back from the stage. Louis ordered drinks as they looked around, noticing that most tables were occupied. Waiters were weaving, almost dancing from table to table balancing drinks on their trays, some doing tricks with empty glasses tossing them in the air and catching them. A group of four men already having had too much to drink were being escorted out of the courtyard, their jovial manner whilst being evicted added to the raucous atmosphere in the courtyard. Rowdy locals singing La Marseillaise, could be heard above the chatter and laughter of rich tourists, these coming from within and beyond the borders of France. Hostesses would flit from table to table lighting customers' cigarettes and with good humour sit on gentlemen's knees making outrageous suggestions. This would cause an uproar of laughter, setting the scene for an unforgettable evening of entertainment. Neither Sam nor Grace had ever seen anything like it. And to spend the evening with French speaking Americans put Grace at ease, allaying any fears she had of feeling out of place. Not that she was out of place but it gave her an insight into meeting strangers that from now on she would. Realising THIS, she told Charlotte, her life had now become one of opportunity.

"You are now in the red light district of Paris", said Louis as he leaned back in his chair. "So, I hope you won't be offended by the scantily dressed ladies that will be performing onstage."

As it was the ladies were not scantily clad, provocative, suggestive, and titillating they may have been while dancing, but scantily clad they were not. The cabaret was an experience to behold, the acrobats, singers, and dancers, especially the dancers ten of them in a line. They wore red dresses with puffed shoulders and fixed to a tiara on their head were long red ostrich feathers. In time to the music, they would lift their dresses along with white petticoats. The girls were tall with slim waists and long legs, these being kicked high in the air and in unison showing black stockings with red garters. Every time this raunchy leg-kicking took place the crowd would applaud with whistles and shouts. The ladies would lift a leg and hold their ankle going around and around, finally falling one after the other to the floor doing the splits. Their performance ending when they turned their backs to the audience and flipped over their backs their red dresses showing their white pantalets, which prompted Louis to declare that in some clubs in Paris the girls didn't even wear those, also saying that their morals were as flexible as the dances they performed.

The following morning the sun shone as it had every morning since their arrival. Grace drew back the curtains the sunlight casting a shadow of her naked body onto the bed, it followed the contours of discarded bed sheets, she looked at her nightdress it had fallen to the floor lying at the foot of the bed still folded. You hussy, she thought smiling to herself, she hadn't worn it once. Sam sat up, "Well Mrs Pryce, and what would you like to do today?"

"Stay in bed," she beamed, "and carry on from where we left off." She squealed as he grabbed her wrist, pulling her towards him. An hour and a half later they descended the stairs walking past the concierge as he greeted new arrivals to the hotel. The rest of the morning was spent walking and sitting outside a cafe people watching and discussing the previous evening's entertainment. A warm breeze rustled the leaves that shaded their table.

Grace played with her wedding ring, Sam's ring. Her old ring, not being that old, she had placed in her jewellery box at home. At first, she didn't know what to do with it. It crossed her mind to place it on another finger or to put it on a necklace, but in the end decided to place it in the box that held the rest of her jewellery. At least she would not lose it, nor would it be a constant reminder to Sam that she had been married before.

"This time tomorrow we will be crossing the channel," she heard Sam say.

"And in four days' time we will be on the big boat," replied Grace.

"You don't know how happy I am about how your mum and dad have been about the whole thing," said Sam after taking a sip of coffee, "And in six months' time they will be coming over to see us, exciting times ahead Grace."

"You must be eager to get back."

"Yes, it seems I have been here a lot longer than I have. I made provisions for every eventuality involving work, but sometimes things happen that you don't have any control of. Thankfully, I have good people who will look after my interests. Coming home was something I had to do, not only to see you but to see my family, I don't know when I will see them again."

"Don't say that Sam," Grace said wistfully, "of course you will see them again."

"I don't know," answered Sam. "As time goes by you feel less inclined to make the trip and that's if you have something to come back to."

"But you have so much to come back to Sam, I don't like to think that you will never see them again."

"Well, that's something we will discuss in another few years."

The rest of their day was spent walking the streets, daring to go down side-streets away from the regular footfall of tourists. They would again stop and listen to the street singers, watch mime artists, painters and anyone who could make a living from their talents, much like New York and probably cities throughout the world. Sam wondered at their bohemian lifestyle, a lifestyle that could only be empowered by the young who knew little of responsibility and accountability relying on the belief that their talents would be their saviour, to some it would, to most it wouldn't. There were also those with money who would play the game. Those who would befriend the people living this life then lay claim that they too were bohemian. This would last until the sun stopped shining and winter came. Then they would walk their brown leather Italian shoes and silk handmade clothes back to the fancy apartments from where they came.

Their last evening in Paris, was again spent in the company of Louis and Charlotte, at another review bar called Joanne Les Pins, again in the district of Pigalle. It was a little more downmarket than the Moulin Rouge and a sight cheaper. The entertainment was just as professional, but what caught their attention was one girl who took to the stage like she was born on it. She looked frail, a tiny girl wearing a black dress. She sang in French and her voice was one that would turn heads. It was noticeable that as she sang, people would stop talking and listen. When she had finished, she walked off stage to a standing ovation, which led Charlotte to remark that that young lady was on a par with the best of them. It was a great evening of entertainment, but it was the young girl who stole the show.

29

As with any holiday there is a time to leave. Sam and Grace said their "goodbyes" to Louis and Charlotte promising to get in touch when they got back to New York. They packed their bags, taking with them gifts for Sam's family and Grace's parents and a little something for Megan, Bill and their children. They caught a train, a boat, then another train to Shrewsbury. There Sam picked up his car arriving back in Bishop's Castle late on the Saturday night. They had three days to prepare for their departure. The arrangements with Grace's parents were that in six months' time they would follow, for a stay of some weeks, staying at Sam's house. Sam had suggested that if they wanted to, he would make enquiries as to them emigrating. Mary was enthusiastic about the idea, saying that all she had in life were Grace and George, and if Sam could do this, she would be indebted to him, if he couldn't, then she was still happy with Grace's move and would be content to visit whenever they could afford to. The following morning, they left George and Mary's home early, opening the door to Sam's home at nine o'clock. Early evening on the day before leaving Sam called at his Uncle Bill's, who had just arrived from work.

"Will you be having your tea before going for your walk Bill?" Megan asked.

"No, I think we'll go for a walk now and have it when I get back." This was a walk that Sam had looked forward to. He had not forgotten the last time they had walked together, the day after Miss Mavis' funeral. It wasn't long before they were leaning on the same gate where Sam had asked if Bill still thought of the war. Bill remembered that day and the question Sam had asked, it was a question that had stayed with him and for whatever reason always would. The subject of the war wasn't mentioned although Bill did say that Jim wasn't the same after it. Bill did ask Sam if he thought he would ever come home again.

"That's a hard one to answer Uncle Bill but if I do it won't be a permanent stay. I have done a lot of things in a short time and the excitement of it all leaves me hungry for more." As they talked Sam looked at the valley below and as they climbed the gate he smiled, "And that's a scene I will never forget, we must do this again."

"Hopefully, we will Sam, hopefully we will."

Sam and Grace said their last goodbyes to Bill and Megan. Their children came running up not wanting to miss out on the farewell. In the sky above them could be heard the drone of an aeroplane.

"It's a DeHavilland Tiger Moth," said Michael nonchalantly not bothering to look up. Michael now at fourteen years of age stood with his outstretched hand not knowing what to say to the man now standing in front of him. He was only eight when Sam first went away and didn't really know the significance of his leaving, it was only in the last couple of years, no, he thought looking at this tall handsome man in front of him, in the last twelve months when his curiosity got the better of him and he had started to ask questions about the man in America. He had read the letters that Sam had written to his parents and had begun to understand the bond that had existed between them. Sam smiled as he shook Michael's hand.

"Well Michael, and what are you going to do with your life?" Michael glanced at his mother and shrugged.

"I don't know, maybe like you, travel a bit and see what's out there."

"Keep me informed on that one," Sam answered as he placed a comforting hand on Michael's shoulder.

Sam's mother cried, fearful that she would never see him again and his father, after placing a bag full of his garden vegetables in the boot of Sam's car never said goodbye he simply said, "I'll see you next time you're home."

They spent their last night at Grace's home and in the morning it was Grace's turn to cry. Their suitcases and as much as they could carry of Grace's belongings were placed in the car. Mary's last words, "we'll see you in six months," and George's, "look after my girl." Then in what seemed like forever the hedgerows of Shropshire fell behind them as they headed for Shrewsbury.

The trip back home to America and the subsequent expense of his six weeks stay had cost Sam a lot of money. Had it been worth it? Every penny. He had seen the people he had gone to see, more importantly he was bringing back a woman whom he loved more than he could say and loving her was easy. As for Grace, to love again was something beyond her dreams, as it was, she could have no more loved again than to have walked the streets of Paris, but she had done both. She threaded her fingers through Sam's as she gazed upon the Atlantic Ocean, watching the white tips of waves crashing back into the sea. It was hard for her to comprehend what had happened in the past six weeks. She clung to the ship's railings with her free hand and looked at Sam, God knows she had not been wrong all those years ago, the young lad who she had fallen for was now her soul mate, her companion, her lover, husband, her everything.

On Tuesday November 8th, six months before Sam had left for England, Franklin Roosevelt became the thirty second President of the United States in a landslide Democratic victory over Herbert Hoover's Republican Party. The depression was at its peak, along with the unemployment number, thousands upon thousands of businesses had gone bankrupt with thousands of banks failing but cash was still king. Curtis was instrumental in looking after Sam's financial interests advising him to buy treasury bills and bonds and not to place all his assets in one place. All cash from Sam's business, apart from weekly expenses, went under Sam's bed. By the time of his return President Roosevelt's new deal was starting to see results, federal money was being spent in a series of public works programmes, financial reforms, and relief for the unemployed and poor. The feeling of despair had been replaced by one of hope.

Willena squealed with delight on opening her door and seeing Sam and Grace standing outside.

"Welcome home Sam," she said as she gave him a big hug, "we have all missed you."

"It's nice to be home Willena."

"And this is your lady?"

"It is, Grace this is Willena."

"I've heard a lot about you Grace, please come in."

Sam had already told Grace that his home was not really his home but Willena's, but would pass to him on Willena's demise. All bags and boxes were brought in and placed in the hallway under the chandelier that Grace's eyes had rested on when having a quick look around. It was two o'clock in the afternoon when Willena sat them down at her kitchen table, she had put the kettle on then asked if they were hungry.

"We had a late breakfast and some nibbles before we got off the ship," Sam said as he took off his coat. After a cup of coffee and a piece of apple tart that Willena insisted they eat they took their cases to Sam's bedroom, Willena having prepared it two days before. Sam gave Grace a tour of the house and when descending the staircase Grace asked about the two portraits hanging on the wall.

"I think I'll let Willena explain the history of those two people."

On the kitchen table were letters addressed to Sam all been opened by Willena, Sam having given her permission to do so. All work related invoices were paid by Willena in cash, as was money coming in, being paid on delivery of goods. Faith in the banking system had all but gone as banks became insolvent with everyone withdrawing their money. But faith and trust was something Sam had in Willena and all his employees. Unemployment being a big factor in his belief that they would look after his interests as by doing that they would be looking after their own.

"I haven't opened this one it came a couple of days ago, thought I'd leave it till you got home." She handed Sam the letter. On the front it read, "To the occupier", Sam turned it over and slit it open, he read the letter and handed it to Willena.

"What is this all about?" she said looking a little confused.

"Well, it seems a development company are interested in buying your house."

"Why would a development company want to buy our house Sam?"

"I have my suspicions," said Sam, "I wonder if our neighbours next door have had a similar letter, I think I'll pop and see." Within ten minutes he was back. The elderly couple living next door had been there for many years and had indeed received a similar letter. They told Sam that as their children had families of their own and lived in another part of New York they had for a long time suggested that their parents sell up and downsize, so it came as no surprise to Sam that they were keen to follow up on the development companies' enquiry. Willena was upset about the letter saying she was too old now to move and that her house was the only place she had ever lived. Sam assured her that they weren't about to sell up, but deep down he knew they were living on prime building land and without telling Willena he would make some enquiries.

The building industry in New York had come to a virtual stop during the depression but now due to government incentive and federal money pouring into the building industry there was a surge in the home building market. Sam was aware of the fall in house prices over the last few years but was equally aware that everything was as relevant as it always was, sell for as much as you could get and buy for as little as possible. On November 11, 1933 a strong dust storm, one of many that year, swept in from the farmlands of South Dakota. It took two days to reach cities in the east such as Buffalo, Boston and New York. With the thousands of folks that had walked off their homesteads over the last few years because of drought, the Mid-West had become a dust bowl. The Great Plains States had become such that no one could earn a living from the land, so the people headed for the large towns and cities to seek a living as best they could.

30

The significance of Grace's appearance in Sam's life led to a lot of rejoicing and congratulations from Sam's friends and acquaintances. For Willena it was a moment of relief, insomuch as he had found a lady to share his future. Grace, she had discovered was an easy going young lady, with ideas for the administration of Sam's business to be one of, "why ever didn't I think of that!" She would ask Willena for her opinion on everything not wanting to appear overpowering. To Willena, Grace was like a breath of fresh air and was more than happy to let go of what little responsibility regarding Sam's business that she had. In the first month Grace had made the acquaintance of most of Sam's friends prompting her to ask how come he knew so many likeable people.

"Because I'm a likeable chap myself," was his reply. Grace was in awe of what Sam had achieved during the six years he had been away. But Sam forever grateful, would always point out that his good fortune was the result of Mrs Doyle's generosity and Willena's faith in him. Sam had made enquiries about the company wanting to buy

Willena's house. As it was, the company had already acquired building land that would accommodate their needs for the next eighteen months to two years but were always looking for prime sites to buy for future speculation. The gentleman whom Sam had spoken to asked if he was interested in selling. Sam's answer to that was everything was for sale at a price and to get back to him in twelve months' time. The gentleman made note of Sam's request saying he would keep in touch. Sam knew that if the building industry were to take off, these people would buy up building plots and sit on them for a few years in the assumption that prices would rise thereby capitalising on the prices that they would have paid for them in the first place.

Driving home Sam thought of the land his workshop stood on. It was a big area and if it were rezoned suitable for housing the land could be worth more than the building on it. Work, work and more work was Sam's priority. He had come back to a changing mentality of the masses. If there was work, people would work, as they would rather eat a roast dinner than dip their bread into a bowl of soup. In the first two weeks that Sam was away and due to increasing demand for cheaper coffins, the boys in the workshop collectively decided to make coffins with inferior timber, timber that was discarded by the sawmills was brought in to be graded and sawn into various widths at the workshop. They would do a trial run to see how it went. The cost to the deceased or their families was the question, making them cheap to buy was the answer.

Cheap, nasty but affordable. Give the people what they wanted was one of Sam's sayings and that is how the boys saw it.

Death being a natural progression of living did not stop because of unemployment and Sam when presented with this turn of events exclaimed, "And I thought it was only me with the bright ideas."

It was an article in the New York Times that Sam's attention was again drawn to. The political situation in Germany where absolute power had been given to Adolf Hitler. Legislators had passed the Enabling Act, *Ermächtigungsgesetz* on March the 23rd, granting Hitler dictatorial power in Germany. There were a couple of columns reporting on this event. Most condemning the position Hitler now held. The British press printed much the same, condemning Germany for its stance against the Jews and in France, according to Louis, the people were dismayed at what dictatorship in Germany would bring. Already sabre rattling speeches by Hitler were being made. But America was a long way from Europe and more pressing things were on his mind.

On the first day of September, being the same day that justice had been seen to be done, three men went to meet their maker in Sing-Sing prison, Grace announced that she was pregnant. Willena, within days laid claim to be the child's nanny saying that the last child to have been brought up in this very home was herself and it would be a fitting end to her advancing years to hear a child's laughter echo throughout the house. Grace's announcement was received by both Pageant and Isabelle. As an added surprise to their own good news. Pageant after giving up hope of ever becoming a mother again declared that she was three months pregnant herself, saying that she hadn't mentioned it before for fear that she could have miscarried like she had twice before. But this time she felt sure she would go full term. Isabelle's good news was her intended marriage to Curtis in the spring. They didn't know for sure if they would be married in Texas or New York State, that, she said depended on her parents as they had mentioned it would be nice to visit New York.

On Monday the 2nd of October Murray Humphreys' men came to pick up for the last time his order of coffins. Maybe it wasn't his men and maybe it hadn't been his men for a long time but someone was picking them up and as long as they were being picked up Sam would make them. There was widespread belief that prohibition would be repealed soon and with Al Capone behind bars for tax evasion and Murray Humphreys becoming public enemy number one things became rather confusing. For the man in the street, the illegal activities on the streets and back alleys of New York were not his concern, most were poor and the wise amongst them kept what they had, not adding to the profits of the mob, for he who had nothing, had nothing to give.

It had started to snow when Sam emerged from the cellar. In his hand was a bottle of sparkling wine.

"Something special," he said as he popped the cork and poured out three glasses of bubbles. He had heard at work that President Roosevelt had announced the repeal of prohibition. Tom had the foresight of what was going to happen and brought along a bottle of bootleg whisky.

"Where the hell did you get this from?" asked Sam screwing up his face on tasting it.

"It was given to me," answered Tom doing the same.

"Well give it back," retorted Sam.

On Tuesday the 5th of December, Sam drove home knowing that, that act of Roosevelt's would change the illegal habits of most Americans, and as he, Grace and Willena chinked glasses he remarked that 1933 would be a year to remember. They drank a toast to everyone and everything that had happened that year and were looking forward to Christmas and another year that would mark their lives like no other could.

Mary and George were overjoyed to receive word of Grace's pregnancy.

"I'm going to be a grandmother," she squealed after reading her daughter's letter. "George get that bottle of port out of the cabinet, I feel like I need a drink."

"At midday on a Saturday!"

"Does it really matter what time or what day it is, get that goddamn port George!"

On the very morning Mary received her letter from Grace two more arrived in Llandyssil, one popping through the letterbox of Sam's home and the other addressed to Bill and Megan Jones. Violet smiled as she placed the letter on the table. Jim was outside gazing at a twin winged aeroplane as it flew over the house.

"You're going to be a Granddad," she said as he came into the kitchen.

"Am I?" he answered looking surprised. Violet looked at the letter on the table, "Well, I'll be damned," he stood for a moment then smiled. "Come and give me a hug Violet," he said, "you must be feeling rather proud of yourself." Violet was amazed at Jim's suggestion but yes, she felt rather proud, and yes, she needed a hug. Tears of joy rolled down her face as Jim held her. It was something he had not done for a long time.

Megan was in the yard helping Michael and Bill saw and split logs for the fire when the postman called and handed Megan Grace's letter.

"It's from Grace," she called out.

She opened and read the letter, "Grace is expecting!"

Bill stopped splitting logs and glanced at Megan's smiling face.

"Good news," he said, he looked at Michael, "do you think we will ever see the child?"

"I will," said Michael almost laughing.

"And how can you be sure?"

"Because I know I will and time is on my side. You remember when Sam was here and he asked me what I wanted to do with my life."

At that moment, the De Havilland Tiger Moth as if on cue, flew over. It banked left heading for the Severn Valley. Then wheeling right, flew between the hills, the drone of its engine grew faint as it disappeared behind a wooded rise.

"Well, I've decided," he looked up, "I want to be up there, I want to fly."

Michael looked at his father and smiled, then he gave him a wink. Bill returned his son's smile and winked back.